Figurative Language

This lively introduction to figurative language explains a broad range of concepts, including metaphor, metonymy, simile, and blending, and develops new tools for analyzing them. It coherently grounds the linguistic understanding of these concepts in basic cognitive mechanisms such as categorization, frames, mental spaces, and viewpoint; and it fits them into a consistent framework which is applied to cross-linguistic data and also to figurative structures in gesture and the visual arts. Comprehensive and practical, the book includes analyses of figurative uses of both word meanings and linguistic constructions.

- Provides definitions of major concepts
- Offers in-depth analyses of examples, exploring multiple levels of complexity
- Surveys figurative structures in different discourse genres
- Helps students to connect figurative usage with the conceptual underpinnings of language
- Goes beyond English to explore cross-linguistic and cross-modal data

BARBARA DANCYGIER is Professor in the Department of English at the University of British Columbia.

EVE SWEETSER is Professor in the Department of Linguistics at the University of California, Berkeley.

CAMBRIDGE TEXTBOOKS IN LINGUISTICS

General editors: P. AUSTIN, J. BRESNAN, B. COMRIE, S. CRAIN,
W. DRESSLER, C. EWEN, R. LASS, D. LIGHTFOOT, K. RICE,
I. ROBERTS, S. ROMAINE, N. V. SMITH

Figurative Language

Figurative Language

BARBARA DANCYGIER

University of British Columbia, Vancouver

EVE SWEETSER

University of California, Berkeley

CAMBRIDGE
UNIVERSITY PRESS

University Printing House, Cambridge CB2 8BS, United Kingdom

Published in the United States of America by Cambridge University Press, New York

Cambridge University Press is part of the University of Cambridge.

It furthers the University's mission by disseminating knowledge in the pursuit of education, learning and research at the highest international levels of excellence.

www.cambridge.org
Information on this title: www.cambridge.org/9780521184731

© Barbara Dancygier and Eve Sweetser 2014

First published 2014

Printed in the United Kingdom by Clays, St Ives plc

A catalogue record for this publication is available from the British Library

Library of Congress Cataloguing in Publication Data
Dancygier, Barbara.
Figurative language / Barbara Dancygier, University of British Columbia, Vancouver;
Eve Sweetser, University of California, Berkeley.
    pages   cm. – (Cambridge textbooks in linguistics)
Includes bibliographical references and index.
ISBN 978-1-107-00595-2 (hardback)
1. Figures of speech – Study and teaching.   2. Metaphor – Study and teaching.
3. Languages, Modern – Study and teaching.   I. Sweetser, Eve.   II. Title.
P301.5.F53D36   2014
808′.032–dc23   2013035759

ISBN 978-1-107-00595-2 Hardback
ISBN 978-0-521-18473-1 Paperback

To our students,
the past ones who inspired us, and the future ones
whom we hope to inspire.

Contents

Figures

Tables

Acknowledgements

Acknowledgements are a moment for considering alternative spaces, since many factors are necessary to a book's development. We must first thank all the colleagues whose work has advanced the community's understanding of figurative language over the last several decades: without them, where would we be? First of all, we acknowledge (though it is almost unnecessary to state) the depth of our scholarly and personal debts to George Lakoff, Mark Johnson, Gilles Fauconnier, and Mark Turner, who have shaped the field – and without whom this book would certainly not have needed to be written. We also owe major gratitude to the research work and collegiality of a great many colleagues in the cognitive linguistics community, of whom we specially note Masako Hiraga, Sarah Taub, Chris Johnson, Joe Grady, Rafael Núñez, Cornelia Müller, Seana Coulson, Karen Sullivan, Irene Mittelberg, Elena Semino, and Ben Bergen.

This book has been a joint endeavor: neither of us would or could have written the same book alone, even with the background of all our years of discussions with each other – and without those years, we wouldn't have undertaken it. Barbara has taught about metaphor and figurative language in English Departments for many years both in Warsaw and at the University of British Columbia, while Eve has been teaching this subject matter to Linguistics and Cognitive Science students at Berkeley. So the book is also the product of several academic generations of interactions with colleagues, teaching and research assistants, and students. Sarah and Chris and Joe and Karen and Mike and our other past students and teaching assistants, many of whom are now faculty: *thank you*. George Lakoff, once Eve's teacher and now the colleague with whom she has alternated teaching Linguistics 106 for almost three decades, stands out as a unique worldwide pedagogical influence: he designed the first cognitive linguistics course on metaphor and has taught it since the 1980s. We know he would have written a very different book (indeed, he has: many of them), so he cannot be blamed for specifics of this one; but he should certainly be thanked.

We have already been fortunate in our readers. Mike Borkent, Karen Sullivan, and Kashmiri Stec generously commented on earlier drafts of major portions of this book, while Kensy Cooperrider and Alice Gaby were both heroically speedy in commenting on Chapter 7. Lieven Vandelanotte's stylistic sense and wisdom about the content are deeply appreciated. Julia Bernd gave us her unique blend of precision, intelligence, and grace under pressure as a copy editor. We are grateful and have tried to heed their insightful words. All the usual disclaimers apply (that is, when and if we didn't listen, it is certainly our own fault). Also, thanks are due to Jan Lermitte for her expert help with indexing.

This book also owes its existence to our editor, Andrew Winnard, who understood what we needed to finish the job.

Eve would like to thank her Berkeley colleagues and students, and in particular her current and past colleagues on the Berkeley FrameNet and MetaNet Projects, and her recent co-authors Seiko Fujii, Paula Radetzky, and Kashmiri Stec. And, always and most of all, Alex – sine quo certe non.

Barbara owes much to Lieven Vandelanotte, and his unfailing support and sober judgment. She also wants to thank Mike Borkent for making work so pleasurable and easy. Above all, she is grateful to Jacek, whose importance no figurative or literal language can adequately describe.

And in fact, we need to jointly thank our families – Jacek, Szymek, and Alex have all three provided not only personal support to us both, but also crucial technical support and lively discussion, not to mention all of the amazing examples they have unearthed for us.

* * *

The Grin Reaper print by Banksy is reprinted with the permission of the artist.

1   Introduction

1.1   Reassessing figurative language

This is a linguistics textbook on figurative language. In the mid- and late-twentieth century, topics like metaphor and metonymy were the province of literature departments, and were primarily studied in their roles as part of literary texts. Figurative language was thought of as being one aspect of what gives a text – in particular, a poetic text – special esthetic value. Shakespeare, in saying, *Shall I compare thee to a summer's day?* (Sonnet 18), conveyed his message more beautifully than if he had literally talked about the subject's personal qualities, such as kindness, charm, and beauty. But did he convey the "same" message he would have conveyed in such a literal description? Intuitively, good readers and literary scholars both feel that he did not. Similarly, irony in a literary text does not just add esthetic value in some generalized way; for example, it may heighten emotional involvement, and that may be exactly the artistic effect intended. A question in both cases might be exactly *how* – how is the metaphoric text's meaning different from a literal "translation," and how does irony work differently from a nonironic recounting of similar circumstances? These already sound like issues of interest to linguists, who care about regular relationships between different choices of form and different meanings. What are the mechanisms by which figurative uses of form create meaning for readers?

In this textbook, we hope to make it clear to readers that figurative structures are far from being just decorative. They are important and pervasive in language and, furthermore, this is because the relevant cognitive structures are important and pervasive in thought – and as a result, figurative meaning is part of the basic fabric of linguistic structure. And this is true *not* just for special literary language, but for everyday language – and it holds for all human languages. The same basic mechanisms are involved in Shakespeare's sonnet as in a phrase like *autumn years*, or one like *taxes rose* (note that nothing literally went upwards).

These are strong claims. Despite important past work on metaphor by major linguistic figures (Roman Jakobson comes to mind), most current basic linguistics textbooks have little or no mention of figurative language. Indeed, the impression they give is that linguists are leaving metaphor, metonymy, understatement, irony, and other "tropes" to deal with after analysts have finished working on topics more central to linguistic structure: in particular, syntax, phonology, morphology, and literal semantics. But the claims underlying that position are also strong, though mostly implicit. Although much evidence has been offered by linguists on both sides of the question of the mutual independence of syntax and semantics, most semanticists have assumed that literal meaning can be fully analyzed independently of figurative meaning, rather than assessing this question systematically.

However, the last four decades of research on figurative language and thought have brought us new understandings of their integral relationship to the linguistic system. An influential and productive wave of scholarship took shape following the 1980 publication of Lakoff and Johnson's *Metaphors we live by*. Cognitive linguistics and cognitive science conferences and journals have seen a proliferation of metaphor studies, and the topic has had an increasingly high public profile. Other traditionally recognized figures such as metonymy and irony (an old topic in cognitive science) have also been productively re-examined during the same period, though with less of the publication volume and public attention which have accompanied metaphor's "star" status. Recent work on irony in particular has been shaped by developments in linguistic pragmatics, the study of the use and interpretation of language in context; this is not surprising, since no linguistic content is ironic on its own, without a context. (It is not ironic in itself for a hero to say the heroine is not pretty enough to attract him, but it is ironic for him to say so when the rest of the novel depicts him as falling deeply in love with her.) This book will be dealing with metonymy in some depth, and irony is not neglected, but both the depth and the volume of the past few decades of work on metaphor are necessarily reflected in our textbook's emphasis.

This book is situated within a particular range of frameworks, a loose family of models often labeled cognitive linguistics. This is both because cognitive linguistic models have been productive in examining the nature of figurative language and because the new current understandings of figurative language have developed within cognitive linguistics, while practitioners of most other linguistic frameworks are not focusing on these problems. Cognitive approaches have quite radically transformed models of everyday literal language and meaning. Recent cognitive models of semantics hypothesize that linguistic production and processing involve *simulating* the situations described: that is, the same parts of the brain are activated (though not identically activated) in imagining or describing a situation as would be involved in perceiving and experiencing such a situation. This *embodied* view of meaning – that meaning is made of the same stuff as bodily experience – challenges the idea of language and thought as abstract. And this theory of meaning offers a context for reassessing the role and mechanisms of figurative language, seeing them as part of language rather than as decorative additions.

Embodied experience is inherently viewpointed – you experience a visual scene from some particular point rather than any other, and you experience situations from your own participant role rather than another. This means that linguistic expression is adapted and developed specifically to express and prompt viewpointed meanings rather than God's-eye ones – and there is experimental evidence to support this view (see Bergen 2012 and Dancygier and Sweetser 2012 for reviews). Figurative language is viewpointed too, for the same reasons – although this issue has not been focused on by researchers. Irony may heighten emotional involvement exactly because it makes readers engage in viewpointed imagination of more than one situation; as we shall be discussing, metaphoric construal is viewpointed too, and thus shapes readers' or listeners' viewpoints.

Before moving on to our main subject matter, we need to discuss some core distinctions and models which have shaped both folk and expert understandings of figurative language. Among these are the literal/figurative distinction itself, the conventional relationship of form and meaning, the relationship between meaning and context, and the nature of embodied literal meaning.

1.2   Metaphor: What does *figurative* mean?

Thinking about figurative language requires first of all that we identify some such entity – that we distinguish figurative language from nonfigurative or literal language. And this is a more complex task than one might think. To begin with, there appears to be a circular reasoning loop involved in many speakers' assessments: on the one hand they feel that figurative language is special or artistic, and on the other hand they feel that the fact of something's being an everyday usage is in itself evidence that the usage is not figurative. Metaphor, rather than other areas of figurative language, has been the primary subject of this debate. Lakoff and Johnson (1980) recount the story of a class taught by Lakoff at Berkeley in the 1970s in which he gave the class a description of an argument and asked them to find the metaphors. He expected that they would recognize phrases such as *shoot down someone else's argument*, *bring out the heavy artillery*, or *blow below the belt* as evidence of metaphoric treatment of argument as War or Combat. Some class members, however, protested, saying, *But this is the normal, ordinary way to talk about arguing*. That is, because these usages are *conventional* rather than novel, and *everyday* rather than artistic, they cannot be metaphoric.

However, there are many reasons to question this view, and to separate the parameters of conventionality and everyday usage from the distinction between literal and figurative. One of these is historical change in meaning: historical linguists have long recognized that some meaning change is metaphoric or metonymic. For example, around the world, words meaning 'see' have come to mean 'know' or 'understand.' Indeed, in some cases that past meaning is lost: English *wit* comes from the Indo-European root for vision, but has only the meaning of intellectual ability in modern English. But in other cases, such as the *see* in *I see what you mean*, metaphoric meanings in the domain of Cognition exist alongside the original literal Vision uses. This KNOWING IS SEEING metaphor is extremely productive: *transparent*, *opaque*, *illuminate*, and *shed light on* are among the many English locutions which are ambiguous between literal visual senses and metaphoric intellectual ones. Do we want to say that because these are conventional usages, they are not metaphoric? In that case, we would have to separate them completely from less entrenched uses which show the same metaphoric meaning relationship: if someone says they have *examined a candidate's record with a magnifying glass*, we probably don't want to say that there should be a dictionary entry for *magnifying glass* listing this usage. Still less would we want to make a new dictionary entry if someone said they had *gone over the data with an electron microscope*. As has been widely argued, starting with Lakoff and Johnson, the most plausible hypothesis here is that while *wit* is no longer metaphoric, *transparent* and *shed light on* are metaphoric – and that it is precisely the habitual use of conventional instances of the KNOWING IS SEEING metaphor which helps motivate innovative uses.

It is thus possible for metaphor or metonymy to motivate conventional extensions of word meanings – and figurative links which are pervasively used in this way shape the vocabularies of the relevant languages. At a first approximation, then, we might say that **figurative** means that a usage is motivated by a metaphoric or metonymic relationship to some other usage, a usage which might be labeled *literal*. And *literal* does not mean 'everyday, normal usage' but 'a meaning which is not dependent on a figurative extension from another meaning.' We will be talking about the nature of those relationships in more detail soon, but of course metaphor and metonymy are not the only motivations for figurative usage.

In this context, we might say that **polysemy** – the relationship between multiple related conventional meanings of a single word – is often figurative in nature. English *see* continues to manifest simultaneously meanings related to physical vision and ones related to cognition or knowledge: *Can you see the street signs?* coexists with *Do you see what I mean?*. Chapters 2 and 3 of this book will specifically focus on metaphoric meaning relationships, conventional and novel.[1]

1.3   Metonymy

Metonymy is a classic trope which has in recent decades played second fiddle to metaphor in the research literature. But as we shall see in Chapter 5, it is even more pervasive than metaphor in human language and thought, and indeed has cognitive underpinnings which appear to be present in other species

---

[1] Gibbs and Steen (1999) gather some major papers from the 1990s on cognitive approaches to metaphor.

as well. It often crucially underlies the evocation of other figurative structures, such as metaphor and blending. It is also quite a diverse category.

Metonymy is sometimes said to be about *part–whole* relationships, and indeed we will cover that kind of metonymy – the kind which allows the same word to be used in many languages for 'hand' and 'arm,' or for 'foot' and 'leg,' or which allows a whole working person to be referred to as *an extra pair of hands*. But more generally, metonymy is about relationships of correlation – things that occur together in experience, so that we associate them and can use the word for one to evoke the other. Salient parts do evoke their wholes, and salient subcategories evoke the larger categories of which they are parts – we may associate tissues with Kleenex-brand tissues and thus use *kleenex* to mean 'tissue.' But perhaps the most interesting kind of associational relationship is the one between entities which are coexperienced in a single setting. Consider a restaurant employee who says to a colleague that *The ham sandwich wants another soda* (example from Fauconnier 1994[1985]). Of course this employee means to refer not to the sandwich but to the customer who ordered it – and in the relevant context, the employees frequently don't know the customer's name but do share knowledge of a unique association between main dish ordered and customer. This is an example of *frame metonymy* – that is, using a label for one entity to refer to another entity which is linked to it in a situation by an association such as that of order and customer.

Continuing our discussion of *see*, we can note that alongside its metaphoric senses, it also has lively *frame-metonymic* senses; that is, meanings which are apparently related to the vision meaning more by situational correlation or association. For example, when we say, *I need to see a dentist*, we don't mean just physically seeing them; nonetheless, it would be very odd to say you have seen a dentist if you have only had e-mail contact, so face-to-face visual contact must be part of the situation referred to. Not every language uses its word for 'see' to refer to visits to medical practitioners (nor do all languages share the same frame for medical consultations). But every language does have a way to refer to vision, and the conventional extensions of *see* in English – some metaphoric, some metonymic – are closely motivated by connection with the visual meaning.

The lexicon of every language is full of polysemous words: multiple related meanings for a word (at least, for any common word) seem to be the norm rather than the exception. And many of the links which hold together these meaning networks are figurative. As well as metaphor and metonymy, irony and sarcasm give rise to new conventional word meanings. English *bad*, for example, has both negative and positive meanings, the positive sense being derived from an ironic usage of the negative one, meaning that someone else (unlike the speaker) would judge this cool or stylish thing negatively. The living and productive presence of figurative processes, constantly creating novel and creative meanings, happens against (and is supported by) a backdrop of widespread conventional meaning networks motivated by the same kinds of processes.

1.4   Broadening our understanding of *figurative*: blending and figurative grammar

We said above that to think of a meaning as figurative, we need to think of there being some literal meaning from which it is "extended" by some figurative relationship. But in this book we will argue that we need to include a broader range of relationships in our definition of *figurative*. There are two major areas where modern research has justified such broadening; one area is certain classes of **blending** and the other is **figurative uses of grammatical constructions**. We will briefly exemplify each of these ranges of phenomena.

As an example of a figurative blend, consider Fauconnier and Turner's (2002) discussion of the press coverage of *Great America II*, a modern catamaran sailing around South America from San Francisco to Boston in 1993, trying to do better than the (then still-standing) record sailing time for that route set by a cargo-bearing clipper ship called *Northern Light* in 1853. Although the two ships were very different in their advantages, and the weather conditions were also of course entirely different, still the 1993 crew wanted to beat the record, and in particular construed their trip as a *race*. News coverage said that the catamaran was *barely maintaining a 4.5 day lead over the ghost of the clipper Northern Light*. *Great America II* did not have (could not have had) a literal "lead" over a ship which passed in that general vicinity 140 years earlier, nor of course did the crew of *Northern Light* ever know that *Great America II* would be making this trip, so they could not have seen it as a competition (although nineteenth-century clipper captains were generally competitive about their travel times over major trade routes). But as Fauconnier and Turner point out, one could even imagine saying that *Great America II is 4.5 days ahead of Northern Light*. And at the end of the trip, the catamaran crew could say not only that they set a new record but also that they *beat Northern Light*.

Fauconnier and Turner label the process involved in these construals *blending*; the topic will be discussed in detail in Chapter 4, but intuitively it seems clear that such usages combine (or blend) two situations, e.g. the situation of the original 1853 trip and the situation of the 1993 trip. Further, when these situations are compressed imaginatively into the same time frame – that is, when we are imagining the trips as taking place over the same time period – then many of the components of a race emerge, even though no race existed in either the 1853 situation or the 1993 one. Two boats, traveling from the same place to the same place *over the same time period*, and both eager to go faster than other boats on that route, sounds like a race.

Although we cannot call this imagined "race" an example of some recognized trope – it is not metaphoric, metonymic, or hyperbolic – nonetheless it is not literal. It requires imaginative reconfiguration to use words like *ahead of* in such a setting – and indeed, Turner (2004) argued in more detail that *ghosts* are imaginative blends of the absence and presence of a dead person. In fact, Fauconnier and Turner argue that both literal meaning composition (putting *cat, mat, on,* and *sat* together to get the meaning of *The cat sat on the mat*) and metaphor are subcases of conceptual integration or blending. Obviously we would not want to say that it is figurative processes which are involved in composing *The cat sat on the mat*. But we probably do want to extend our definition of figurative meaning to include nonmetaphoric combinations of elements from different scenarios to create a new scenario which is not an instance of either, such as the race between *Great America II* and the ghost of *Northern Light*.

Another area where scholars have not traditionally talked about figurative usage is in their treatments of extended meanings of grammatical constructions. We don't think of a transitive construction, for example, as having the possibility for both literal and figurative meanings. But note that in English we can say that *Line's sister knitted her a sweater*, meaning not only that Line's sister knitted the sweater (created it by knitting) but also that she did so with the intent that Line would be the *recipient* to whom she would *give* the sweater. Goldberg (1995) argued that this meaning of 'giving something to a recipient' is a characteristic of the English Ditransitive Construction (here very loosely defined as Verb Object-1 Object-2), rather than of any of the words in the sentence (certainly not the verb *knit*). But Goldberg noted that this construction is equally applicable to metaphoric "exchanges" such as linguistic communication, where there is nothing literally given or received – as we can see in *Marie told Joe the story*. As we shall see in Chapter 6, grammatical constructions as well as words frequently carry figurative extended uses. Grammatical constructions, like words, have networks of related meanings – and related by many of the same principles, which (for words and constructions alike) license both relationships between conventional meanings and novel extensions to new uses.

As we shall also see in Chapter 6, grammatical constructions are crucial in prompting figurative construals, even when we might not want to say that the constructions are themselves figuratively used. We note here the importance of copula constructions (*X is Y*) in prompting metaphoric mappings, or the role of the *X is like Y* Comparison Construction in building simile.

1.5   Figurative language, cognition, and culture

Examination of figurative language uses demands consideration of how such uses differ between languages – and that brings up the general question of how linguistic and cultural patterns are related to cognition. In Chapter 7 we will tackle this question, taking spatial metaphors for time as our sample case. Some metaphors seem in fact to be remarkably stable across languages and cultures: for example, there are innumerable languages where More is metaphorically Up (as in English *prices rose*, meaning 'prices increased in quantity'), but no attested examples of MORE IS DOWN. And others seem remarkably specific to time and place: Gloria Yang informs us that Taiwanese speakers of Mandarin use the metaphor ROMANTIC-RELATIONSHIP MANAGEMENT IS KITE FLYING, which is not obviously accessible to English speakers, and would presumably be entirely opaque to members of cultural and linguistic communities where kite flying was unknown. However, we might also note that many languages lacking this metaphor do have the metaphor RELATIONSHIPS ARE PHYSICAL TIES or LINKS – and when it is explained to an English speaker that the woman is the kite flyer, and that her management of the boyfriend is understood as the kite flyer's physical manipulation of the kite (strategic letting out and pulling in of the string), the English speaker might find the metaphor quite comprehensible, though still novel.

As stated above, figurative language usages appear to be pervasive in all languages – and the reason is apparently that they reflect patterns of human cognition. Some of those patterns, such as the basic experiential correlation between More and Up, emerge fairly unproblematically from crosscultural patterns in everyday experience; other cognitive patterns are quite culture specific. But the potential for figurative patterns is a universal, as are some of the basic classes of figurative patterns. A good deal of cognitive science research over the last few decades has shown that metaphor is not "just" linguistic; rather, linguistic patterns reflect cognitive ones. Although this is a linguistics textbook and not a cognitive science one, these issues are important for linguistics, and basic treatments of some of them will be presented later in the book, particularly in Chapters 2 (on the cognitive underpinnings of metaphor), 5 (on metonymy), and 7 (on crosslinguistic patterns).

Multimodal evidence is often crucial in examining the relationship between figurative thought and language, and has been a crucial component of crosscultural comparison of figurative uses as well. Art, architecture, and other cultural artifacts show figurative uses as pervasive as those found in language: The Statue of Liberty metaphorically represents (*personifies*) the abstract concept of Liberty, and an icon of a crossed spoon and fork (objects whose central uses are in the frame of Eating) may frame-metonymically identify the location of a restaurant on a map. In general, there is a close relationship between linguistic figurative uses and the structures to be found in these nonlinguistic representations and artifacts; it is therefore illuminating to study them together, and we will be doing that throughout the book. Another area where nonlinguistic modalities are closely related to linguistic ones is the structure of co-speech gesture, which will come up mostly in Chapter 7, since differences in gestural patterns often provide remarkable support for the cognitive status of metaphors also manifested in language. Surprisingly to English speakers, speakers of Aymara (an Andean language) gesture forward in talking about the past and backward in talking about the future – and they also talk about the future as behind them and the past as in front of them (Núñez and Sweetser 2006).

1.6   The uses of figurative language

Finally, as with any kind of language, the question arises as to *how* various kinds of figurative language serve human purposes, whether everyday communicative purposes in some speech setting, or purposes more specific to some genre of communication, or of course artistic and creative purposes in poetry and fiction. As linguists, we are very much aware that language is a multilectal phenomenon; people speak and write differently depending on their social group, audience, setting, and other contextual factors. Good creative writing draws on and extends the uses familiar from more everyday usages, as well as from past artistic usages. So on the one hand, as Lakoff and Turner (1989) make clear, literary metaphor is by no means some foreign category separate from speakers' everyday metaphoric usages – indeed, novel literary metaphor and blending is usually comprehensible to readers precisely because it draws on familiar structures. And on the other hand, the metaphors of Shakespeare or Emily Dickinson – or the blends of Jonathan Raban – are unique and brilliant creations, and indications of the human cognitive ability to extend and innovate from conventions. High-quality literary texts should thus be of immense interest to both linguists and cognitive scientists – though neither group of scholars seems universally aware of the value of literature as data.

Not just in literature, but in value-laden domains such as Religious and Political Language, and in more "prosaic" domains like Scientific Discourse, figurative cognition and language are pervasive as well. And frequently these discourses have their own domain-specific and genre-specific figurative usages. Only in politics do *left* and *right* refer to particular sociopolitical opinion ranges; in chemistry they might bring to mind dextro- and laevo- ('left-handed' and 'right-handed') molecules whose structures are related in that they are mirror images of each other. The political uses of *left* and *right* began apparently as frame-metonymic associations between opinion groups and seating arrangements in the Assembly following the French Revolution; this is now largely forgotten, but the terms have taken on lively metaphoric meanings, as can be seen in a joke where a Chinese leader tells his driver to *signal left, turn right*, meaning that rhetoric should remain framed in terms of Communist values, but actual policy should accommodate capitalism.

Fields such as stylistics and discourse studies have examined figurative aspects of style and discourse along with other aspects: much work on literary texts, particularly on metaphor, has also made productive use of cognitive and cognitive linguistic approaches. In Chapter 8, we will examine a number of the themes that emerge from examining the discourse role of figurative language. Figurative usages clearly do not serve the same purposes as their literal "translations" – they are there for a reason and achieve goals for the writer. Even the *means* of evoking a figurative construal – for example, the choice of direct comparison (*Shall*

I compare thee to a summer's day?) as opposed to leaving the connection to the reader (Dylan Thomas does not overtly identify *night* as referring to Death when he says, *Do not go gentle into that good night*) may be considered stylistically important.

And finally, it is no surprise that the field of rhetoric has long shown an interest in figurative language, as far back as Aristotle. Traditionally, an important aspect of rhetoric was persuasive discourse, which consists in bringing someone else around to your viewpoint on a situation. As we said above, cognitive and linguistic structures are pervasively viewpointed. But many very general ideas and frames are neutral as to viewpoint: for example, I can imagine an Election frame without personal identification with one or another candidate or party. And although the cognitive frame of Anger involves an aggrieved party and some cause (possibly a person) responsible for the grievance – and thus the possibility of taking one of the two viewpoints – the mention of *anger* does not automatically involve the speaker or listener in identification with one of these two parties rather than the other. However, that does not mean that most discourse about anger is neutral; on the contrary. Talking about an extreme expression of anger as *blowing up* or *exploding* certainly suggests the viewpoint of the addressee or onlookers of the scene, since people more naturally take on the viewpoint of a human than an explosive device. And this in turn means making at least some negative emotional assessment; explosions are harmful or at least dangerous to those present – and angry shouting may damage social relations. As Lakoff (2009) has pointed out, political framing is equally pervasive in establishing viewpoint. Using a metaphor such as *tax relief* presumes that taxes are an affliction or a burden from which citizens need "relief"; one does not need relief from the right to participate in one's government institutions, or from duties which are not onerous or coercive.

Metonymy creates viewpoint too: although the person in question may or may not resent it in particular circumstances, being viewed as *another pair of hands* does not mean that your cognitive and emotional viewpoints are being included in the construal. You are being seen as a worker or tool relevant to someone else's viewpoint and project plans. And not only does blending often involve viewpointed scenarios, it may also may create new viewpoint structures. The crew of *Great America II* not only built up a Race frame with two possible opposing viewpoints out of two separate one-participant events, but also of course took the viewpoint of their boat as contestant, not that of the long-ago crew of *Northern Light*.

So, as figurative language is shaping cognitive construals in discourse, it is typically shaping viewpoint on the relevant content as well. This happens at every level from the most wild and creative innovation to the most pedestrian usage (like *tax relief* or *angry explosion*), and in ways which may be blatantly obvious or completely under the listener's conscious radar. Understanding discourse crucially involves understanding these processes.

1.7   The basic tool-kit: categories, frames, and mental spaces

In order to give precise and technical accounts of metaphor, metonymy, irony, and blending in general, we will need some of the basic concepts of cognitive science and cognitive linguistics. These concepts are needed not just for figurative language – they are generally needed for any discussion of cognition and language. **Human category structure** has been a major object of study in cognitive science, and remains of major interest to linguists – after all, words name conceptual categories. So in order to understand how categories can be extended figuratively, we need to understand literal categorization. Metonymy in particular rests on this foundation – without some understanding of *how* subcategories relate to larger categories, or how categories are related to salient members, we would have a great deal of trouble understanding potential usages such as *She's the new Margaret Thatcher*, which relies for possible interpretations on Thatcher's prominent membership in various categories (e.g. British conservative, female political leader).

We will also need to make use of work on the **frame-based** nature of cognition and linguistic meaning. The Thatcher example shows this too; the name *Margaret Thatcher* is not being used here just to name an individual (there is only one such individual, so there cannot literally be a new one) but to evoke her role in the kinds of structured situations in which she played a part. Just the phrase *Prime Minister* fully evokes one of those frames, that of Parliamentary Government. Frame structures are crucial in understanding metaphor as well as metonymy. How can one simply map a domain as complex and various as Mind onto another one as complex as our understanding of the Body? We noted above that KNOWING IS SEEING is one particular mapping which is basic in many cultures and languages – but this maps much more specific structures than Body and Mind. Mind might include our models of phenomena such as emotions, meditation, decision making, speculation, and much more; Body obviously includes many other situational frames besides Vision. Indeed, we also find mappings between Body and Mind such as UNDERSTANDING IS GRASPING (*I can't quite grasp that idea; it keeps slipping away from me*), which again maps more specific frame structures from the broad domains of Body and Mind.

And finally, both for metaphor and for nonmetaphoric blends such as those described above, we will need to bring in the Theory of Mental Spaces, originally built up by Fauconnier (1994[1985], 1997) and further developed by Fauconnier and Turner (2002) into the Theory of Blending. The imagined boat race between two crews 140 years apart begs the questions of what kinds of conceptual structures can be inputs into such creative blends, and what principles constrain the combinations. Random conceptual combinations might well simply be nonsensical: could I conceptualize, say, human reasoning as brushing my teeth? Perhaps, but it doesn't seem obvious what sense it would make, or how it could serve my discourse goals. Mental Spaces Theory will help us to see the structured and systematic nature of blending and figurative language; even the most creative usages harness the same kinds of systematic processes.

1.8   The road ahead

Readers can now see the basic shape of our book, and we shall plunge into the examination of the various categories of figurative usage mentioned above, using the analytic tools of cognitive linguistics. The book as a whole is intended to give an overview of both cognitive motivations and linguistic uses, and therefore necessarily to redefine *figurative* to include new data which had not been observed by the authors of earlier lists of tropes. It is also intended to show the integral relationship between figurative and literal: to the extent that we do not understand linguistic meaning in general, we cannot develop any reasonable understanding of figurative meaning, and a view of literal meaning which does not provide a basis for figurative uses is too limited. This is all the more true given that not only words but also grammatical constructions contribute to both literal and figurative meaning building. Not just linguistic forms but concepts, and therefore their linguistic expressions, are tied to figurative senses.

Along the way, we will be helping readers to develop analytic techniques and judgments; metaphor analysis in particular has been a field where a great deal of loose argumentation has prevailed. What kind of data are needed to support an analysis? We will also be developing a typology of figurative language, which will help analysts by showing what kinds of structures are common or generally observed and what kinds of variation exist among figurative usages. We would like to see the field move towards more rigorous analysis – even while we would also like to see it use wider ranges of data, including literary data, and more closely examine the metaphoric systems of non-European languages.

2   The basics of metaphor

In this chapter, we will outline the very basic underpinnings of the Theory of Conceptual Metaphor. We will start with introducing the concept of a mapping, and will then connect that concept with two areas of study: frame semantics and the experiential grounding of figurative thought. In the next chapter, we will offer further explanation about the nature of mappings and the relations among them.

2.1   The concept of a mapping

Thinking about figurative expressions requires that we develop hypotheses about how words can provide access to concepts which are not literally associated with them. For example, using the verb *attack* outside of a specific context usually evokes a scenario of physical activity in which the agent intends to physically harm the patient. One can imagine the verb being used in a news item reporting events in which someone is physically hurt. Another natural context would be a description of historical events where countries or groups of soldiers engage in a military conflict (which also intends to inflict bodily harm). But one might also hear the verb in the context of a political debate, a discussion in the press, etc. where no physical harm is at stake, but where there is nevertheless a clear sense of opposing intentional agents acting against each other.

We should note that such vocabulary choices are not random, but are often very systematic. A person likely to talk about her views being *under attack* is also likely to talk about *defending* her position, using *strategies* or *weapons*, planning *campaigns*, or even being a *casualty* in some ideological conflict. This entire range of vocabulary items, basically associated with military conflict or combat, can be used to talk about situations where the conflict is at the level of ideas. This kind of usage has been described by referring to two conceptual domains, in this case Argument and War, and postulating a **mapping** between them, such that some of the conceptual structure of one (military conflict, its participants, the tools and processes involved) is projected into the other. An event such as a Dispute, Debate, or Argument involves its own Event Structure and participant roles; it is oppositional in nature, but it is otherwise unlike physical fighting. But it is nonetheless often metaphorically construed as Combat or War, and it seems clear that such a construal is different from literal usage: calling a debater's verbal behavior a *blow below the belt* provides new inferences (e.g. it was behavior to which the addressee was personally vulnerable, and it was somehow outside the "fairness" conventions of the debate setting). A **conceptual metaphor** is a *unidirectional mapping* projecting conceptual material from one structured domain (in this case, War), called the *source domain*, to another one, called the *target domain* (Argument). When we say that the mapping is unidirectional, we mean that the construal is asymmetric: these usages construe Argument events as War or Combat events, and are not construing War as verbal debate or Argument.

> Metaphoric mapping: a unidirectional relation between two conceptual domains (the **source domain** and the **target domain**) which sets up links (mappings) between specific elements of the two domains' structures. A conceptual connection of this kind may be further reflected in metaphoric expressions, linguistic usages of source-domain forms to refer to corresponding aspects of the target domain.

The existence of such a conceptual connection licenses a range of vocabulary choices which rely on connecting aspects of the two domains linked by the mapping. We can therefore talk about verbal disputes in terms of *winning* or *losing*, *being a casualty*, or *having a secret weapon*. These linguistic choices are a consequence of the conceptual metaphoric mappings.

One could well argue that there are limits on how much of the source is actually available for use in referring to the target. Would it be natural to talk about nuclear war as a model of a debate? Would we refer to the military hierarchy (say, foot soldiers vs. generals) in portraying an oppositional verbal exchange? Certainly, the choice of an expression like *He viciously attacked my views* seems more natural than an expression like *I sent my troops on a suicide mission* when talking about a debate. The latter expression, however, is not entirely impossible in a context where the war metaphor has already been elaborated, creating some expectation that further aspects of the domain could be applicable. What such cases suggest is that the usage involved is not just a matter of the choice of individual words, but of the contextual accessibility of the domains (of both War and Argument) and the nature of the unidirectional mapping between them.

To distinguish them from cited examples, mappings are typically represented by analysts using the sequence TARGET IS SOURCE written in small caps, while the names of domains are otherwise conventionally capitalized (Argument, War). The mapping discussed above was originally described in Lakoff and Johnson (1980) as ARGUMENT IS WAR. We would like to point out here that the actual labeling of the domains is a matter which needs to be decided in the context of attested usage and in comparison with alternative labels. For example, the label War may seem too strong, given that the linguistic expressions involved are primarily focused on the physical nature of the conflict rather than on the political and international implications which are part of the concept of War. In fact, some analysts find it more appropriate to label the mapping ARGUMENT IS

COMBAT. This question does not imply that metaphoric mappings in themselves lack specificity, but rather that our formulation of them necessarily depends on the linguistic labels we find most appropriate to represent the conceptual content involved. It is therefore all the more important to realize that terms such as War or Combat are primarily representations of *frames* – knowledge structures we use in processing language. (Frames are discussed in detail in the next section.)

Returning to ARGUMENT IS WAR, there are ready mappings available between the oppositional stances of the two participants in the two scenarios. But these mappings are not alone in licensing the construal whereby the 'weapons' in an argument are ideas expressed by the opponents. There is a much more general mapping which motivates this specific one. Very generally in English, the IDEAS ARE OBJECTS metaphor gives object status to an abstraction and has therefore been called an **ontological metaphor** because it so radically reframes the ontological status of the abstraction (Lakoff and Johnson 1980). (Chapter 3 will further elucidate this concept.) In general, not just in argumentative settings, a speaker can *toss out an idea*, which one's interlocutor may *catch onto*, or it might just *go right past them*. The specific case where argumentative ideas are understood as weapons or projectiles is motivated not only by the ARGUMENT IS WAR mapping but also by this very general IDEAS ARE OBJECTS mapping.

It is rare for a complex domain to be understood metaphorically via only one set of mappings. Since a debate or an argument is a communicative event, it is also partially structured by other mappings, specifically those that allow us to construe the concept of communication. One of the mappings that was discussed in detail even before the Theory of Conceptual Metaphor had been formulated was the COMMUNICATION IS EXCHANGE OF OBJECTS metaphor, originally known as the Conduit Metaphor (Reddy 1979).[1] This metaphor represents acts of communication as acts of physical object transfer, in which the speaker and the addressee give or send objects to each other, taking turns. The objects exchanged are linguistic meanings, while the containers in which they are exchanged are the linguistic forms; the "containers" filled with meanings are sent to the addressee, so he can unpack the meanings at the other end of the communicative channel. Reddy suggests that the Conduit Metaphor explains the cohesiveness across expressions such as *I can't **put it into** words!* and *Did you **get** what I said?* – not to mention graders' comments (observed by Reddy on essays) such as *You're **packing** too much **into** this paragraph*, *This sentence is **empty***, or *I didn't **get** anything **out of** this section*. This metaphor was discussed by Lakoff and Johnson (1980, 1999) and has been reanalyzed by subsequent cognitive linguists, most notably Grady (1998).

---

[1] It is difficult not to observe here that the Conduit Metaphor seems to underlie many early and still-current theories of meaning and communication. Only now, when there has been much significant work on the contextual nature of communication, can we say that the conduit model is becoming outdated.

The two metaphors discussed here share structure, in that both the Conduit Metaphor and the war metaphor involve construing communication as sending objects which reach the addressee and have an effect. The Conduit Metaphor also includes an understanding of the relation between meaning and form (forms are containers for meaning), while the war/combat metaphor adds the adversarial nature of the exchange. But it is important to note that there are underlying conceptual patterns which can reappear in the context of different mappings; that is, mappings are not necessarily fully independent of each other. Conceptual structure can be more or less richly detailed, or specified. We might therefore say that there is a very schematic – i.e. not detailed – conceptual structure that is shared between the ARGUMENT IS WAR and the COMMUNICATION IS OBJECT EXCHANGE metaphors: the schematically shared target-domain structure is that of (not necessarily argumentative) communication, and the schematically shared source-domain structure is that of objects being moved from one participant to another (not necessarily either containers or projectiles).

The choice of which label to use to represent a metaphoric domain thus needs to take many aspects of the mapping into account. On the target-domain side, one could say Argument, Dispute, or Debate. And on the source-domain side, crucially, the choice of War or Combat discussed above reflects certain assumptions about the types of situations and roles available for projection. While War may have broad international or legal implications (and so license expressions such as *signing a peace treaty* or *war diplomacy*, assuming we could imagine them to have counterparts in the target domain of Argument), the concept of Combat most prototypically involves conflict between two individuals, where bodily harm and strength may be of primary importance. If we look at more conventional English usage, *losing ground* or *gaining ground* in an argument sounds more like War, since warfare is often about territory ownership, while *a blow below the belt* sounds more like individual Combat. Both choices leave room for a whole range of expressions, though not necessarily the same expressions. It might sometimes be justified, then, to pick a broad term for a domain, while knowing that other, more specific concepts would perhaps represent the mapping better, but would also narrow down the scope.

This question of how to determine which domain label is best suited to the representation of the linguistic usage has generated much discussion among metaphor theorists. For example, Turner 1991 attempted to narrow down the scope of the mapping discussed above by choosing the label RATIONAL ARGU- MENT IS COMBAT BETWEEN INTENTIONAL AGENTS. While such a formulation is justified for a certain range of usages, it also limits the mapping, as Clausner and Croft (1997) observed, to rational forms of debating. But irrational "fights" over seemingly unimportant issues happen as well, often in an even more aggressive way, and so Clausner and Croft consider the choice of War over Combat to be justified.

Given these debates, it might seem that metaphor analysts are making some- what arbitrary choices between labels, but the issue is in fact different. Domains are labeled with available expressions, representing specific construals. The choice of construal licenses a range of linguistic expressions, but the structure of conceptual frames and categories is complex, and there is much potential overlap between them. The fact that categories often have not just a boundary, but a core and a periphery (Rosch 1977, Mervis and Rosch 1981, Lakoff 1987) already means that a given category label may apply better or worse (rather than completely or not at all). And, as we shall see in the next section, aspects of structure may be shared between categories. For example, *protesting*, *criticizing*, and *arguing* are not the same, nor is one a subcase of another, but they do share conceptual structure which none of them share with *praise* or *agreement*. War and Combat share some quite specific conceptual structure, much more specific than objects being exchanged. War does normally involve the entire scenario of Combat, and a given combat could be part of, or develop into, a war. Neither can be described as right or wrong as a metaphor for argumentation events, except within the context of the specific mappings observed in the discourse.

Furthermore, the choice of the domain label is also a choice about the level of schematicity; such choices may range from using highly schematic concepts like Up to more detailed and fleshed-out frames such as Journey. We will show in Chapter 3 that some of the most crucial choices between domain labels are between more and less general labels. In Section 2.2, however, we will consider the nature of a domain in more detail.

2.2   Frames and domains

The concept of a **domain** is basic to the formulation of metaphor as a unidirectional mapping, but we have so far refrained from defining it except as a conceptual structure which can be used as a source or a target in such a mapping. A domain, in this understanding, is a chunk of conceptual matter which either contains structure to be projected into another domain or receives such a projection. As we saw above, however, determining the content or limits of a domain without ambiguity may present problems: something as broad as Cognition could be thought of as a "domain," as could something as narrow as Tests, or something intermediate such as Education. A number of theorists, from Croft and Cruse (2004) to Sullivan (2013), have thus preferred to talk about metaphors as mappings between **frames**. The term *frame* was introduced to linguistics by Fillmore (1982, 1985) to represent a "prefab" chunk of knowledge structure; a **lexical frame** is a frame paired with a lexical item or lexical items that represent it. Crucially, the definition of a *frame* also involves gestalt structure: that is, an expression referring to some aspect of a frame structure gives conceptual access to the entire structure, so that evoking one aspect of a frame provides access to the entire frame, and individual frame components are understood in the context of the entire frame. For example, the word *husband* cannot be properly understood other than in the context of the frame of Marriage, which (in its conventional heterosexual version) also includes a wife, a legal and spiritual bond between them, other family relationships (such as in-laws), financial implications, etc. Mentioning *husband, wife, divorce,* or *in-laws* requires reference to the entire frame: there can be no marriage without spouses, no spouses or in-laws or divorce without marriage. More specific frames such as Wedding are parts of the Marriage frame; specifically, the Wedding frame is understood to constitute the normal initiatory step in the larger Marriage frame. The reader will have noted that names of frames, like names of domains, are conventionally capitalized: thus "marriage" in our text refers to the meaning of the word *marriage* (cited forms are italicized by linguists), while "Marriage" refers to the cognitive frame involved in that meaning.

Frames are thus tightly linked chunks of conceptual structure which get evoked together. Lexical frames are of course frames that are evoked often enough to be given names – which means they are general enough or schematic enough to be needed recurrently by language users. Typically, complex frames have roles, and relations between those roles: in the Marriage frame, roles such as Husband or Wife or Mother-in-Law are filled by different individuals.

Frames display various levels of specificity, complexity, and cultural embed-dedness. One might have more specific subframes of a Wedding frame, e.g. for an Orthodox Jewish wedding or an Episcopalian wedding. In many countries, the Marriage and Wedding frames are currently the focus of a cultural reframing concerning the partners eligible to enter into a married state – so that such part-ners do not have to be of different sexes. The dispute involves the relationship of Marriage to other frames (Moral, Religious, Gender, etc.). Two roles for Spouses remain parts of the frame, but the gender specifications attached to those roles are altered in making a frame of Same-Sex Marriage. This example shows clearly that frames are deeply engrained both in linguistic knowledge and in the cultural context, but also that they are potentially subject to change.

The concept of a frame is quite close to what Schank and Abelson (1977) discussed under the term *scripts*, although the literature on frames has focused more on the roles frame elements play with respect to each other. For example, the standard schema of a Commercial Transaction contains the same roles whether it is discussed as a frame or as a script: there needs to be a Seller, a Buyer, Goods (an object transferred between them), a Price, etc. But the concept of a frame stresses additionally that the very mention of any aspect of the transaction evokes the transaction frame – so that mentioning *the price* brings up the seller, the buyer, and the object sold/bought. Literature on both scripts and frames also mentions the example of a Restaurant frame, with roles for the Customer, the Food, the Waiter/Waitress, Tables, Menus, Checks, etc. We will be returning to the discussion of the complexity of frames throughout this book.

A broad conceptual domain is thus by no means equivalent to a single frame. As Sullivan argues, a metaphoric source or target domain may involve many lev-els of frames and subframes: while some frames involved in the broader domains of Sex and Gender are certainly evoked as parts of the frame of Marriage, there are probably aspects of the larger domain of Sex (e.g. differential susceptibility of men and women to medical conditions) or Gender (e.g. reading "masculine" or "feminine" literary genres) which are not evoked directly in understanding Marriage. What is useful about frames for our analysis is that we know something about their structure, whereas a *domain* is simply a term for a connected piece of conceptual structure, of any kind. And structure is what gets mapped in metaphoric mappings, so the more we know about the structure of the source and the target, the more precisely we can define and motivate the mappings. For example, a frame of Combat is evoked by any expression describing physical conflict, including literal expressions such as *He was attacked by a brigade of enemy soldiers*. The sentence clearly refers to a bodily conflict in which there are two opposing sides and one of them wins. But a very similar sentence, *He was attacked by a brigade of angry philosophers*, maps the Combat frame onto an Academic Dispute frame. It would not be very helpful to say that this maps the general Military domain onto the general Academic domain, for example; we might find other frames which could be mapped onto each other (perhaps a university president might be described as a general, mapping rank hierarchies between the two domains), but those would not be the relevant ones. We will thus define mappings in terms of the source and target frames which they connect, though we may use the term *domain* for the sake of simplicity when it is not clear exactly what the identities of the frames are – or, of course, when we mean some larger multiframe entity. As we shall see, it is frames which are relevant to other figurative structures, as well as to metaphor.

Frames thus provide a clearer way to identify the aspects of domains involved in metaphoric mappings. Another benefit of relying on the concept of a frame is that it is easier to show the levels of schematicity involved in mappings. For example, many published analyses rely on the KNOWING IS SEEING metaphor in explaining any usage that draws on the domain of light in referring to cognition or understanding. The conclusion one might draw from this is that any metaphoric expression related to light uses the frame in the same way, but, as Sullivan (2013) has shown, this may not be the case. We will consider Sullivan's work in more detail in Chapter 6, but let us note here that the presence of light is only one aspect of a rich frame. A concept can be metaphorically treated as a source of light, as when we talk about *a bright idea* or *a bright person* or about someone *shedding light* on a problem, but when a participant reaches understanding without external help, *a light bulb* inside her head can provide illumination, in very much the same way (she is her own light source). Also, a participant can be understood as uncovering objects and exposing them to light, so others can see/understand them (as in *Her lecture **uncovered** new meanings of the concept* or *The teacher put the problem **in a new light***), in which case concepts can be seen as objects viewed with the aid of illumination. Further, a participant's ability to see can be used to represent their ability to understand, as in *He was **blinded** by prejudice*, *He is still **in the dark***, or *He **saw** my point right away*, while the level of transparency of a medium may be used in representing the thinker's access to comprehension (*The argument was **murky/clear/transparent***). Each of these usages maps different aspects of the broader domain of Vision onto that of Cognition or Understanding.

A particular example discussed by Sullivan is that of the English words *bright* and *brilliant*. *Bright* can refer to both intelligence and cheerfulness; a *bright student* is intelligent, while a person described as *bright and cheery* is not specified as being intelligent, only as cheerful. However, *brilliant* can only refer to intelligence, not to cheerfulness: *she's brilliant and cheery* could only mean 'intelligent and cheery.' At first glance, we might have thrown up our hands and said we couldn't explain the quirky word-specific patterns of meaning involved here. However, Sullivan points out that, in fact, there are deeper regularities underlying this contrast. In the domain of Physical Light, *bright* can refer to both the subframes of Ambient Illumination (*a bright room*) and Intensity of Light Source (*a bright lamp*). *Brilliant*, on the other hand, refers specifically to Intensity of Light Source; one could not say *a brilliant room* to refer to a 'very bright room', but *a brilliant spotlight* is a normal usage. A way of expressing this generalization might be to say that INTELLIGENCE IS A LIGHT SOURCE is a frame-to-frame metaphoric mapping, while CHEERFULNESS IS AMBIENT LIGHT LEVEL is another such mapping. Since *bright* participates in both of the two source-domain frames in the complex Light / Vision domain, it can also take part in both of these two metaphoric mappings; since *brilliant* does not refer to Ambient Light Level, it can only participate in one of these two kinds of metaphoric usages.

Notice that we haven't explained why the literal senses of *bright* and *brilliant* are what they are – why can't *brilliant* refer to Ambient Light Level? But as metaphor analysts, it is important to know that literal senses (quirky or not) are what provide the point of departure for metaphoric usages. If we had stuck with very broad domain labels, we might not have been able to see what the generalization was in this case. Source-domain frames are what get mapped onto target-domain frames – so we have to look carefully and precisely at those source frames. This point has also been made forcefully by Croft (2009) in his analysis of English metaphoric extensions of the vocabulary of Eating.

In Chapter 1, we argued for the importance of viewpoint in metaphoric as well as literal construals. This importance is not unexpected, since frames (the inputs to metaphoric mappings) are themselves viewpointed. There are many ways in which viewpoint may be involved in figurative uses of frames, in metonymic as well as metaphoric usages. For example, the Restaurant frame mentioned above is commonly used from the viewpoint of a restaurant customer. When a customer says, *We ate out last night. The service was awful*, the expression *ate out* evokes the restaurant frame. It also shows that the speaker evaluates the event from the point of view of the customer – so it is no surprise that it is followed by assessment of the helpfulness or timeliness of the service. And this kind of viewpoint can be present in a metaphoric usage: evaluating a conference as *an attractive smorgasbord* seems to be from the viewpoint of a conference participant who finds the offerings attractive and also appreciates the freedom of choice. But when a waitress tells another waitress that *Table 5 needs more water*, this is a metonymic reference to the customer(s) at that table; and it is a reference which could only be made from the wait-staff's viewpoint. Only the wait-staff know which table is Table 5, and indeed they are precisely the ones whose job is Food Delivery, a separate subframe of the Restaurant frame from Food Selection or Food Consumption.

The viewpointed use of frames is also visible in some extended uses of proper names. Dancygier (2009, 2011) has argued that proper names obtain their special semantic status as pointers to unique individuals not just on the basis of a special type of reference or Identity relation, but primarily because, in discourse, they represent frames so rich that they identify referents as unique. For example, the expression *Mount Everest* represents more than a name of one unique mountain, but also its rich frame – the highest peak and the ultimate achievement in climbing (even though other mountains can be harder to climb, the tragic history of early attempts to conquer the peak give Everest its special framing). But when a person has finished a university degree which was very hard to obtain and is enjoying the sense of a great success, she might say, *This MA was my Everest!* In this context, two important frame-related facts should be pointed out. First, the expression *Everest* here refers not just to the mountain, but to the frame which the mountain has acquired over the years – that of being the highest achievement, reached thanks to much effort and perseverance; the referring part of the frame (the Mountain) is not used. Second, this is largely due to the genitive viewpoint marker *my*, which makes it clear that such a use of the frame is profiled from the experiential perspective of the speaker – finishing her MA was as hard for her as it was for Hillary and Tenzing to conquer the highest peak. The Top Achievement part of the frame is applied to the experience the speaker is trying to describe.

The word *Everest* can be used in many such situations, since its frame is widely known. But if we imagine that the speaker completed an MA degree in history, while her sister had earlier obtained a PhD in physics with much sacrifice and effort, within the family someone might describe her success as *her PhD in physics*. The principle is the same – a contextually available frame of Hard-Earned Success is used to frame a new situation. In all cases, such a viewpointed use of the frame yields a meaning which is dependent on more than just the identity of the referent, and which may then enable metaphoric mapping (an MA is not literally a mountain). Chapter 6 will further discuss these uses, and the relation between metaphor and metonymy. It should be clear at this point that mappings depend on frames, but how exactly the frames will be used in contexts (and what domains linguists will need to postulate) is a matter of theoretical importance.

2.3   How mappings are grounded in experience

All frames and domains are not equal: when it comes to figurative usage, some domains are commonly (even pervasively) used in conceptual mappings, while others are not, and some of them are more likely to appear as source and others as target. While a debate can be construed as Combat, it would seem far less natural to construe it as a process of applying makeup to one's face; also, we do not find regular linguistic uses which structure Combat in terms of a debate, or Objects in terms of ideas. In fact, we need to ask whether there are any restrictions on which domains can be linked by metaphor – if all connections were possible, the variety of metaphors in use would be so broad that it would be hard to find common ground across speakers. These questions cannot be properly addressed without seeking an explanation in terms of conceptual structure – for, as we hope to have shown, metaphors are not a linguistic phenomenon, but a cognitive one.

Many earlier theories either postulated that no restrictions were needed and any metaphor was possible (the wilder the mapping, the more poetic, and therefore the better), or spoke (rather vaguely) about "similarity" between domains. Both of these approaches are problematic. What does it mean to say that *Achilles is a lion* brings to mind "similarities" between the two entities? Achilles's reputation of being a ferocious, invincible warrior is what the metaphor appears to refer to, but this does not imply a "similarity" between a Greek hero and an animal such as a lion. And in the case of less conventional metaphors, amusing though novel mappings may be, they are not as unrestricted as one might think.

What we need to consider is the ways in which the conceptual patterns (and their linguistic representations) are rooted in human embodied experience and how they are constrained by human cognition. Lakoff and Johnson (1980) suggested that the mapping MORE IS UP is so common because it is motivated by our experience of More as being correlated with higher levels, in a container, a pile, etc. Crosscultural constraints will be further explored in Chapter 7, but suffice it to say here that since *Metaphors we live by* suggested an experiential basis for such metaphoric mappings, researchers have yet to locate a language where MORE IS DOWN is current rather than MORE IS UP. In fact, Lakoff and Johnson (provocatively, at the time) claimed further that many metaphoric structures may be based on correlations between the source and target domains in human experience. One such class of metaphors they noted in English are Orientational Metaphors, such as MORE IS UP, LESS IS DOWN, or GOOD IS UP, or FUNCTIONAL IS UP – all cases where the up/down vertical dimension is mapped onto more abstract domains. How can this shared concept of verticality help to shape a range of metaphoric mappings?

In the rest of this section, we will consider various aspects of experience and the ways in which they influence the range of metaphoric mappings in common use.

2.3.1   Image schemata and experiential correlations

The first concept to be considered is that of an **image schema** (originally introduced and described in Johnson 1987) – a schematic or skeletal structure representing a spatial configuration (such as verticality) and/or the various forces that affect a human body (e.g. pressure, gravity, etc.). Crucially, these schemata do not elaborate many aspects of the scene – such as what kinds of objects are located above or below each other. They are "skeletal" – not filled in with rich propositional content – but they help us structure more elaborate concepts in ways linked to experience. Humans share a gravitic environment with other life forms, and are therefore inevitably and (except for astronauts) constantly experiencing Up/Down as part of the spatial structure of our environment. This very schematic structure is instantiated in our experience in many different, more specific situations such as standing up vs. falling down or lying down to sleep, being a toddler and looking upwards towards adults, standing at the top of the stairs and looking down, and so on. And Up/Down seems to be an image schema shared across cultures – unsurprisingly, since all human cultures share a pervasive experience of gravity.

Another image schema which is apparently of major relevance in many cultures is the Container schema, a very schematic cognitive representation which involves an Interior, an Exterior, and a Barrier separating the Interior from the Exterior. Not only do all cultures seem to have containers (bowls, sacks, dwellings), but our bodies are in fact containers (we take air into our lungs, and we take food into our stomachs via our mouths). Again, there are a great many more specific situations which instantiate this schematic structure: being in a crib and trying to get out, being outside a room with a closed door and trying to get in, or opening a box.

We point out here that image schemas are, like categories in general, abstractions from specific instances of experience. Humans never encounter Up/Down schematically, any more than they encounter the "Platonic" cat or book. They encounter specific instances of cats and books, and specific instances of vertical relationships in space, just as they only encounter specific containers from specific viewpoints, never a schematic Container. From these specific instances, they abstract more schematic categories and schemas.

Other basic schemas we could list are Path, Force, Counterforce, Balance, Control, Cycle, In/Out, Center/Periphery, Link, etc. (see Johnson 1987, Lakoff and Johnson 1999). They rely on our very basic sense of the spatial positioning of our body with respect to the environment and also the ways in which the environment may affect us (by exerting force) and call for a counterforce to be applied. It would be a mistake to suggest that we could enumerate human image schemas in some list, but it is important to note that spatial position and force dynamics are central to both our deepest sense of how our bodies function and to the way we experience concepts at higher cognitive levels. It is also important to note that this is an area of cognitive structure which we may well share with other species; many other animals are good at assessing spatial relations, and chimpanzees may lack other human cognitive abilities (such as metaphor), but are excellent at solving spatial problems.

> Image schemas: basic, skeletal conceptual structures emerging out of the spatial and force-dynamic sense of our bodies. They are not fleshed out with propositional content, but participate in the construction and emergence of more elaborate concepts, such as frames.

Image schemas constitute the very most schematic level of conceptualization of experience, but they do connect to frames. They are only the bare bones of frames – they are structural commonalities which can be noticed between richer, more-filled-out frame structures. They are apparently abstracted from experience, which is inevitably richer and more detailed; we never experience a generic container, but only specific ones. The schema for Path is an abstract line which delineates movement from one location to another. But it participates in a wide range of frames. Obviously, it underlies the frame of a Path(way), understood as a visible trail or pathway in space, marked by a different surface, a lack of objects on it, suitability for human use, directionality, etc. But it also underlies the more complex frame of Travel, where the path may be imaginary (an itinerary drawn on a map), or involve means of moving along a path (means of transportation); and the concept of a Race (with two or more trajectors moving along a real or imaginary path towards a destination, each trying to get to the destination faster).

In metaphor analyses, the distinction between different levels of specificity in mapped frames is crucial. We often talk about various forms of competitive behavior in terms of a Race (for example, releasing a product first, publishing research results ahead of others, gaining the affection of a desired person first). But the mapping we would propose would be COMPETITION IS A RACE, not COMPETITION IS A PATH, because the Path schema is a component of the Race frame, and it is the Race frame as a whole which explains the inferences transferred in this metaphor. Path alone does not profile the destination or the participants moving towards the destination in any detail, let alone the desire to get there first; it thus does not give us the relevant inferences about Competition. But the Path schema is a necessary component of the Race frame. The issue is thus the appropriate level of schematicity and complexity – the central consideration in metaphor analysis.

Lakoff and Johnson's claim was that these very schematic structures correlate with other aspects of human experience in ways that result in pervasive metaphoric mappings. Orientational metaphors are an example. Humans very early experience correlations between Up/Down and power, control, or authority. Adult caregivers are larger and taller than small children, and not only loom over them physically but have control over them – a small child's utmost physical efforts cannot prevent a caregiver from carrying him off to bed. The physically lower position of the child correlates with lack of control or authority, and the adult's greater control correlates with greater height. Similarly, the child will learn at a young age that not only does height give a power advantage in a struggle, but being in a higher location (standing on a stair, for example) gives an advantage in a struggle with someone your own size – not to mention that the victor in the struggle will end up on top, the loser at the bottom. The child thus correlates Power with Up. The child will also learn that sleeping people (and, she will eventually discover, dead animals and people) cannot stand upright, while live waking animals and people stand and move around actively; sick people also lie down, and well ones move around upright. Active Functioning is thus correlated with being Up. Happy people are upright and energetic and bouncy, while unhappy people are lethargic and less upright; Happiness is thus correlated with Up and Sadness with Down. And since we prefer, all else being equal, to be alive, healthy, functioning/mobile, winning, happy, and powerful to being dead, sick, immobile, losers in a struggle, sad, and powerless – therefore, from this composite of preferences all correlated with vertical position, GOOD IS UP.

Such correlations in experience also produce metaphoric mappings which have been identified as *Primary Metaphors*. They constitute the topic of the next section.

2.3.2   Primary Metaphors, conflation, and MIND AS BODY mappings

Grady (1997, 1998) and Johnson (1997) developed the Experiential-Correlation Theory of metaphor into an understanding of two closely related concepts: *primary scenes* and Primary Metaphors. Primary scenes are early and pervasive correlations – often specifically between physical experiential input and subjective judgment or assessment. For example, the physical experience of being lower than your adult caregiver correlates with a subjective experience of being less powerful; physical observation of an increase in height of a liquid within the same container correlates with an assessment of increased quantity. Some of these scenes involve highly *valid cues*, in psychologists' terms: we judge height easily, and use it as a cue for the less readily assessable dimension of quantity. This is true in other domains as well as Height: the physical sensation of being warm, for a baby, correlates with affection from caregivers, in the primary scene of cuddling, which involves both warmth and affection. Hence the Primary Metaphor AFFECTION IS WARMTH.

Primary Metaphors result from these primary scenes, as small children pull apart the paired experiences of height and power, or height and quantity. As Johnson observes, there is significant evidence that small children are not think-ing in terms of separate domains in these cases (in contrast to the natural adult ability to distinguish a debate from combat). Height and Quantity is a clear example of a cross-domain correlation which is *conflated* at earlier stages of development; children only gradually learn that they are independent parame-ters, and that water poured from a tall, thin glass to a short, fat glass is the same quantity of water, even though the height is different (this is one of the classic Piagetian "conservation tasks" (Piaget 1985[1975]) used by many psy-chologists to assess children's cognitive development. We can see how easy this conflation would be, particularly for a small child using the same cup every day, so that the height of the liquid was a one-hundred-percent-valid cue for quantity.

> Primary Metaphors: metaphoric mappings emerging directly from correla-
> tions in experience, in primary scenes. Primary Metaphors do not rely on
> frame-rich domains; instead they build on cross-mapping of domains of
> experience (for example, the correlation between volume and verticality
> yields MORE IS UP).

Another crosslinguistically common metaphor, which is also basic to the structure
of English, is KNOWLEDGE IS VISION or KNOWING IS SEEING. The correlation, in
the case of sighted children, is obvious: a great deal of our cognitive assessment
of our surroundings is based on visual experiential input. The visual cortex is very
large, and thanks to links to other areas of the brain, it provides assessments of
likely tactile, motor, and other affordances of objects. Johnson (1997) used data
from the CHILDES corpus to track uses of *see* by and to young children, showing
that early uses referred to both visual and cognitive events: *See the ducks!* means
both 'visually attend to the ducks' and 'be cognitively aware of the ducks'; *Let's
go see what mom's doing* is suggesting that we obtain both visual access to mom
and resulting information about her activity. Only at about eight years of age
do children start using truly metaphoric examples such as *See what I mean?*
where there is nothing to be visually processed and *see* refers only to intellectual
experience. It seems that children do conflate closely correlated parameters of
experience in different domains, and then later pull apart that conflation and
recognize two separable domains.

   Of course, the experiential correlation in the primary scene does not go away
once the children separate the domains. On the contrary, adults constantly use
height of contained liquid as a cue for quantity, and visual experience as a basis
for new cognitive assessments. But for the adult, these correlations are close links
between two distinct frames in two domains. Only then can metaphor be said to
have come into existence.

   An important question is why the direction of these mappings is so frequently
from a physical experiential domain as source to a more subjective one as target. One might here appeal to the needs of communication. Domains such as
Physical Perception are understood (despite philosophical uncertainty about any
actual identity between the qualia of those perceptions) to be relatively intersubjectively accessible, while internal judgments, cognitive states, and emotions are
"invisible," accessible only to the experiencer if not expressed. Why not use the
language of the shared to express what we are not sure is so easily shared with
an addressee?

   But another point made by Lakoff and Johnson (1999) is that, for Primary
Metaphors, the direction of *cuing* parallels that of metaphoric mapping. And
this is true even in cases where both of the two domains are physical, such as
MORE IS UP. Both volume and height are physical parameters. But we constantly
and easily judge height and find it an easy cue for volume when the container
is a constant, while we do not use an assessment of three-dimensional volume

(which is much harder to judge) as a cue for the assessment of height. This is equally true for the physical/subjective or concrete/abstract mappings, such as KNOWING IS SEEING: infants quite early learn to follow adult gaze and visual attention, and then to direct adults to share attention with them. This is naturally often a clue as to the cognitive input being processed by the person looking, while cognitive input is not accessible as a cue to visual data. The same might be true of AFFECTION IS WARMTH, POWER IS UP, and other Primary Metaphors; it is exactly the asymmetric cognitive use of these primary scenes which leads to asymmetric cognitive connection, and (by hypothesis) to asymmetric metaphoric mappings. The relationship of abstract and concrete domains in metaphor will be further discussed in Section 3.4.

Well before Grady's and Johnson's work on Primary Metaphors, it had been noted (Lakoff and Johnson 1980, Sweetser 1984, 1990) that many pervasive metaphors involve understanding a more abstract domain in terms of a more concrete one (for an extensive discussion of this pattern, see Chapter 3). Given Grady's and Johnson's hypotheses about paired physical and subjective-experiential structures, we would expect Primary Metaphors specifically to have this asymmetry. And we might restate this, as Sweetser suggested and Grady and Johnson argue, as understanding a more subjective and less mutually accessible domain in terms of a more intersubjectively accessible domain. I can see what you see (and that you see it), but not what you know (or that you know it).

Lakoff and Johnson (1980, 1999) presented a wealth of examples of social and cognitive structure being understood in terms of physical experience; Sweetser (1984, 1990) gave the family label MIND IS BODY metaphors to some of these. However, it is certainly not the case that MIND IS BODY could ever have been thought of as a single systematic set of mappings. To give an example of the problems this would pose, let's look at KNOWING IS SEEING (*I see what you mean*) and UNDERSTANDING IS GRASPING (*I caught on to what she meant, I grasped the general idea*) side-by-side. The frames of Seeing, Grasping, Knowing, and Understanding are more complex than skeletal image schemata; rather, they are generic event or situation structures, with familiar roles and relations.

Tables 2.1 and 2.2 show the mappings between Seeing and Knowing, and between Grasping and Understanding. In a multiframed scenario which is more

Table 2.1 *Selected mappings from Seeing to Knowing*

Source: Seeing	Target: Knowing
Visual experiencer	Knower
Objects/events seen	Content known
Light source	Factors enabling knowledge
Barriers to vision	Impediments to knowledge

Table 2.2 *Selected mappings from Grasping to Understanding*

Source: Grasping	Target: Understanding
Grasper	Understander
Objects grasped	Ideas understood
Firm grasp or hold (*I have a firm grasp of that theory.*)	Good understanding
Catching hold of object (*I caught on to the idea.*)	Coming to understand
Loss of grip on object (*I thought I understood, but it slipped away.*)	Loss of understanding
Failure to grasp	Failure to understand

complex than the schemas examined by Johnson (1997), a person might well (1) hold an object specifically in order to (2) visually inspect it, and *thus* to (3) find out more about it; it is even possible that these three domains are partially conflated in some infant experience (consider babies grabbing their toes in order to look at them, as they explore their bodies). But you don't necessarily need a light source to grasp something firmly; nor do you need to use hands to see a well-lit object. So if you grasp something, it doesn't necessarily follow that you see it, or vice versa. These metaphors are not parts of a single coherent mapping of mind to body: rather, they are two distinct mappings, where the frame of physical vision is mapped onto that of knowledge acquisition, and where the frame of grasping physical objects is mapped onto that of comprehension. This includes mapping of causal and aspectual structure: your causal control over holding onto an object corresponds to your control over a concept you understand, and coming to understand something is catching hold of an object when you didn't previously have hold of it, while ceasing to understand something is losing hold of an object. Seeing is about visual access, and that access could be removed at any point if the source of light fails; KNOWLEDGE IS VISION maps causal and aspectual parallels here too. This is why *Light dawns* or *I'm starting to see* don't imply as much causal control over one's own knowledge or understanding as *getting a firm grasp* does.

Furthermore, even within our visual experience, there are a number of separate structured frames, and not all of these are mapped. As we noted above (and despite the label), it is not all of vision, but specifically the visual frame of a light source shedding light on objects, which is mapped in KNOWLEDGE IS VISION – not, for example, the assessment of ambient light in a space. The mapping is quite coherent; it can be extended to talk about *opaque* vs. *illuminating* presentations (the latter *shed new light* on some content). But the source frame is all about whether light from a source reaches an object, not about general ambient light.

Emotions are another area where subjective experiences are frequently described in terms of (often correlated) bodily experiences. Anger is perhaps the best-explored example in English, with studies by Kövecses (1986, 2000) and Lakoff (1987). It seems clear that a pervasive metaphor in English is ANGER

Table 2.3 *Selected mappings from Container to Self*

Source: Container	*Target:* Self
Liquid contents	Emotions
Heat, pressure	Anger
Degree of heat, pressure	Degree of anger
Allowing steam to escape	Expressing anger
Explosion	Sudden, violent rage

IS HEAT AND PRESSURE OF A CONTAINED LIQUID. An angry person can be said to be *simmering, boiling,* or *steaming with rage*; and in the end this person might *blow her top* or *explode*. It is indeed the case that body heat and blood pressure rise in angry people, which is the basic experiential correlation. However, of course they don't rise to boiling, steam-producing levels which could physically harm adjacent people. It is the *social* expression of anger which is *socially* harmful to adjacent people, just as escaping heat and steam from an exploding container are *physically* harmful. Table 2.3. shows some of the mappings involved in this metaphor.

As Lakoff points out, there is not just physical structure but inferential structure being mapped here; many Americans believe that *venting* or *letting off steam* (expressing anger in a "safe" way, often not to the person you're angry with) will help prevent serious social damage from uncontrolled *explosions* of anger. This is mapped from the source domain, where letting off pressure in a controlled way may prevent explosions of a heated pressurized liquid. Not all cultures believe that expressing anger in a controlled setting helps prevent social conflict; this metaphor would not work for them, since the source-domain frame of Pressurized Liquid is not culturally variable in the same way, and therefore might give rise to culturally wrong inferences about the target domain of Anger.

The role of experience may affect the mapping in more partial ways as well. Other metaphors of anger include ANGER/AN ANGRY PERSON IS A WILD BEAST; one can immediately see that the inferences here are very different, since you won't make a wild beast less dangerous by letting it growl, for example. You just have to protect people from it, or cage it. So the inference here might be that people should not show anger. Note, however, that the pervasive SELF IS A CONTAINER mapping surfaces here too: you would need to keep your anger *shut up inside* if it were a beast. The Self is also a container of knowledge (which is "in" your head), of emotions at large (*What do you feel inside you?*) and other aspects of cognitive/emotional experience. Thus the example shows that correlations in experience are not necessarily found only in Primary Metaphors, but may constitute a part of metaphoric mappings in which richer frames (such as Pressure Cooker or Wild Beast) are used. We will return in Chapter 3 to the relationship between more general mappings such as SELF IS A CONTAINER and more specific metaphoric mappings. And in Section 2.3.4, we will explore how metaphoric mappings (and especially Primary Metaphors) can influence patterns of meaning change.

2.3.3   "Two-directional" metaphors

How basic to metaphor is this idea of asymmetric, unidirectional mapping? We have just been arguing that, for Primary Metaphors, there is an inherent asymmetry between human experiences of the source and target areas: MORE IS UP is a cognitive universal, and UP IS MORE is not, precisely because humans necessarily assess quantity in terms of vertical height and not the reverse. The traditional idea that metaphor is using language from one domain to talk about another certainly sounds unidirectional; even though it is talking only about cross-domain linguistic usage rather than referring to cognitive mappings, it still conceives of the relationship as an asymmetric one. But many traditional understandings of metaphor also describe it as involving some kind of *similarity* between the two domains, which sounds much less asymmetric. Of course, similarity is itself a viewpointed and asymmetric phenomenon – that is, it typically involves a landmark against which something is compared. It seems more ordinary to say *Sue looks like her mom* than *Sue's mom looks like her*, because we think of parent–child resemblance as a comparison of the child to the parent, both because the parent's genetic makeup is assumed to cause the child's and because a small child's rapidly changing appearance is not as good a landmark as the adult's more stable one. But in the right context, choices of landmark may shift, and when Sue's mom comes past the college dormitory to pick up her daughter, a friend may recognize her because *She looks like Sue*, whom the friend already knows and is using as a landmark. And furthermore, anyone talking about resemblance, no matter which person is the landmark, will be pointing out actual features of Sue's and her mother's appearances which are *in common* between the two (they're both tall, or short; both long-nosed, or short-nosed).

But are metaphoric mappings as reversible as literal comparisons? The answer is no. Let's take a look at a metaphor which might seem to be "reversible." PEOPLE ARE COMPUTERS and COMPUTERS ARE PEOPLE might be taken as such a case, given that I can say *my memory banks are scrambled* to mean that I'm confused, and also say that *My computer is being stubborn and difficult today.* These are both real metaphors – and they are a clear example of the problems with talking about metaphor as always being "from concrete to abstract." Both computers and people are physical entities, and both have a lot of abstract structure which is not directly physically experienced but may be inferred from their behavior.

However, better labels for these two metaphors might be HUMAN COGNITIVE PROCESSING IS COMPUTER INFORMATION PROCESSING and APPARENTLY ERRATIC ASPECTS OF COMPUTER BEHAVIOR ARE EMOTIONAL MOOD-BASED ASPECTS OF HUMAN BEHAVIOR. The single most important and pervasive metaphor for human cognition is computer processing; this metaphor has filtered from the expert artificial-intelligence community into popular use. Even though extremely complex software systems can't be understood completely by any one human cognizer, the designers of computer systems still understand computer processing and information retrieval better than anyone understands human reasoning and memory. So this is an alluring metaphor.

On the other hand, apparently inexplicable or erratic responses from computer systems, although ultimately explicable (we assume) in terms of hardware, software, and differences in human input, are in the immediate situation problematic: why did the computer "do something different" when I "did the same thing" as input? And as humans, we have extensive experience of indidivual humans responding differently to the same input at different times – and knowing what makes our own responses variable, we ascribe some of other humans' behavioral variability to moods, differences in emotional state. This makes moods or whims a cognitive "handle," or at least a coping mechanism, for frustrated humans dealing with variable responses from computers. Of course, it is a limited coping mechanism, since basically the only strategy transferable from human moods is to accept that they happen, and hence to accept that computers won't respond consistently. Other human mood-coping strategies don't help much, since the average frustrated nontechie will not be able to imagine strategies for "cajoling the computer out of its bad mood."

The point here is that we do not try to understand human *emotional response* in terms of computer structure (although we may mock humans who are not emotionally responsive by calling their behavior *robotic*). And even though computers are anthropomorphized via some of the same cognitive mechanisms which are applied to other kinds of objects and systems, what is primarily being mapped are *specific frames* related to humans and computers. Those are not the same frames for the HUMANS ARE COMPUTERS mappings as for the COMPUTERS ARE HUMANS mappings.

2.3.4   Metaphoric meaning change

One of the most important and established achievements of linguistics in the 1980s and 1990s was the recognition of well-worn paths in meaning change. And some of these are one-way streets. As mentioned in Chapter 1, over and over again in the Indo-European language family and in many other languages outside it, words meaning 'see' have come to mean 'know,' but words for cognition don't come to mean physical vision – or grasping (Sweetser 1990). Similarly, Fleischman (1982) recognized a Romance-language pattern in which GO + INFINITIVE comes to mean Future Tense, a pattern also found in English *gonna*; again, the reverse does not happen. The former semantic trend appears to exemplify the KNOWLEDGE IS VISION metaphor, and the latter the Event Structure Metaphor (discussed in detail in Chapter 3).

It seems clear that many of the best-recognized "superhighways" of meaning change are precisely cases where meanings are related by Primary Metaphors – that is, they are cases where there is a strong correlation between the two meanings. However, once a metaphor is productively in place, it seems clear that no specific situational correlation is needed for a new metaphoric meaning of a particular form to emerge. For a language with a strong KNOWLEDGE IS VISION metaphor, the use of the basic vision verb to mean 'know' or 'understand' may still have its developmental origin in experiential conflation of domains, only later emerging in older children's usage as metaphoric – that is, as referring exclusively to the cognitive rather than the visual domain. But once that mapping is broadly productive for a speaker, it seems highly unlikely that uses like *sheds light on an issue* are being derived from experiential correlation between light emission and theoretical clarification; rather, uses like this – and other uses of visual vocabulary such as *illuminating discussion, transparent motives*, and *opaque prose* – are metaphorically motivated by the overall pervasive and entrenched metaphoric mapping between the two domains.

This is not of course to say that individual meaning changes within particular languages can only move in the directions seen in these strong historical trends. It is crucial to realize that there are multiple possible metaphoric construals of any important target domain, both within and across languages. Although, crosslinguistically, KNOWLEDGE IS VISION seems not only common but also pervasive, Evans and Wilkins (1998; see also Wilkins 1996) have shown that in some Australian languages verbs of hearing are more commonly used to refer to knowledge and comprehension than verbs of seeing. This contrasts with the uses of verbs of hearing in Semitic and Indo-European languages, where (as Sweetser [1990] pointed out) they often develop into meanings related to successful social "understanding" and obedience, more than into meanings related to content comprehension. But of course, although vision is the very top overall data-gathering sense for sighted humans, hearing correlates well specifically with information intake via language. So both correlations are primary ones, but the Vision–Knowledge correlation is even stronger, and it is no surprise that it turns up in so many of the world's languages. Similarly, although motion in space correlates with changing time for all humans – as an entity moves along a path, successive locations correspond to successive temporal moments – we shall see in Chapter 7 that different aspects of this correlation motivate different metaphors of time, and indeed many languages have more than one such system (as Lakoff and Johnson pointed out, English says both *We're coming to the end of the semester* and *The end of the semester's coming up*).

It is also important to remember that a productive metaphor only motivates expanded uses of of forms; it does not force historical-change processes to spread a new meaning to the level of a broad convention, nor to erase an earlier meaning. As Traugott (1982, 1989) and Hopper and Traugott (1993) have pointed out, older literal meanings very frequently coexist for long periods of time with their metaphoric counterparts: conventional English uses like *I see* or *opaque prose* have not wiped out the visual meanings of *see* and *opaque*, nor has the *gonna* future wiped out the deictic-motion sense of the verb *go*. And motivation of extensions is one thing; conventionalization of those extensions is another. Even in the case of a very basic shared metaphoric mapping between domains, individual lexical items may have their own historical developments. As mentioned in Chapter 1, in English, the Indo-European **weid-* root meaning 'see' has given rise to both *witness* (which still retains a visual sense, of someone who actually saw an event) and *wit* (which now has no visual sense, but only a cognitive one). We might say that in modern English, almost any linguistic form related to vision can be understood in some usage as referring to cognition. *Political astigmatism*, *theoretical blinders*, and other metaphoric uses attest to this. But every extension is not a new conventional word meaning. Do we want to list in a dictionary a special sense of *peripheral vision* because we can understand such a usage as *Joe's great asset as a stockbroker is his peripheral vision; he can always see the trends in other areas of the market that are going to affect the area he's dealing in?*

As we have just noted in the case of *wit*, a particular word may lose its source-domain meaning and thereby refer only to one domain (the original target domain); that is, it may lose the metaphoric motivations for its meaning, even while the general metaphor remains productive. Of course, reanalysis of a linguistic form – particularly in the case of borrowing between languages – may also cut off its original metaphoric motivation. Lakoff and Turner's (1989) classic example of this is English *pedigree*, which comes from the French *pied-de-grue* 'crane's foot,' an image metaphor for the shape of a genealogical tree. Since English speakers mostly did not know that this French form meant 'crane's foot,' they only conventionalized the target-domain meaning 'genealogy' and the metaphor was lost.

In still other cases, a culture can lose a metaphor which was once active (either locally or with broader productivity), and thus cut off word meanings from their original metaphoric motivations. An example of this might be the Italian *cardinale* (used, like English *cardinal*, for both 'cardinal numbers' and Cardinals of the Catholic church), which has a clear relationship to the Italian *cardine* 'hinge.' General Primary Metaphors might still meaningfully link these words (DEPENDENCE IS PHYSICAL SUPPORT; hinges *support* doors, and other numbers *depend on* cardinal numbers for their definition?). But most Italian speakers cannot reconstruct the Roman image metaphor that initially gave rise to these meanings: the *main* road through a Roman military camp was called the *via cardinalis*, because it divided the square camp into two halves like those of a hinge. Hence *cardinale* came to mean 'primary, most important.'

Far from being the only force involved in meaning change, metaphor is one of many – and other forces may obscure its results. (Later chapters in this book will talk about some of those other forces.) When an etymological metaphoric motivation is no longer accessible to speakers for a given word (though of course, this accessibility may differ between speakers at a given time), we can say that a particular metaphoric connection is "dead" for that lexical item. This is an entirely separate question from the general productivity of the metaphor within the language: the fact that *wit* no longer has a visual sense does not diminish the general productivity of KNOWLEDGE IS VISION in English.

In this book, we cannot try to offer a fuller account of the role of metaphor in meaning change, but the cases discussed above should make it clear that salient mappings, especially when supported by correlations in experience, affect polysemy patterns in important ways. The examples discussed above also raise an important issue. We are explaining the emergence of metaphors, including their motivation through correlations in experience. This might make someone think that because these correlations are shared among humans, the mappings could also be expected to be universal. Indeed, certain metaphoric pathways of meaning change have been described as "superhighways" precisely because of the pervasiveness of experiential roots of such changes. But no linguist we know would expect patterns of polysemy to be universal. As in other areas of the study of metaphor, in this case we are talking about meanings being *motivated* – but this does not mean they are predictable. Correlations in experience *motivate* the emergence of new meanings in various languages, and when we examine the correlations in detail, we can talk about the patterns that emerge.

2.4   Conventional or creative?

Before reading this book, some of our readers may have assumed that many of the examples we have looked at so far are so conventional that they no longer count as metaphor. Many people associate the term *metaphor* with a figurative, possibly literary, trope, in opposition to colloquial, literal, everyday use of language. It might seem that *I see your point* cannot be metaphoric because it does not feel poetic or novel in any way – it is, in fact, one of the most worn-out expressions in English. Perhaps an even stronger example might be the temporal uses of spatial prepositions (*from nine to five, at three* PM), which are not simply highly conventional, but often indeed the only way to refer to such temporal relations.

However, we argued in Chapter 1 that the distinction between literal and figurative language, as it has been used both by literary analysts and other researchers, is misleading, or heavily dependent on the a priori definition of literalness as pedestrian and figurativeness as remarkable. Like literal language, figurative language is necessarily grounded in experience and cognition; the difference is in the structure of the grounding relations. Metaphor involves two conceptual structures and a set of projections between them, while metonymy, personification, irony, hyperbole, synesthesia, and oxymoron rely on different, but equally conceptually motivated, patterns. It is the presence of this inter-frame mapping pattern (once we describe it) that determines whether a linguistic expression is metaphoric or not. Also, as we suggested in Section 2.3, we can examine how these patterns motivate synchronic polysemy patterns, independently of our examination of how they motivated past meaning changes – though we are bound to find similarities since polysemy patterns are the results of historical extensions of meaning.

The level of conventionality of an expression is a criterion totally independent of the nature of figurative thought and language. Some of the conceptual patterns we call metaphor are fully conventionalized, for example when calling independent-study educational material a *study guide*. The expression relies on the domain of Travel, where the presence of a guide simplifies the process of reaching the destination; in the domain of Studying, reaching a satisfactory level of knowledge and understanding can be facilitated by appropriate texts, so they can be called *guides*. But the same pattern can be used in a less predictable context, as when Romeo addresses the vial containing poison as *bitter conduct* and *unsavoury guide* (Romeo and Juliet V.iii.116). This usage would be generally recognized as a metaphoric expression. Romeo is committing suicide, and so the poison is metaphorically going to "lead" him to death, his Purpose and hence his metaphoric Destination. So the metaphor is appropriate, but this is not a typical construal of what poison does. In these two instances, the same pattern explains two expressions that differ widely in their level of conventionality.

Idioms are another important area of interest for studying the relationship between conventionality and metaphoric structure. Many idioms are metaphoric. Some are so obscure in history as to be completely opaque to contemporary users, e.g. *red herring*, while others retain some aspects of their metaphoric roots, e.g. *let sleeping dogs lie*, where the concept of not disturbing a bodily state such as sleep (associated with inaction, lack of communication) is used to talk about problems which we prefer not to bring to activity at the moment. Although idioms may be processed as indivisible wholes, analyzable idioms have been shown to evoke both source and target domains in processing (Gibbs 1994): processing *spill the beans* evokes an image of a container and beans, not just the target-domain concept of Revealing Secrets. This is a clear case of a hyperconventional usage which is evidently still metaphoric. If the image metaphor originally motivating *pedigree* is dead (as argued above) because English speakers can no longer access its source domain, *spill the beans* is not dead but remains metaphoric.

Conventionalized metaphors have often been termed "dead," presumably because the patterns they represent no longer motivate *new* expressions. But, as Müller (2008) has observed, all metaphor use relies on a certain level of activation in the context of use, and so such metaphors are often better described as "sleeping," as they can easily awaken and become newly productive. This is certainly true of ordinary conventional metaphors such as KNOWING IS SEEING, but even in the case of idioms, which are presumed "dead," we can imagine someone saying something like *The cat is now out of the bag; and a big, ugly cat it is too*. In such cases, the opaque conceptual pattern is revived to be enhanced – reactivated – with a level of detail not typically present in the expression. This shows that, though dormant, the pattern is still alive.

2.5   Experimental support for Cognitive Metaphor Theory

The question of conventionality, as outlined above, touches upon another important theoretical conundrum: for conventional cases where clear polysemy exists between original source- and target-domain senses (as with *I see the cat* and *I see what you mean* in English), what is the cognitive reality of the polysemy relationship? From the beginning, experimental psychologists have been interested in testing the cognitive claims made by Cognitive (or Conceptual) Metaphor Theory. At the same time, many linguists – among others – have found it extremely hard to believe that, in particular, idiomatic or fixed metaphoric usages were "live" metaphors, and processed as such. How could processing *high quantity* or *prices rose* really involve an active conceptual processing of vertical height? Surely (the argument was) that is just the normal (hence literal) way we talk about quantity-change, even if less conventional usages like *went through the stratosphere* might have a bit more vertical conceptual content, and actually involve mapping between frames.

But there are a number of serious problems with this noncognitive view of conventional metaphors. One is that if the everyday idiomatic metaphors are not "conceptual" but just linguistic, we need some other explanation for how they help us to understand related novel and poetic metaphors. English readers faced with the sentence *It would take an electron microscope to find the point of that paper* readily figure out that the point of the paper (1) is difficult to know or identify and (2) may also be insignificant or unimportant once identified. A simple hypothesis would be that such usages are piggy-backing on the cognitive structure used in dealing with more conventional usages like *It's a small point* (UNIMPORTANT IS SMALL) or *It's hard to see your point* (KNOWING IS SEEING). If they are not, then we need a special cognitive theory of metaphor for the creative uses – and it also means they are very unlike other creative aspects of language use, which generally do play on or extend conventional structures.

Experimental psychologists and psycholinguists have begun to test the cognitive reality of metaphoric usage. Gibbs (1994) was among the first to test processing of metaphoric idioms, and he found quite solid evidence that subjects were processing source-domain images as well as target-domain meanings. For example, he gave subjects similar stories about someone with a secret, one of which ended *He let the cat out of the bag* and the other *He spilled the beans*. Knowing that these sentences referred to revealing the secret, and knowing that in that target domain the revelation is irreversible, subjects who heard *spilled the beans* reported images of messy, goopy beans or widely scattered beans, which could not be picked up and put back into the can or pot. Gibbs also showed that subjects processed metaphoric sentences such as *She blew her top faster* if the story had earlier included other vocabulary referring not just to anger, but in particular to the Heat/Pressure metaphor for Anger (e.g. *She was simmering*).

The same sentence was processed more slowly if the preceding story had instead included other activations of the Anger frame (e.g. describing the character as pacing or growling). If *blow one's top* is simply a literal description of anger, with no metaphoric connection to the domain of Heat and Pressure, it is hard to see why it should be differentially primed specifically by other expressions involving metaphoric usage of heat and pressure vocabulary to refer to anger.

More recently, there have been even stronger lab results suggesting that metaphoric source and target domains are cognitively linked to each other. For example, Boroditsky (2000) and Boroditsky and Ramscar (2002) have shown that, at least for experientially based metaphors, an experience in the source domain will prime particular choices of mapping to a target domain; in this case, they found that actual physical-motion experiences (with no linguistic expression related to time or space) affect subjects' choice of time metaphors. We will cover Boroditsky's results in more detail in Chapter 7, where we will be discussing the conceptualization of time across modalities and languages. Other investigations of the role of spatial cognition have also consistently demonstrated its role in processing abstract concepts. Matlock (2004) has shown that reading about actual physical journeys with different characteristics (driving along a straight, easy road as opposed to a long, winding road through a wilderness) affects the time that subjects take to process very conventional metaphoric motion usages. *The road runs from X to Y* involves no literal motion, only so-called *virtual* or *fictive* motion, but such a sentence nonetheless takes longer to read if you've just read about a long, hard trip. This suggests that subjects are engaging in imagined visual scanning of spatial motion to process this metaphoric motion.

Looking at the cognitive connection between verticality and emotion, Casasanto and Dijkstra (2010) asked subjects to move marbles downwards from a higher rack to a lower one, or alternatively upwards from a lower rack to a higher one, while telling stories about their childhoods. They told happier stories when moving the marbles upwards, and sadder ones when moving them downwards (metaphorically, HAPPY IS UP, SAD IS DOWN). Similarly Williams and Bargh (2008) found that subjects given a warm drink are more likely to say that they like a person they are introduced to during the experiment, as opposed to subjects given a cold drink (AFFECTION IS WARMTH), and Jostman et al. (2009) found that people handed heavy objects to hold are more likely to judge a new opinion they are exposed to as important than people holding a light object (SIGNIFICANCE IS WEIGHT). These abstract/concrete correlations in actual behavior are giving much support to the hypothesized cognitive nature of metaphoric mappings.

In his recent account of the ways our brains respond to language, Bergen (2012) gives an overview of brain-imaging studies which appear to show mixed results. It seems to be generally the case that literal meaning is simulated in the brain; that is, processing a literal description of letting a cat out of a bag will activate centers for processing motion in space, etc. In some contexts, subjects respond in the same way to hearing or reading motion expressions used metaphorically, but in other cases the motor areas suggested by the source-domain language do not "light up" in the brain. Possible explanations for the non-activation include a certain level of "bleaching" of idiomatic expressions (which would stand in contrast to the studies by Gibbs summarized above) and differences in how the stimuli are processed under different conditions. It was observed that source-domain simulation effects are more likely to occur in the brain when sentences are presented more incrementally, so the speed with which the linguistic expressions are processed appears to be a factor. But, perhaps more importantly, the kinds of simulation involved may be different. If we hear or read about grasping actual physical objects, the brain can simulate the situation in all its rich detail, including the concrete object being grasped (a key, or a glass, or a book). But when we hear or read about *grasping an idea*, this usage probably does not trigger a fully simulated image of an object. Bergen's conclusion is that simulations of metaphoric expressions in the brain are *weaker* – because less richly simulated – than simulations of fully concrete situations. However, it is clear that there is some observable effect in the brain. Obviously – and, we could add, as always – more studies need to be done.

Overall, it seems clear that, at least in many specific cases – particularly cases involving Primary Metaphors in particular – there is strong evidence of co-activation of source and target domains in cognition. This includes examples such as HAPPY IS UP, AFFECTION IS WARMTH – and, as we shall see in Chapter 7, temporal metaphors such as FUTURE EVENTS ARE MOVING TOWARDS EGO. Interestingly, much less work has been done on the processing of highly creative poetic metaphors – so in fact, we have the clearest evidence for cognitive reality in cases which were originally thought to be so conventional as to be essentially literal. This does not of course mean that any given metaphoric mapping is accessible for every speaker; any of the factors mentioned in the previous section (linguistic or cultural) could cut off access to metaphoric aspects of meaning.

But experimental work does show clearly that, in the relevant cognitive domains, the metaphoric connection is not just linguistic; it is cognitive. Patterns of mapping exist independently of linguistic evocation: warm or cold drinks, or heavy objects, evoke social like or dislike and cognitive importance, with no linguistic mention of the source domain. It is true that many of the same observations have been made specifically about the processing of linguistic forms: brain areas associated with one domain are activated by language from another. But language is only one of the possible ways of evoking a cognitive metaphoric mapping. In Chapters 5 and 7, we will further discuss the ways in which these cognitive forms show up in visual and other nonlinguistic media.

2.6   What is transferred between source and target?

In ending this chapter, we pause to revisit the relationship between source and target domains. We said above that it probably would not be useful to have a metaphor treating argument as putting on one's makeup, or drinking coffee, rather than as war or combat. Intuitively, a workable metaphor needs source and target domains that "match," for mappings to work out. In Chapter 3, we'll talk in more detail about how those mappings work. But certain constraints seem clear: for example, the temporal structure of the two domains has to be compatible, and mapped appropriately (we can't map the *end* of a combat onto the *beginning* of an argument, or vice versa). Correlated scales also often seem to shape mappings. For example, the full scale of possible levels of liquid in a container and the full scale of possible volume quantities for the contents of a container are already correlated in experience, so of course the top Height level in MORE IS UP corresponds to the greatest Quantity.

Nonetheless, for a salient abstract domain, humans often end up with a multiplicity of metaphors, all of which are apparently workable. And different metaphors for the same target domain can produce quite different inferences, as we saw in thinking about different metaphors for Anger. If ANGER IS HEAT AND PRESSURE OF CONTAINED LIQUID, then "venting" your anger is good, since letting off excess pressure in a hydraulic system is good; if ANGER IS A DANGEROUS WILD BEAST, perhaps it would be better to conquer or kill the animal, and therefore better to control or destroy your anger. With conventional metaphors like these two for Anger, we may be so used to the inferences that we don't stop to ask whether they are inferences about the Anger frame on its own or whether they are "imported" inferences from the relevant source frame.

We argued in Chapter 1 that viewpoint is an inherent part of metaphoric usage. In concluding this chapter, we would like to discuss in more depth the ways in which viewpoint interacts with, and is produced by, metaphoric mappings. Metaphor is not just thinking but *reasoning* about one domain in terms of another. As we have argued, metaphoric mappings crucially involve mapping not just objects and qualities and relations, but also inferences about causes, results, and other aspects of the structure of the two domains. *Viewpoint* on a situation does affect inferential structure, so viewpoint on a source domain should affect which inferences are mappable to the target.

As we pointed out in Section 2.3.2, our metaphoric understanding that ANGER IS HEAT/PRESSURE OF A CONTAINED FLUID leads to a whole list of inferences. The degree of anger is the degree of heat and pressure; this kind of mapping between two scales, like that in MORE IS UP, is often called a *paired-scale* mapping (Lakoff and Johnson 1999). Since the higher the pressure, the greater the danger of an explosion, the inference is that the more intense the anger, the greater the risk of socially upsetting behavior. If pressure can be relieved harmlessly through release of gas or liquid from the container, a potentially harmful explosion can be avoided; so if anger is expressed in a socially harmless way (perhaps not to the person it is directed at), social damage might be avoided. Therefore, *venting your feelings* can be a good thing. And, as we commented above, a culture which did not think expressing negative feelings was a good idea at all would not find this metaphoric model's inferences appropriate.

An important question, and one less frequently addressed, is *whose* inferences are involved? In the exploding-boiler frame, viewpoint is almost automatically aligned with the person who doesn't want the boiler to explode; this is no surprise, since very few people deliberately explode boilers, and those that do are not seen as behaving normatively. Viewpoint cannot be readily aligned with the boiler, which has no consciousness and doesn't care. In the Anger frame, however, there are multiple possible alignments. The person at whom anger is directed does not want a socially disruptive expression of that anger, and bystanders are often upset by such disruption as well. But the anger scenario involves a history where the angry person sees herself as having been harmed in some way by the person at whom the anger is directed. The angry person's viewpoint may therefore be that the guilty party *deserves* to suffer social disruption in retaliation for doing past harm – and in a given case, some bystanders might take this viewpoint too. However, by seeing anger as the heat and pressure of contained liquid, we are pushed into taking the viewpoint of those who object to the social disruption, against the viewpoint of those who think it justified.

Another such case is the attested example which Lakoff cites as one of the original sparks leading to the writing of *Metaphors we live by*. In the late 1970s, a woman student in a Berkeley classroom expressed distress because her boyfriend had said their relationship was *a dead-end street*. It was instantly obvious to everyone in the classroom that this was a negative judgment of the relationship – hence the girlfriend's distress. Stepping back, however, one might wonder why that should be. In a rental listing, location on a dead-end street (or cul-de-sac) might be seen as a plus – dead-ends may be quiet places with less traffic and pollution. Some American neighborhoods have even built street barriers on small residential streets that effectively create dead-ends for cars while maintaining through streets for bicyclists and pedestrians. So from the viewpoint of a resident, a dead-end might well be associated with desirable inferences.

But of course, the drivers who can't get through those street barriers are less happy than the residents; *they* see the dead-ends as a problem. And indeed, as Lakoff and Johnson (1980) documented, that entire Berkeley class clearly understood the boyfriend to be taking the viewpoint of a traveler trying to get through. The Event Structure Metaphor, in particular the subcase LIFE IS A JOURNEY, was in play. When you have turned into a dead-end street by mistake, you are frustrated because you cannot go any further in the direction you were trying to go; your physical movement towards that goal is impeded, and you may be forced to turn back in order to look for another route which will take you in the desired direction. A RELATIONSHIP IS A SHARED JOURNEY, and therefore involves shared life goals (PURPOSES ARE DESTINATIONS); the boyfriend is apparently seeing the relationship as one which does not allow Progress towards Purposes, and feels he may need to stop participating in the relationship (abandon the joint journey, by stopping being co-located with the fellow-traveler) in order to make progress towards at least his personal goals.

The subconscious complexities of metaphoric inferential transfer are particularly on display in this example. No wonder the girlfriend felt cognitively trapped. To counter the boyfriend's inferences, she would have had to unpack all this metaphoric structure, which flowed smoothly and automatically from his chosen mapping, given their culture's conventional metaphoric understandings of Life and Relationships. We might add that Lakoff and Johnson (1980) didn't suggest the resident's viewpoint on dead-ends as a contrasting option – naturally enough, since the traveler's viewpoint was so obviously the one in play in the actual dialogue reported by the girlfriend. The processing of metaphoric linguistic usages, like that of most linguistic usages, is largely done below the conscious level, and this is why it enables such insidious inferential transfers.

2.7   Conclusions

As Lakoff and Johnson (1999) emphasized, metaphor is neither a special "superrational" artistic mode of thought nor a "subrational" artistic muddling of understandings which might be better modeled more literally. It is part and parcel of our everyday rationality; it reflects reasoning patterns and viewpoint. Conventional metaphors are inferential "shortcuts" in everyday reasoning. New metaphors are of course creative, but since they are shaping basic reasoning patterns, that creativity can turn out to be brilliant science, as well as brilliant art.

Above all, metaphor is a cognitive phenomenon. It is reflected in visual art (graphs whose lines go downwards for diminished quantity, for example) as well as in general cognitive patterns – more of which will be discussed in the course of the book. It has been of particular interest to linguists and literary scholars, however, because of the pervasive metaphoric linguistic patterns which express cognitive metaphoric mappings. Literary scholars have been more interested in creative and novel metaphoric uses, and linguists in regular and conventional ones, but linguistic change is constantly turning more novel instances into conventional ones, so they are part and parcel of the same fabric.

In Chapter 3 we will explore the ways in which metaphors are related to each other and combined with each other productively. In that discussion, it will be important to remember that metaphors can normally combine only if their inferences are compatible and their broader structural mappings are not in conflict. We will necessarily be drawing on our discussion of schemas and frames, as we examine what makes for compatibility.

2.8   Summary

In this chapter we have given a broad introduction to figurative mappings to be discussed in detail in the chapters to follow. Primarily, we have highlighted the following points:

- figurative construals depend on preexisting knowledge structures called frames; consequently, the processing of such usage relies on general understanding of

meanings evoked by linguistic expressions, but also on the re-construal of
meanings for figurative purposes

- links between frames and domains exist on multiple levels of schematicity;
analyzing figurative meanings requires that schematic levels be clearly recognized
- figurative forms do not depend only on specific frames and patterns, but also
on more schematic and experientially motivated aspects of meaning (image
schemas, primary scenes); this adds an important level of schematicity, but
also helps us understand the link between language and cognition
- at the same time, some figurative patterns are conventionally fixed in language
use, leading to figuratively based patterns of polysemy
- finally, experiments investigating figurative forms help us see their connection
to literal meanings on the one hand, and their different status on the other.

3   Metaphoric structure: levels and relations

We have shown that metaphors map structure and inferences between domains, but *how* does this happen? What relationships have to exist between the domains, and how do humans build mappings systematically between them? And – crucially for any metaphor analyst – what are the relationships among the metaphors themselves? Such relationships are the topic of this chapter. We will first consider the levels of schematicity which various mappings operate at, and look at how metaphoric mappings combine. We will then return to discussing the various ways in which metaphor structures and connects abstract and concrete concepts.

One thing which needs to be clear from the start is that specificity and concreteness are two quite different parameters. *Tree* and *black oak* are equally concrete object names, but *black oak* names a more specific and elaborated subcategory of the more general category of *trees*. Similarly, *ponder* is more specific than *think*, though both are equally abstract. Relationships between metaphors are largely *categorial* relationships between more and less specific mappings, or relationships between mappings which are both subcases of the same more general mapping. But this is made more complex, as we shall see, by the fact that a single specific metaphor may be a subcase of more than one more general metaphor; these will be called *complex metaphors*. Relationships between the source and target domains of a metaphor are often (though not invariably) structured by a contrast between concrete and abstract – by degrees of concreteness, rather than degrees of specificity.

3.1   Inheritance and compositional relations between metaphors

In Chapter 2 we laid out some of the motivations for, and the constraints on, metaphoric structures. Among other things, we discussed primary scenes and Primary Metaphors, and suggested that these very basic construals can then become building blocks in more complex and abstract conceptualizations. In this section, we will consider some of the ways in which a system of Primary Metaphors can connect very general and skeletal spatial schemas with more complex social and cultural concepts – and the proliferation of metaphors which can result.

We will focus on three image schemas: Force, Directed Motion along a Path towards a Destination, and Holding an Object. We usually understand force as a physical influence on objects and bodies, which may result in these objects moving, being held in place, or changing shape as a result. When we align ourselves with the two types of participation the schema profiles, we can either imagine exerting force over other entities ourselves or being subject to it. In some cases, we can also imagine ourselves as the mover and the moved at the same time, which is a very different experience from being either one in a two-participant experience, and we can then talk about self-propelled motion. In general, because any application of force affects the object to which the force is applied, there is an experiential correlation between Causation and Force which gives rise to the metaphor CAUSES ARE FORCES. This metaphor is exemplified in sentences such as *They squeezed the confession out of him*, while related mappings such as CAUSATION IS FORCED MOVEMENT and ACTIONS ARE SELF-PROPELLED MOVEMENTS can be seen commonly in the metaphoric usage of force verbs such as *push* or *drag* and some motion verbs, as in *He was pushed into this deal*, *They won't even budge under pressure*, or *I dragged myself through the application process*.

The image schema of Directed Motion along a Path is even richer. Regardless of the actual shape of the route to be taken, it assumes a line leading to a destination, possibly with some obstacles along the way, and a participant following the path, intending to reach the destination in the most efficient way. Metaphorically, PURPOSIVE ACTION IS GOAL-DIRECTED MOTION. Locations, whether along a path or defined independently of it, map onto different situations encountered by the participant in an action, while the path can be mapped onto the means allowing the participant to achieve her purposes. Moving forward or backward along the path is mapped onto Changes of State; when reaching the destination is considered desirable, moving forward to a location closer to the destination constitutes progress towards achieving a purpose. Various aspects of this schema can then be projected into activities which can be experienced as involving a Purpose. In other words, these mappings rely on the Directed Motion along a Path schema and view states of body and mind, as well as purposeful activities, in terms of motion towards a spatial location. Importantly, as noted above, the combination of Force and Motion allows even more complex mappings onto the domain of activities.

Some example usages are given here, with the relevant mappings:

(1)   That's *the only way* to get her to agree. (MEANS ARE PATHS)

(2)   We are *stuck here*. (STATES ARE LOCATIONS, DIFFICULTIES ARE IMPEDIMENTS TO MOTION)

(3)   We need to *reach the next stage* quickly. (ACTIONS ARE SELF-PROPELLED MOVEMENTS, STATES ARE LOCATIONS, PROGRESS IS FORWARD MOTION)

Table 3.1 *Selected mappings from Location/Motion to Event Structure*

Source: Location/Motion	*Target:* Event Structure
Locations	States
Motion (change of location)	Change of state
Self-propelled motion	Action
Destination	Purpose
Forward motion	Progress in purposeful action
Inability to move	Inability to act
Impediments	Difficulties
Crossroads	Choices about action

These mappings jointly profile a complex metaphoric schema, usually known as the *Location Event Structure Metaphor* (Location ESM). The source is built out of the ingredients of the two schemas defined above, Force and Directed Motion along a Path, while the target may be any static situation, any case of causation, or any purposeful activity. Importantly, the range of situations to which the schema can apply is very broad, as the particular nature of the target activity or state is not specified. More specific mappings – PURPOSIVE ACTION IS GOAL-DIRECTED MOTION – still apply to any target domain that is purposive and proceeds through some stages (it can be a research project, an educational process, a relationship, following a recipe, or cleaning up the attic).

> Location Event Structure Metaphor: a mapping between States and Locations, and Change or Action and Motion. Table 3.1 lays out the mappings.

The specific subcase of the Location ESM which comes under discussion the most in metaphor literature is the range of metaphoric mappings from the Journey frame. The Journey frame profiles a number of components such as Traveler(s), a Destination, Obstacles, a Route, and even Vehicles. Since it is a more detailed subcase of the Directed Motion on a Path frame involved in the Location ESM, it has a very broad range of rich target domains which it can be applied to, such as Life, Relationships, and Recovery from Illness – in fact, almost any long-term human activity. In each case, what the metaphor highlights in the target is the purposeful nature of the endeavor, the stages of progress, and the difficulties and choices along the way. Because the Journey frame is a subframe of Directed Motion along a Path, the Journey metaphors are subcases of the Location ESM (see Lakoff 1993, Sullivan 2013); they add to that more general mapping more specifics about the nature of the involvement of the participant. Travelers are more aware of their chosen routes and destinations than other people moving along a path, and this maps onto the idea that Life, or a Career, or a Relationship are human activities in which participants are saliently aware of their situations, their purposes, and their means for achieving those purposes. The difference between the Location ESM per se and metaphorically construing some domain or activity as a Journey is primarily in the level of schematicity.[1]

We find particular justification for the idea that domain enrichment simply builds a more elaborated subcase, rather than creating a new and separate metaphor, when we consider some common choices of wording in the Location ESM. *Being stuck* in a situation or *dragging oneself* through a purposeful activity are descriptions which inherit every aspect of the more schematic ACTION IS MOTION metaphors; nothing is left out (moving entity, path, obstacles, etc.). What is added by *being stuck* is the experiential viewpoint of the participant who cannot leave her location (mapped onto the experiencer who cannot change her situation). Physical dragging is more difficult than accompanying a person, and is usually only necessary for agentive patients when they are unwilling: so *I dragged myself through the application process* suggests that I was reluctant and the activity was difficult. These effects could be thought of as added mappings – for example, MANNER OF ACTION IS MANNER OF MOTION, INABILITY TO ACT IS INABILITY TO MOVE. But they do not change the basic STATES ARE LOCATIONS, ACTION IS MOTION mappings. They do, interestingly, add viewpoint. When we think of someone unable to move, we don't just think of their physically static location, but of their frustration at being static when they want to move – which is certainly attributed to the person who is *stuck* in a situation.

More specific metaphoric mappings (and linguistic expressions) are thus best understood as more elaborated instances of more schematic ones, as Lakoff (1993) argued. We do not have to restate all the mappings that are part of the Location ESM in describing LIFE IS A JOURNEY, or in talking about the description of a particular unwilling and effortful action as *dragging oneself though the application process*. And we do not have to debate as to whether we should say that *She's still looking for her path in life* is an instance of LIFE IS A JOURNEY or whether it is an example of PURPOSEFUL ACTION IS MOTION; it is both, since one is a more elaborated instance of the other.

The more complex the linguistic expression, often the more complex the mappings involved, and the relations between levels. In a sentence such as *She successfully navigated her way through the divorce negotiations*, the experience of the participant referred to is being described from many angles, as different component parts of the form contribute different metaphoric mappings. The verb *navigated* may be claimed to suggest a journey (LONG-TERM PURPOSEFUL ACTIVITIES ARE JOURNEYS), since literal uses of the word *navigate* are normally about longer trips. But *navigate* also specifically focuses on the careful choice of a path (MEANS ARE PATHS), suggesting obstacles (DIFFICULTIES ARE IMPEDIMENTS TO MOTION); the idea of the activity as difficult is further confirmed by the choice of the adverb *successfully*, which both refers to the achievement of a purpose

---

[1] Lakoff and Johnson (1999) list the mapping LONG-TERM PURPOSEFUL ACTIVITIES ARE JOURNEYS as one of the (sub)mappings of the Location ESM. They mean by this precisely that it is at a less schematic level.

and also brings up the alternative possibility of failure. The prepositional phrase *through the divorce negotiations* construes the time spent negotiating as a bounded region which needed to be crossed from one side to the other, and thus implies that the goal is located beyond the boundaries of that region – the successful final state of the purposeful activity is beyond the temporal bounds of the activity. Finally, the experience seems to involve a self-propelled movement (although the participant could still be self-moving under compulsion) – which suggests independent purposeful activity. All in all, this sentence does indeed profile much of the Location ESM – but it is not enough to notice this. Each individual word or phrase has its own role in contributing (sometimes overlapping) mappings. And some of them add experiential viewpoint as an essential component of the construal.

Such complex elaborations of Primary Metaphors are common, as are compositional combinations of mappings involving distinct but compatible metaphors. For example, an expression such as *He fell into depression* profiles a cluster of metaphors. *Depression* is understood as a bounded container, thanks to the *in* of the preposition *into*, and the participant whose state is described is presented as falling into it. The addition of the Container schema to STATES ARE LOCATIONS gives us STATES ARE BOUNDED REGIONS or CONTAINERS. Since containers are barriers to movement between inside and outside, we infer that someone in a container may not be able to get out; this maps onto the understanding that, from the point of view of a person suffering from depression, it often seems difficult to change one's state to a less depressed one. Being physically contained could also mean that the person restricted cannot fully experience the world either in terms of perception or interaction and motion towards goals; this corresponds to the social and psychological disadvantages of being in a depressed state. The verb *fell* refers to uncontrolled or unintentional downwards motion – which might be understood as having a negative effect on the person falling (at least her activities may be disrupted, and also she could get hurt). These map onto the uncontrolled nature of becoming depressed, and the damaging nature of depression. But the downwards directionality of *fell* also evokes other primary orientational metaphors such as GOOD IS UP, HEALTHY IS UP, and HAPPY IS UP, all of which involve mapping *worse* situations onto lower spatial positions. Even the etymological meaning of *depression* is 'pushing down,' which could foreground the negative aspects of the state further, for those aware of the word's history. Crucially, the evocation of such Location ESM subcases as CHANGE IS MOTION does not in itself require upward or downward motion being mapped onto a situation getting better or worse. But these other Primary Metaphors are perfectly compatible with the Location ESM metaphor because they are also spatial; they can be integrated with it and allow *fell* to mean 'changed to a negative state from a more positive one.'

A complex expression may thus activate many mappings at once – and we will not accuse it of being a "mixed metaphor" as long as those mappings are compatible with each other. Rather, it is a **compositionally complex** metaphor, built up of compatible components. We refer to this as *compositional* structure.

Just as grammatical constructions are composed of multiple mutually compatible structures which are simultaneously instantiated – a sentence may be passive and a question at the same time, for example – similarly, multiple compatible metaphors can be simultaneously instantiated in more specific examples such as these.

> Compositionally complex metaphor: a metaphor which is a fully specified instance of more than one higher level (less specific) metaphoric mapping. This may mean that multiple Primary Metaphors are involved.

Additionally, all uses of the Location ESM at least imply the passage of time. And indeed time, as well as events and activities, is primarily conceptualized in terms of motion through space. The primary experiential correlations are clear, since all motion actions are activities in both space and time. In many Location ESM examples, time is specifically profiled, as in *He went from happy to sad in minutes* (Change, but a fast change) or *That's where we are now and it's a long way to go*, which construes the location (situation) both in terms of time and with respect to the current stage in the process and also suggests that the goal (purpose) is distant both temporally and in terms of the stages which still need to be accomplished. As Fauconnier and Turner (2008) have suggested, it is difficult to separate Event Structure both from Temporal Structure and Experiential Structure. Our examples support their conclusion. We will postpone further discussion of metaphoric construals of time until Chapter 7; for the moment, we will just observe that the temporal structures on the two sides of a metaphoric mapping need to be compatible: it could not be the case, for instance, that the end of a life could be the start of the journey onto which the life is mapped, or that the start of the life could be the end of the journey. This is part of what has been proposed as the Invariance Principle (Lakoff 1993), which will be further discussed in the next chapter. Certain structures are "invariant" across metaphoric mappings: in particular, temporal sequence and aspectual stages must be mapped coherently between the inputs in a metaphoric blend.

At the beginning of this section, we mentioned another low-level schema that can be exploited as part of our understanding of Event Structure – that of Holding an Object or having it. This schema gives rise to the Object Event Structure Metaphor, in which attributes such as bodily states are described in terms of a participant "having" them (so one can *have good looks*, *have a sense of humor*, or *have pneumonia*). Some of these attributes can then be transferred to others, which can be a matter of simple movement or intentional transfer – in the latter case, we can also talk about causation as transfer of possessions. The Object ESM is so named because it treats events and situations as objects rather than locations. In some ways it is the inverse of the Location ESM: the Object ESM treats attributes or situations as mobile objects which can be acquired, while the Location ESM treats them as fixed locations to and from which participants move. The Object ESM is common, and is an interesting example of reliance on ontological metaphors, such that attributes are conceptualized as physical objects which can then be possessed or given away. There are classes of situations which can be referred to by both ESMs: a person can **have** *a serious depression* or **be in** *a serious depression*, **have** *a good relationship* or **be in** *a good relationship*. Levels of schematicity seem to play an important role in the construal of this metaphor as well; for example, *leaving a relationship* is rather less specific than *abandoning* or *ditching a relationship*.

In this section, we have argued that metaphoric construals can share structure but differ in their degree of specificity, that combinations of linguistic forms frequently evoke compositional combinations of metaphors. We examined in particular the interaction between locational and orientational Primary Metaphors. And we noted that even individual lexical forms (such as *fall*) can simultaneously instantiate more than one Primary Metaphor. This in itself should keep us from wanting to say that a linguistic expression – whether a word or a larger phrasal structure – is "a metaphor" – a shorthand frequently used by writers from many disciplines. Calling a linguistic expression *a metaphor* can give us the misimpression that there is a one-to-one mapping between metaphors and forms. But of course, the linguistic form itself is not a metaphoric structure; it is its usage in context which prompts a metaphoric construal rather than a literal one. And a linguistic expression may, in context, express one or many metaphoric mappings – the *metaphors* are those cognitive mappings.

In the next section, we will discuss schematicity in the context of a more elaborate example.

3.2   Levels of complexity

In this chapter so far, we have been looking at relationships between levels of conceptualization. Here, we will show how these levels interact in a complex system of mappings. We stressed in Chapter 2 that metaphoric mappings build up from the lowest level of embodied conceptualization to more complex, often culturally shaped mappings. In this section, we will illustrate that process by analyzing a family of mappings which has been known since Lakoff and Johnson (1980) as IDEAS ARE FOOD, many aspects of which have also been analyzed by Croft (2009). The crucial point here is that the connections between the domain of mental constructs and processes (for which Ideas can be used as a rather general label) and the domain of, broadly defined, human nutrition (Food) exist at many levels of conceptualization, for there are multiple frames and subframes involved. The Food domain, being the source, brings the complexity of its frames into our understanding of mental life. The subframes range from those related to the food itself (its Nature, Taste, and Availability, Preparation Techniques, etc.) through the role of Nutrition in Health and Well-Being, to the viewpointed processes of Absorbing and Digesting Food. The complexity of the subframes is also the basis on which this broad family of mappings builds up a complex construal of mental processes. Some of the subframes can in fact be organized hierarchically, in the sense that most of them inherit a schematic ontological metaphor IDEAS ARE OBJECTS mapping, in the specific subinstance of IDEAS ARE EDIBLE OBJECTS. Edible objects are typically evaluated in terms of Nutritional Value, Attractiveness, and Stage of Preparation, and each of these subframes yields interesting expressions in the domain of Mental Activity.

For example, expressions such as *a wholesome idea* or *solid food for thought* refer to the intellectual value of the thoughts in question; the ability of food items to allow the body to remain healthy and strong is mapped onto the 'nourishment of the mind.' Similar meanings can be expressed using more elaborate expressions such as *The lecture satisfied all my appetites* or even *He drew a lot of intellectual proteins from what he heard.* All such expressions can be explained in terms of a metaphor THE INTELLECTUAL VALUE OF AN IDEA IS THE NUTRITIONAL VALUE OF FOOD. The presentation of ideas also yields a submapping THE APPEAL OF AN IDEA IS THE APPEAL OF FOOD, represented by a wide range of examples including *an appetizing thought, an idea that makes your mouth water, a skillfully garnished idea with little merit,* etc. The subframe of Stage of Preparation (yielding STAGE OF DEVELOPMENT OF AN IDEA IS STAGE OF PREPARATION OF FOOD) is commonly used in expressions such as *a half-baked theory, raw ideas, refried concepts,* and so on. Finally, presenting or preparing to present ideas can be metaphorically represented as serving or cooking food: *He cooked up the whole proposal in a day, The conference was a very attractive spread/a smorgasbord.*

The reader has most likely noticed that this broad range of metaphors depends both on the basic mapping allowing us to think of ideas as edible objects and also on another basic family of mappings that allows us to think about the functioning of the mind in terms of the functioning of the body and to present mental processes as bodily processes (described in detail in Sweetser 1984 and 1990 and in Lakoff and Johnson 1999). Recall that we said in Chapter 2 that MIND IS BODY is not a single metaphor, but a name for a whole range of metaphors which conceptualize humans' mental and emotional selves in terms of their physical selves acting in the physical world. In this case, we are mapping a range of bodily functions, such as requiring nutrition and eating, onto a range of mental functions such as considering, believing, remembering, and rejecting ideas. Our vocabulary for dealing with ideas thus includes a number of verbs which represent what Croft (2009) describes as the three parts of the Eating frame: Intake, Processing, and Ingestion. These verbs range from *bite* or *bite off* through *chew* and *swallow* to *digest,* and even include the verbs representing the reversal of Ingestion, such as *spit out, regurgitate,* and *throw up.* All such verbs can be naturally used to represent various stages of acceptance (or lack of acceptance) of thought content, via metaphors such as MENTAL CONSIDERATION IS PROCESSING FOOD BY CHEWING, INTELLECTUAL ACCEPTANCE IS SWALLOWING, UNDERSTANDING IS DIGESTION, REMEMBERING WITHOUT UNDERSTANDING IS REGURGITATION, etc. Thus we can *swallow an idea without thinking* or *thoroughly digest it,* or we can *regurgitate it upon demand* for a test.

A number of metaphoric expressions for cognitive processes and reactions also describe a participant's response to food – *being nauseated, savoring the taste, gorging on X, finding X tasteless*, etc. Another subframe which is mapped is the whole range of taste sensations as correlates of one's response to ideas presented; here, it is quite natural to talk about *bitter thoughts, sweet delusions*, or *sour irony*. As Croft points out, eating is also associated with social sharing and serving of food (so that one can *serve a whole banquet of new proposals* or *offer ideas on a silver platter*). The range of expressions associated with food and eating is enormous, and a remarkably wide range of such expressions either have been used or could be used in the description of intellectual or esthetic tastes and interactions with thought content of all kinds. In fact, listing all of the appropriate metaphors would be difficult and, in some sense, even pointless.

What the above examples make clear is that the complexity of the domains involved in metaphor and the complexity of the resulting range of metaphoric usages depend in a direct way on the complexity of the frames involved, which is in turn proportional to the frames' importance in human experience and culture. The complexity may be an effect of the range of subframes (which is very broad in the case of food), and the result may be quite a varied array of meanings. The source frames in IDEAS ARE FOOD range from very direct embodied experiences of Hunger or Taste (we can be *hungry for new ideas*, and we know how *a bitter thought* is different from *a sweet one*), through more specific aspects of bodily experience like Chewing, to general experiences with objects (e.g. whether they are edible or not). These more general frames also interact with culturally and socially available frames involving, in this case, food serving, cooking traditions, dietary choices, the place of food in social events, and so on. Saying that a workshop is an *appetizer before the coming conference* will only work if the listener knows the role of appetizers in a meal schedule.

Importantly, multiple subframes can be metaphorically exploited at the same time, and the ones which are more salient culturally depend in many ways on the more directly embodied ones: for example, our *appetizer* example demands cultural knowledge of conventional orders of serving but also evokes the idea that appetizers are supposed to be attractive and make guests eager to eat. Practically the entire range of metaphors discussed above relies on the more schematic mapping IDEAS ARE EDIBLE OBJECTS in combination with the broad ontological family of mappings, MIND IS BODY. The complexity of the range of mappings previously summarized as IDEAS ARE FOOD thus emerges out of the complexity of bodily experiences connected to food and nutrition.

It is also important to note that, even with the kind of complexity involved in the mappings of frames and subframes discussed above, there are still subframes of the Food domain which are not mapped onto the realm of the relationship between minds and ideas. Croft has observed, on the basis of corpus data, that the frame of Eating specific to humans is largely independent of the frame of Animal Eating; the latter yields its own types of mappings, as in expressions that describe unfair or brutal exploitation. For example, in *The press has been feeding on his election disaster for weeks*, we take *feed on* to mean 'exploit' or 'profit from' rather than 'intellectually assimilate'. But Human Eating can also serve as a source for expressions describing reinforcement, as in *feeding the rumors* or *feeding the outrage*.

And as we have pointed out before, any important area of abstract experience can be thought about in many different metaphoric ways. Ideas are not just edible objects, but malleable objects (*The reviewer **twisted** my ideas all **out of shape***), moving, graspable objects (*The idea **came to me** last night, I finally **grasped** what he was talking about*), objects that are building blocks for more complex structures (*That idea is the **cornerstone** of my theory*), and so on. Any metaphor we consider is thus situated in a complex network of other mappings – mappings from the source domain to other target domains, more or less schematic mappings which underlie or extend the mapping we are considering, and mappings from other source domains onto that target domain.

We argue that these connections between mappings are crucial to the role of metaphors in conceptualization. We should expect links and relations among metaphors to be the core feature of metaphoric thought, directly related to the conceptual power of metaphoric mappings. The connections across mappings can emerge on various levels. They can be based on the more schematic levels of embodiment and ontology, so that, for example, ideas can be viewed as either edible objects or as malleable objects; however, in both cases, the mind also has to be viewed as a body and thus capable of interacting with whichever types of objects in appropriate manners. At the other end of the spectrum, the rich cultural content of metaphoric domains may yield very specific mappings (as in *serving a whole buffet of theories, an intellectual feast*, etc.). However, the richness of the concepts of a *buffet* or a *feast* in fact relies on both more schematic and more specified levels of framing and conceptualization: the exceptional nature of a feast or the variety involved in a buffet are culturally specific, but they rely on the basic understandings of food and eating, of material objects and the functions of the body. To sum up, each of these metaphors participates in a hierarchy of mappings, and their power is significantly based in the human ability to connect the body and its material interactions to complex cultural scenarios. Metaphors are thus connected, not only vertically (with the eating and digestion metaphors relying on the underlying Primary and ontological Metaphors of physical interaction with objects), but also horizontally (with many metaphors relying on treating mental constructs as different types of material objects, and treating the mind as a body in different ways).

There does not, however, appear to be a *single unified* system of coherent mappings between Ideas and Food. Croft's (2009) model explicitly maps lower level frames: not IDEAS ARE FOOD, but INTELLECTUAL ASSIMILATION IS DIGESTION or INTELLECTUAL ACCEPTANCE IS SWALLOWING. The wisdom of sticking to these more specific mappings becomes clear when we see that one might be able to say of the same intellectual proposals that *I've thoroughly digested Jones's ideas* and at the same time that *I can't swallow Jones's ideas*. If there were a single global mapping of eating onto our interaction with new ideas, this would be impossible.

One cannot, in the domain of Eating, digest something without swallowing it! So it would be better to say that we have evidence for more specific metaphoric mappings between subframes. IDEAS ARE FOOD is not the statement of a single metaphor, but a convenient label for a group of partially independent metaphors that map food consumption onto cognition.

Relationships among mappings also affect metaphoric construal of specific domains in more than one way. Croft observes that there are metaphoric uses of food vocabulary which cannot be explained through a single unidirectional projection from the source to the target. For example, expressions like *feeding data into a computer* do not have direct literal correlates, in that it would be strange to talk about *feeding the formula into the baby*. As Croft argues, such examples display different argument structure because they rely on the framing from *both* the source and the target. This connects the IDEAS ARE FOOD metaphors to other frames in which the preposition *into* profiles the flow of material into a container. Croft's conclusion is that metaphoric mappings, while asymmetric, should include the contribution of both the assumed source and the assumed target.[2] Similar arguments have been made by Sullivan (2009, 2013) who has also noted the importance of the details of source and target domains in determining mappings, as discussed in Chapter 2. Not only the level of complexity and the level of schematicity of the mappings, but also the structures of both of the two input domains are important aspects of how we represent figurative conceptualizations.

3.3   The experiential bases of complex mappings

There seem to be no obvious primary scenes linking Ideas and Food, despite the primary experiential basis for ACQUIESCENCE IS SWALLOWING – and yet the complex metaphoric links between the domains were built up. We would now like to examine a case where there seems no experiential basis for the proposed complex metaphor as a whole, but the complex metaphor seems plausibly grounded in multiple primary experiential correlations. The THEORIES ARE BUILDINGS metaphor is an excellent example of this kind of structure. It is also an example of the messiness of the opposition between "concrete" and "abstract" – an issue to which we will return in a detailed discussion in Section 3.4. And, finally, it is a salient example of the ways in which inferences and mappings flow by inheritance from more general metaphors down to more specific subcases.

THEORIES ARE BUILDINGS was proposed by Lakoff and Johnson (1980) based on examples such as *My theory has a **solid foundation***, *Do the data **support** that theory?*, *That theory is now **in ruins***, *The **cornerstone** of any philosophy of language is an understanding of representation*, *They are slowly **building** a new theory of subatomic physics*, and *Einstein was the original **architect** of relativity*

---

[2] This claim is a revision of the standard approach to metaphor, but it is worth noting that Croft should not be understood as fully endorsing the blending approach discussed Chapter 4.

theory. Grady (1997) noted, however, that this metaphor does not have an obvious experiential basis, at least not a direct one. We don't really think small children first learn about the workings of theories via a pervasive correlation between their initial experiences of theory structure and architectural structure.

Further, there seem to be a lot of vacant areas in the mappings which that formulation of the metaphor might have suggested. Buildings normally have doors, windows, bathrooms, even furniture and appliances inside. None of these things are mapped onto Theories. Lakoff and Johnson noted that architectural style can be mapped; a theory can be *baroque*, or *modernist-minimal*, possibly even *gothic*. They even suggested an extension to exterior ornamentation, imagining a *gothic theory with gargoyles* – but it still makes no sense to talk of theories' paint, wallpaper, and none of the examples they found discussed plumbing. So, as with IDEAS ARE FOOD, it seems that THEORIES ARE BUILDINGS may not actually reflect a single metaphoric mapping between the two domains as wholes.

As Grady pointed out, the primary aspects of Buildings which are pervasively mapped onto Theories are physical support relations and the creation and destruction of those support relations: cornerstones, foundations, supporting, architects, builders, undermining, collapsing, and so on. We might extend this list to include structural integrity at large; theories can be *watertight* or *full of leaks*. Grady therefore suggested that some Primary Metaphors might well underlie the Building metaphor – and that these Primary Metaphors motivate the mappings we do find, and not the ones we don't (see also the analysis of Clausner and Croft 1997).

The first of these Primary Metaphors is DEPENDENCE IS PHYSICAL SUPPORT. One can easily see how small children would experience this correlation: as they learn about physical support, they also learn that the location of a supported object is causally dependent on that of supporting objects, while the reverse is not true. The location of the top block in a pile *depends* causally on the position of the lower blocks, not the other way round, and that is because the lower blocks *support* the higher ones. Also relevant to THEORIES ARE BUILDINGS is the Primary Metaphor which Grady labels PERSISTENCE ('continued existence') IS REMAINING ERECT. Again, there would be plenty of experiential examples of this for small children: a card or block structure ceases to exist when it is no longer upright because it was knocked down. Even plants are likely to bend down or topple when they die.

A third crucial Primary Metaphor is ABSTRACT ORGANIZATION IS PHYSICAL STRUCTURE. Even very small children are ready to sort objects into physical collections by category, creating a pile of books and another pile of clothes; around them, they see adults developing and maintaining such patterns constantly. We enable ourselves to find objects by mapping various abstract categorial structures (e.g. tableware, cooking tools) directly onto divisions of spatial storage. Abstract family relationships may be manifested in table-sitting arrangements with parents at the head and foot and children along the sides. And abstract causal-relation structures are frequently the basis for the structure of complex objects: the child will figure out quite soon that without an electrical cord or a battery in its physical structure, a device as a whole will not work.

Of course, a human-constructed building is a very salient and central example of a physical structure which only persists while it is upright, and whose persistence is causally dependent on transitive physical support relationships, and which manifests complex conceptual structure (mutually dependent plans and purposes) in its complex physical structure. And a theory is a salient and central example of a complex cognitive entity which involves successive levels of causal dependencies (between component premises and conclusions), which may have a large number of such interrelationships between conceptual components, and which does not continue to function or exist if the necessary causal-reasoning dependencies fail. So it is not at all surprising that we would find a group of mappings (the one which has been labeled THEORIES ARE BUILDINGS) which inherit structure from the more general Primary Metaphors. However, there are no Primary Metaphors relating paint, carpets, or bathrooms to frames involved in the domain of Theories. The frame of Building Support Structure is mapped onto the frame of Epistemic Dependence Relations in theories; the frame of Building Remaining Erect is mapped onto the frame of Functional Persistence of the Theory, and the frame of Complex Part–Whole Structure in the building is mapped onto the frame of Complex Cognitive Structure in the theory. In each case, the Primary Metaphor is inherited in full by the particular subcase. Further, these mappings are entirely coherent with each other. And the relevant frames are certainly among the most essential ones involved in the two domains. So even if the entire Building frame (which has subframes for plumbing, electrical connections, and interior decoration) is not mapped, we could say that the label THEORIES ARE BUILDINGS is not entirely inappropriate, so long as we keep in mind that it is shorthand for this group of mappings between salient subframes.

THEORIES ARE BUILDINGS is thus both a nice example of the principle that metaphors frequently construe abstract domains in terms of concrete ones and a nice example of the limitations of that generalization. Although THEORIES ARE BUILDINGS is not itself a Primary Metaphor, the direction of its mappings is determined by Primary Metaphors which are based on primary experiential correlations between *physical experiences* (of support, uprightness, complex spatial structure) and *attendant subjective evaluations* such as judgments about ongoing existence, attributions of causal dependence, and so on (Grady 1997, Johnson 1997). Even though it is not itself a Primary Metaphor, it is deeply motivated by Primary Metaphors – whereas there would be no motivation for the reverse mapping BUILDINGS ARE THEORIES, because there would not be Primary Metaphors on which to base that more specific one.

THEORIES ARE BUILDINGS is also an example of the relationship between more skeletal, general metaphors and their more specified subcases. Primary Metaphors are by nature extremely general, and motivate potentially huge numbers of subcases; as we saw earlier, the Location ESM permeates almost all of our understandings of human actions and states. STATES ARE LOCATIONS and DISTINCT STATES ARE BOUNDED LOCATIONS, SO LOVE IS A CONTAINER (you can be *in love*). ACTION IS MOTION, DIFFICULTIES ARE OBSTACLES TO MOTION, and PURPOSES ARE DESTINATIONS – SO LIFE IS A JOURNEY, A LOVE RELATIONSHIP IS

A SHARED JOURNEY, and A CAREER IS A JOURNEY. And the metaphoric Journey can be specifically a car trip or a rail trip; you can be *spinning your wheels* at this stage of your career, or your career can be *derailed*. All of that follows from the more skeletal Location ESM plus the characteristics of the more specific domains, just as the characteristics of the THEORIES ARE BUILDINGS metaphoric mappings follow from the more schematic metaphors and the specific case of a Building, with its specific physical structure.

Also, in THEORIES ARE BUILDINGS as in other metaphors, inferential structure is transferred. That is inevitable in Primary Metaphors, which are about "cuing" inferences in one domain from data in another. So also in these submappings, we know what it would mean to have your theory *come down around you*, to have to *rebuild from the foundation*, or to have *even the foundations undermined*. We know that in the case of undermined foundations, more rebuilding is needed than in the case where a building's foundations still survive; and we transfer that inference to an assessment of the extent to which theorizing needs to be redone.

Causal and aspectual structure is also preserved across mappings, as predicted by the Invariance Hypothesis. If you are *building a building*, it isn't yet complete, and if you're *building a theory*, it is still being developed. Causing the physical structure to be stronger or higher or broader corresponds to making the theory better reasoned or more ambitious or more extensive in coverage; damaging the physical structure corresponds to making the theory less convincing or less likely to continue to be believed. These mappings could not go in the opposite direction: physical damage to the building could not correspond to improvement of the theory, for example. In the case of metaphors with primary experiential bases, this kind of causal and aspectual coherence is ensured by the correlation between the input domains. For MORE IS UP, the gradually increasing height of liquid in a container just *does* correlate with increasing quantity, not with decreasing quantity; the scale of heights (say, on a graduated measuring cup) corresponds to the scale of quantities, and adding more liquid causes the level to go up, while removing liquid causes it to go down.

The power of the THEORIES ARE BUILDINGS metaphors, despite the relatively unelaborated lower level mappings between the two domains, is shown in scientific discourse, for example in the following quote from the mathematician Henri Poincaré:

> Le savant doit ordonner; on fait la science avec des faits comme une maison avec des pierres; mais une accumulation de faits n'est pas plus une science qu'un tas de pierres n'est une maison. [The Scientist must set in order. Science is built up with facts, as a house is with stones. But a collection of facts is no more a science than a heap of stones is a house.][3]

---

[3] Henri Poincaré, *Science and Hypothesis*, vol. 1 of *Foundations of Science*, trans. George Bruce Halsted, New York and Garrison, NY: The Science Press, 1913.

Table 3.2 *Selected mappings from Journey to Love Relationship. (Roles in boldface are not inherited from the higher-level schemas.)*

Source: Journey (Inherits from Location/Motion)	Target: Love Relationship (Inherits from Event Structure)
Location	State (life situation)
Destination	Purpose
Impediment to motion	Difficulty
Vehicle	**Relationship**
Passengers	**Lovers**
Co-location in vehicle	**Participation in relationship**
Shared destination	**Shared purpose**

The Metaphor Analysis team led by George Lakoff as part of the MetaNet project[4] has coined the term **cascades** to talk about the kind of inheritance relationships that link levels of metaphoric structure. The term is borrowed from neuroscience, but in metaphor theory it means something like the following. We don't need to restate the mappings STATES ARE LOCATIONS and CHANGE IS MOTION at every level of metaphoric structure. We have strong, highly conventional links which constitute the Location ESM. It is sufficient to activate those mappings; there is no need to separately state the ESM at every level of the network of metaphoric mappings. Its structure "cascades" downhill to lower-level, more specific structures, such as LIFE IS A JOURNEY, LOVE IS A SHARED JOURNEY, and A CAREER IS A JOURNEY. Of course, for example, in LIFE IS A JOURNEY, the relevant states are specifically Life Situations, and the relevant changes are purposive changes in one's life situation. The primary characteristics of cascade relationships between metaphors are that (1) higher, more schematic structure is fully inherited by lower more elaborated subcases and (2) one specific metaphor can inherit fully the structures of multiple higher level metaphors (as we saw with our earlier example of *falling into depression*). Table 3.2 shows some of this structure for A LOVE RELATIONSHIP IS A JOURNEY; keep in mind that the more schematic mappings are understood to be present in the more elaborated ones.

Notice that basically each mapping between the Journey and Love domains is a subinstance of the mappings cited in Table 3.1 as characterizing the more general Location ESM. The Journey's Locations, Destination, and Impediments are subcases of these general categories; but a Journey adds, for example, possible

---

[4] MetaNet is an IARPA-funded project bringing together linguists, neuroscientists, and computational analysts at the University of California, Berkeley, the International Computer Science Institute, UC-San Diego, Stanford, UC-Merced, and the University of Southern California. Although most of the data and analysis are not yet publicly accessible as of the time of writing, interested readers can visit the MetaNet project website at www.icsi.berkeley.edu/icsi/projects/ai/metanet.

Table 3.3 *Selected mappings from Physical Structures to Theories*

Source: Physical Structures	*Target:* Theories
Complex physical structure	Complex cognitive structure
Support relations	Epistemic dependence relations
Remaining erect, not falling down	Continued existence

roles for a Vehicle, Passengers, and a Shared Destination for the passengers. Similarly, a Love Relationship is a subcase of generic action and Event Structures: like them, it involves Situations, Purposes, and Difficulties. But it has added roles for the Relationship, the Lovers, and their Shared Purposes. Just as the more specific frames are elaborated versions of the more schematic ones, the more specific metaphor is an elaborated version of the more schematic one.

Similarly, in talking about the THEORIES ARE BUILDINGS metaphors, we have no need to separate them from the PERSISTENCE IS REMAINING ERECT or the DEPENDENCE IS PHYSICAL SUPPORT metaphors. Those cascade naturally downwards to participate in the more specific metaphors, and are included in their structure. We should therefore not be surprised that some details of building structure (paint, plumbing, windows) don't seem to be incorporated: they are not present to be inherited from the Primary Metaphor structures. In Table 3.3. we can see that even though the mappings are schematic primary ones, there are not really any added mappings in the THEORIES ARE BUILDINGS metaphor to elaborate it beyond those inherited mappings.

One very interesting fall-out of this kind of approach to levels of metaphor is that we can see why it is so rare to encounter a truly novel metaphor. What we generally encounter instead are either *elaborations* and/or *compositional combinations* of known metaphors. The classic example *the fast lane on the freeway of love* is an elaboration of LOVE IS A SHARED JOURNEY – specifically, one in which love is a journey in a speeding car on a freeway, so the (uncertain) ultimate outcome (= Destination) will happen *soon*. Interestingly, even these subcases still have their own inferences, added to the inferences available from the more general mappings: the *risk* and emotional excitement which go with very fast speeds (and possibly breaking the speed limit) emerge from this specific case, and suggest that the love relationship is risky and exciting. (We'll talk more about this in Chapter 4, when we get to blends.) But we can't say this is a brand new metaphor.

More interesting, perhaps, are compositional cases such as *glass ceiling*, a phrase which became current in the 1980s. It refers to the situation where women and minority employees somehow never get promoted above a certain level (in particular, into the higher levels of management) – but where the reason is not obvious, since the companies hire women and minorities at lower levels and generally appear to be open in their employment and promotion policies. Note that to understand this metaphor, we must compositionally combine A CAREER IS A JOURNEY (itself a subcase of LIFE IS A JOURNEY) with AUTHORITY IS

UP, a combination that also yields *the career ladder* and *climbing the corporate ladder*, where PROMOTION IS UPWARDS MOTION. The ceiling is a barrier specifically to upwards motion, and DIFFICULTIES ARE OBSTACLES. But we need another piece too. The reason the ceiling is "glass" is that you don't know it is there: the social exclusion is *unnoticeable*, like a physical barrier that is transparent and thus invisible. And this requires KNOWING IS SEEING. No wonder this metaphor was readily comprehensible as soon as it was coined; all the compositional inputs are deeply conventional for English speakers. They all cascade into, as it were, a single new compositionally complex metaphor. The new metaphor is more specific, and more imageable, than most of the motivating "upstream" metaphors. But those upstream metaphors are present in its structure.

So, again, innovative metaphoric usages are usually either (1) elaborations (subcases) of conventional higher-level metaphors, or (2) compositional combinations of conventional higher-level metaphors. This makes them easy to learn, since they don't need really new conceptual foundations. Further, since many of the Primary Metaphors are based in primary scenes, the higher up you go in the metaphor hierarchy, the more likely you are to find crosslinguistically shared structures. We will get to this in Chapter 7 – and we certainly don't mean to say that any one language, let alone all languages, has only one possible way of looking at some important domain metaphorically. But there seems to be a limited range of ways that cultures can choose to look at Time in terms of Space, for example; variation between metaphoric models is not unconstrained, either within a language community or crossculturally.

3.4   Image metaphors

We have not yet talked about **image metaphors**, the kind of metaphors that involve mapping specifically of images from one domain onto another, like *hourglass waist* or *apple cheeks*. Image metaphors appear to be differently motivated, and subject to different constraints, from conceptual metaphors. Human perceptual structure is constantly mapping inputs onto each other, without necessarily involving inferential structure or broader categorial generalizations. We also map *between* sensory modalities – the mappings are there in the brain, even for those who don't have the neurological condition of synesthesia in the clinical sense. So someone can have a *velvety voice* or a *clear voice* or a *sweet voice*. Lakoff and Turner (1989) cite an example from Indian poetry, describing a river whose level has gone down during the dry season, which maps it onto clothing sliding down the body of a lover (the water being mapped onto the clothing and the light-brown river banks onto the body). The image metaphor *hourglass waist* is not surprising in a culture (such as certain nineteenth-century European cultures) which has hourglasses and happens to idealize a very narrow-waisted but large-breasted and large-hipped female figure. But this metaphor doesn't seem to have significant structure mapped beyond the image similarity – no inferences about hourglasses beyond the shape are transferred to the female figures so described. Nor does there seem to be any broader network of metaphoric mappings into which this one fits or from which it inherits structure, as LIFE IS A JOURNEY inherits from the Location ESM. Not a great deal is known about image metaphors as a class, but they are clearly structurally distinct from conceptual metaphors.

Another way in which image metaphors are different from conceptual metaphors is that they don't tend to have a basis in experiential correlation. Primary Metaphors need primary scenes – correlations in experience – to motivate them. And that motivation is passed on downwards to the complex metaphors which inherit Primary Metaphor structures. There is no experiential correlation at the specific level between, say, discriminatory promotion practices and transparent glass ceilings in buildings. But there are primary experiential correlations between vision and knowledge, between verticality and authority, and between motion/barriers and purposive action/difficulties. These primary mappings cascade downhill to motivate the specific case of *glass ceiling*, even though it has no direct correlational motivation of its own. Image metaphors don't seem to work this way. There not only is no experiential correlation between hourglasses and waists, or sweet flavors and harmonious sounds, there doesn't need to be. The brain's structure connects these shapes, and these modalities.

And this brings us to *synesthesia*. In language, it is a frequent phenomenon for vocabulary from one perceptual domain to be used to describe phenomena in another perceptual domain, as in *sweet sound, smooth wine, sharp cheese, quiet color*. The connections across domains of perception are difficult to classify in terms of concrete or abstract meanings, but what such uses share with metaphor is the pattern whereby a domain basic to human experience (*smooth* refers to touch) yields a conceptualization applied to another such domain – although the target domain in this case is also an area of basic experience (such as taste, in *smooth wine*). Such mappings have been talked about as *synesthesia*, clearly in reference to a clinically recognized condition in which experiences in one area are received in another as well. Symptoms vary, but various forms of the condition link color and numbers, color and letters, touch and hearing, sound and color; that is, subjects physically perceive, for example, the color blue when processing a particular numeric value. There is obviously a significant difference between having synesthesia in this dramatic way, and the kinds of associations which result in synesthetic linguistic usages. But all humans seem to have some crossmodal associations, and most languages seem to lexicalize at least some such associations.

Importantly, the category of synesthetic metaphor is often broadened from cross-perceptual-domain mappings to include the use of perception vocabulary to talk about emotions (as in *bitter sorrow, black despair, sweet indifference,* etc.). The connection between mood and emotion on the one hand and perception of taste or color on the other is an interesting way of using an experiential source domain to describe a more elusive target domain. But, as we have seen, it is not unusual for bodily sensations to be used in descriptions of emotional states. And there is evidence that there are some shared associations crossculturally. Humans are wired to find sweet tastes pleasurable and bitter tastes unpleasant, so it would be surprising if the English uses of *bitter sorrow* and *sweet love* were reversed, although we cannot predict these specific lexicalizations. And although words for the color blue do not universally refer to sadness (as in English), crossculturally blue and COOL colors are associated with less active and calmer emotional states (including sadness), while red and WARM colors are associated with active and stimulated emotional states (anger, lust). Thus at least some of these crossmodal metaphors have correlational metonymic bases.

One way of thinking about some of these synesthetic metaphoric linguistic usages is to say that they follow not an asymmetry of concreteness but an asymmetry of accessibility; that is, in general a more intersubjectively accessible domain is used to talk about a less intersubjectively accessible domain. Although one cannot experience either someone else's sorrow or someone else's taste experience of a food, and despite the fact that taste is proverbially variable as a sense, still we have a better guess that other humans will find sugar sweet and coffee bitter (which is why children have to acquire that taste) than we do about emotional states. And likewise, in tasting a wine, the subtleties of the taste are not at all clearly shared or communicable; we don't even have a definite shared vocabulary beyond *sour, sweet*, and such basic words. We do have an idea that others will find the same objects smooth to the touch that we do; this aspect of tactile sensation is thus more intersubjectively accessible than the kind of taste sensation referred to in calling a wine *smooth* (Lehrer 1983 gives extensive analysis of wine-tasting language). We will be discussing intersubjective accessibility further in Section 3.5.

It is interesting to note that poetic forms may build on newly established synesthetic links, as in Bashō's haiku:

(4)   The sea grows more dark
           with the ducks' voices sounding faintly white

It is often the case that sounds become more clear when visibility grows low. This effect is captured in example (4) with the image of the voices of birds coming into contrast with the darkening color of the water.

In sum, images are readily mapped in the brain within sensory modalities and even across them. We should expect that new sensory images, whenever they arise and particularly when they are generally and conventionally accessible, will potentially give rise to new image metaphors. But we do not expect the same kind of innovation to arise in conceptual metaphor networks. It seems possible for a linguistic system to undergo a reorganization of preferences with regard to Primary Metaphors: for example, a language's speakers could start favoring FUTURE EVENTS ARE MOVING TOWARDS EGO (as in *Thanksgiving is coming soon*) over EGO IS MOVING TOWARDS FUTURE EVENTS (as in *We're approaching Thanksgiving*) – and indeed, the differing preferences for these mappings in actual different language communities presumably result from historic developments of this kind. But even these are closely related metaphors, both subcases of TIME IS RELATIVE MOTION IN SPACE. In order to give birth to really novel conceptual metaphors, as opposed to new compositional combinations and subcases, new primary experiential scenes would have to arise and motivate new Primary Metaphors. This is not, of course, impossible, but it is a much higher bar than for innovation in image metaphors. Rather, inheritance and recombination of extant structures are the essence of ordinary conceptual metaphor innovation.

3.5   Constraints on source–target relationships – is it about concrete and abstract?

We have been talking at length about relationships of specificity between schematic higher-level mappings and subcases of those mappings – that is, relationships between metaphors. We now return to another basic issue, namely the relationship between the source and target frames within a metaphor. As we have said, the idea that metaphor treats abstract concepts in terms of concrete ones is a recurring theme in metaphor studies. There is an assumed cognitive benefit to a construal which allows us to visualize and mentally manipulate abstract ideas in ways that resemble our embodied interaction with the concrete world. Recent research on simulation (Bergen 2012; see also discussion in Gibbs 2005) confirms that our brains do indeed simulate many abstract concepts in terms of concrete ones, but the linguistic instantiation of this tendency is a question we need to consider in detail.

3.5.1   Objectification and personification

Making abstract concepts concrete can take very basic paths. As Lakoff and Johnson (1980, 1999) have pointed out, abstract concepts can be talked about from various perspectives if they are treated as physical objects or people. Ontological metaphors are examples of mappings where an abstract entity is *personified* (made into a person) or *reified* (*objectified* – made into a thing) as a more concrete entity. (Recall that these are called *ontological metaphors* because they saliently reframe the ontological status of the abstract entity in question.) Examples of such usage are common. Social Groups are objectified as Containers (*the in crowd, kick someone out of the club*), or personified as People (one nation can be a *good neighbor* to another, or can be an *outlaw* or *rogue* nation). The male Uncle Sam personifies the United States (and shares the nation's initials), while the beautiful female figure Marianne is a personification of the French Republic. The personification metaphor of CORPORATIONS ARE PEOPLE is taken extremely seriously in the American legal system in particular, where corporations – which always had some of the same legal status as people, for example being able to sue or be sued in court, or having to pay their bills – have recently been officially given by the Supreme Court the free-speech rights which were previously understood to be reserved for literal individual people.

Abstract qualities are also personified; it seems that some of these conventional personifications go back a long way in Indo-European cultures, where gods and goddesses were imagined to represent many abstract qualities. The Statue of Liberty is a monumental statue of a woman that represents the quality of Liberty, given in recognition of the shared national democratic values of France (the donor nation) and the United States (the recipient). The French noun *liberté* and its Latin source *libertas* are both feminine nouns, and this French personification continues the Latin tradition of a female goddess Libertas. Justice, similarly a Latin feminine noun (*Iustitia*), was already a goddess in Rome as well, and some of her modern attributes as Lady Justice on courthouse doors (the scales in particular) go back to a Greek goddess Dike, whose name is also a feminine noun meaning 'justice.' Even classical gods who did not have quality-noun names often represented abstract qualities or situations: Athene, for example, represents reason and wisdom, while Ares personifies war and Aphrodite beauty and sexual love.

Personification of abstractions and groups achieves, among other things, what Fauconnier and Turner (2002) refer to as *compression to human scale*. It is impossible to interact directly with a thousand, much less a million, people – we can't even conceptualize a million. But once a nation is understood not only as a unit but as a person, one can reason about it in terms of human behavior, and about international relations in terms of human relationships. Mappings become possible where advantageous trade agreements may be seen as personal favors, bad diplomatic relations due to past conflict are construed as grudges, good diplomatic relations are friendships, disputes are arguments, and so on. Cartoons depicting Germany and France as personified by their leaders at the time (Angela Merkel and Nicolas Sarkozy) allowed us to consider the problems of international relations in terms of the difficulties of a friendship (or marriage) between the prosaic, practical, and economically conservative Merkel (who is understood as sharing "character" with Germany), and the more "flamboyant" character of Sarkozy (and, in this model, of France). Thinking of gods as people similarly allows humans to imagine patterns of interaction with the intangible Divine, as evidenced by religious traditions involving praising gods (presuming they have positive social face, like humans), giving them offerings (presuming they can participate in exchanges of goods and favors, like humans), and so on.

Examples of personification and objectification are very common in language and art, which demonstrates pervasive importance in cognition. Personification allows speakers to attribute volitional behavior to abstractions, and also to represent the ways in which the speaker is affected by them. If one says, *Greed makes me angry*, *Envy breaks people's lives*, or *This idea makes me happy*, the crucial effect is to allow us to talk about how humans are affected by events, emotions, and the behaviors associated with them. Giving *this idea* the power to have an effect (for example on one's mood) is primarily useful in describing that effect, rather than conveying any details of how the effect is achieved. As a result, personifications of this kind are frequently used with verbs of causation and other transitive verbs which attribute agenthood to the subject. The examples given here thus clearly show that analysis of metaphoric usages requires close attention to the sentential patterns they promote.

Objectifications, in comparison, are most common in descriptions of how we mentally manipulate abstractions. In a sense, it is the flip side of personification since, instead of providing a construal of an effect something has on us, they offer a construal of our (often agentive) interaction with something. *Unpacking, constructing, digesting, grasping,* or *throwing away an idea* are expressions which help us describe mental processes rather than the abstractions themselves. Adjectives used to describe these metaphoric objects indicate the properties of the abstract entities, in terms of the physical properties of physical entities. Ideas can be *appetizing, fragile, malleable, impermeable, unwieldy,* etc., in each case presenting human minds in interaction with objects. From the perspective of linguistic choices, objectification and personification play important roles in more complex construals of causation and mental activity, and are thus frequently components of other metaphors: if we could not construe Ideas as Objects, we could not construe Communication as Object Exchange.

As a final note, it is crucial to distinguish metaphoric personification and objectification from metonymic processes which have been labeled *objectification*. Social theorists (e.g. Chen 2012) have discussed "objectifications" such as referring to a woman as a *cunt,* a *pair of boobs,* or a *piece of ass,* i.e. referring to her by (usually pejorative) names for parts of a female body. Most people prefer other people to be interested in them as whole people, rather than being interested only in particular parts of their anatomies (even when the words themselves are not pejorative, as in *a pretty face*). So these usages are indeed dehumanizing, but belong in a different category from *metaphorically* objectifying, for example, a category as a container, or a country as a household. In a way they are doing the opposite of personification. Personification of Liberty, like anthropomorphizing your computer or your car as a metaphoric person, construes the inanimate as human, sentient, even social. But metonymically referring to a person as *a pair of boobs* construes the human social being purely as physical body parts – body parts which have no social or cognitive processes. Metonymies involving human body parts are extremely common; they will be discussed in detail in Chapter 5.

3.5.2   Making the abstract concrete

Once we get beyond personification and objectification of abstract entities, however, it is much less obvious that we should be talking about metaphor as "thinking of the abstract in terms of the more concrete." In Chapter 2 we suggested that, for Primary Metaphors, the asymmetry between source and target domains is not really just one of concreteness, but is based in the cognitive asymmetry between the two domains. Vertical Height is not more concrete than Quantity, but it is more assessable than Quantity and serves as a cue for assessing Quantity, rather than the other way around. Of course, not all conceptual metaphors are primary: many of them are more complex and can be described as subcases or combinations of Primary Metaphors. However, they will naturally inherit cognitive asymmetries, including target–source differences in degree of concreteness, from their components. For example, Gibbs's (1994) examples of *spill the beans* and *let the cat out of the bag* are both examples of SECRECY IS CONCEALMENT, a more specific submapping of the very basic Primary Metaphor KNOWING IS SEEING: if knowing is seeing, then preventing something from being known is preventing something from being seen. As we noted briefly above, it is important to distinguish here between *degrees of concreteness or abstraction* and *degrees of specificity*, which we have also been discussing with reference to comparison between metaphors. Letting a cat out of a bag is much more *specific* than the rather generic idea of bringing an object out of visual concealment, but both are *concrete* physical scenarios that can be used to express something about the abstract ideas of secrecy and knowledge. The specific choice of a source domain may be a better or worse match for a specific target-domain inferential structure: in this case, a cat let out of a container may be impossible to get back into it, and that maps onto the impossibility of making an idea secret again once it has been told. There is nothing in the general source domain of Concealment which would specify this, since it is easy to hide an object again.

As we pointed out in Chapter 2, Grady (1997) and Johnson (1997) both refer to the basis of Primary Metaphors as being a correlation between a more directly sensory domain and a more subjective-assessment domain, where often the more concrete sensory domain ends up being the source domain in the metaphor, and the subjective-assessment domain is the target (MORE IS UP, AFFECTION IS WARMTH, ACQUIESCENCE IS SWALLOWING). And as Sweetser (1990) observed, the concrete/abstract contrast in metaphor is really about more and less *intersubjectively accessible* domains. Not only do we experience height physically, but *because* we do so, we expect others to assess height using the same input we use, and to predictably share our assessment of relative heights, while assessments of quantity or volume are both more difficult and less likely to be shared. We assume that heat and cold are commonly accessible to the participants in the same physical situation, while the degree of affection is something much less directly accessible through physical perception. This is equally true with the cat-out-of-the-bag example: looking at a scene, it might be difficult to know whether someone had just revealed previously secret information; but a cat's presence inside or outside of a bag is a very intersubjectively stable fact. This asymmetry of accessibility frequently leads to an asymmetry of concreteness between source and target – also present in the secrecy and cat-escape scenes, and observed by many researchers.

We have given examples where two concrete domains (Vertical Height and Quantity or Volume) are linked by experiential correlation and become source and target domains in a Primary Metaphor: target domains certainly do not have to be abstract. Nor do source domains need to be concrete. Conceptual metaphors can rely on source domains which are not immediately construable as concrete. Consider the Moral Accounting Metaphor, in which social interaction is understood as object exchange, even as financial exchange. (This metaphor was first examined by Taub, whose analysis was more extensively developed by Lakoff and Johnson [1999].) Examples of conventional references to social interaction using this metaphor include *I'm deep **in your debt***, *You **owe** me*, *I can never **repay** you*, and *I'll **pay** you **back***. It would be hard to claim Morality is self-evidently more or less abstract than Accounting, though one might well argue that repayment of a monetary debt – although abstract – is surely more intersubjectively verifiable than the precise moral equivalence of good or bad actions. And certainly there is a deep and pervasive moral aspect to monetary exchanges (paying debts is a moral thing to do), and (asymmetrically) not so necessarily a financial aspect to all moral exchanges. Small children do not of course understand money; but they early understand exchange of objects and reciprocity of favors – laying a groundwork in primary scenes for the adult Moral Accounting Metaphor.

So even for metaphors with a clear experiential basis, there are immediate difficulties in maintaining the idea that metaphors are about understanding the abstract in terms of the concrete. Consider ARGUMENT IS WAR – or ARGUMENT IS COMBAT, depending on our choice between labels for overlapping metaphors discussed in Chapter 2. Of course it is true that War and Combat involve physical force and fighting, while Argument can be entirely a linguistic communicative activity. But this does not fully resolve the problem of abstraction. Certainly an argument is more linguistic and social than a physical fight – though the two certainly can co-occur, providing a clear experiential basis for the metaphor. And we can even say this is related to a primary mapping: that is, disagreement can lead simultaneously (in little children's frequent experience) to argumentative communication and to physical struggle, which are thus correlated in a primary scene.

But there are added complexities to consider. Some fights – and organized wars in particular – have a great deal of abstract conceptual structure (strategy, purposes, social relations within armies and between governments, and so on). And both arguments and wars typically involve people who have conflicting desires and beliefs about some situation, so there is real shared structure in the domain of participant intentions. Because of this shared structure, we are not surprised to find examples such as *a border squabble between two nations*, which suggests that beside ARGUMENT IS COMBAT/WAR, there is a WAR IS ARGUMENT metaphor. This is true – although the function of that metaphor is entirely different from that of the ARGUMENT IS WAR metaphor. *Border squabble* (referring perhaps to a relatively minor military skirmish along an international border) makes use of the NATIONS ARE PEOPLE metaphor mentioned above, and in particular trivializes the military action by treating it not just as an argument, but as a minor argument between kids, a squabble. As with the domains of Computers and Humans, we have here two domains each of which has both concrete and abstract structure, and we may pick different frames in the two domains and build different mappings between them.

An added crucial point is that not all these metaphors have equal degrees of experiential grounding. The Primary Metaphor is clearly something more like ARGUMENT IS COMBAT, not ARGUMENT IS WAR. Small children experience correlation between communicative disagreement and physical struggle, not between verbal disagreement and organized warfare. Soldiers fighting a war may never even talk to each other. So the Primary Metaphor here is, again, a mapping from concrete to abstract. But how do we know when *nonprimary* mappings like ARGUMENT IS WAR will arise, and what they will be?

3.5.3   Metaphor families

To make things more complicated, consider cases such as SPORTS ARE WAR and WAR IS A SPORT. Morgan (2008) developed the concept of **metaphor families** to describe cases where a group of domains includes shared frame structure, which permits mapping back and forth among that group of domains. One such family is united by the Competition frame, which is part of the structure of such varied domains as War, Combat, Argument, Business Competition, Elections, Sports Competition, and Predation. The Competition frame involves at least two parties, consciously acting towards incompatible goals: only one of the parties can achieve her desired result. Both competing sports teams can't win a game, and only one athlete gets the Olympic gold medal in a given sport; in Predation, either the prey escapes or the predator gets fed; in Business Competition, multiple competing businesses cannot all get the same desirable contract or sell a car to the same customer; in Elections, one candidate is elected and the others are not; in War or Combat, it is understood that one side's victory is the other side's loss (they can't both have the desired territory, for example); and in Argument, it is equally understood that the winner's views will prevail and perhaps shape group decision making, while the loser's will not.

We might now rephrase this metaphor family relationship partly in terms of inheritance, since the general Competition frame is inherited by all of the subdomains. But there is something more here. Within a metaphor family, we can see metaphors mapping in a number of directions between domains, with some of those mappings being more productive than others. Competitive Team Sports are particularly likely to be seen as War – and this is most true of sports such as rugby or American football, which share a lot of structure with physical combat. Thus we find mappings like *The Vikings slaughtered the Raiders* (note that these attested team names are themselves evocative of combat situations), or references to a top player as the team's *secret weapon*. But Morgan also notes that organized Warfare is also understood as Competitive Team Sports: one could speak of the *game plan* for a military raid, or imagine a military unit saying they *scored a goal* against the enemy. And both Sports Competition and War

Table 3.4 *Selected mappings among the Competition family of frames*

Competition	War	Team Sports
Competitors	Combatants	Players
(Groups competing)	National armies	Teams
Incompatible purposes	Can't both own land	Can't both win game
One participant succeeds	Military victory	Winning a game
Successful participant achieves purpose	Gain in territory	Status as winner

Political Election	Business Competition	Predation
Candidates	Businesses	Predators/prey
Parties	Groups of employees	(Packs of predators)
Only one candidate can take office	(Only one business gets a given customer)	Preying and escaping incompatible
Getting the most votes	Getting customers	Preying or escaping
Taking office	Gain in profit	Survival

are metaphors for Business Competition: a company could *take out its heavy artillery* in competing with another; Business Competition can be *cutthroat* or *take no prisoners*, and you could equally have a *game plan* and *score points* against the competition. Further, Predation is a model at least for Team Sports and Business Competition; in both of the latter domains, one can say *it's dog eat dog* or *survival of the fittest* (and note the frequency of "predator" sports-team names such as Sharks, Wolverines, Tigers, and Bears). Moving to politics, an election can be seen as a Race (perhaps the most basic metaphor for Elections in American English), a competitive Team Sport (Candidate X *scored points against*, or *made an end run around*, Candidate Y), a War or Combat (candidates *advance*, *hunker down*, *bring out the big guns*, and *land punches*), and possibly Predation as well.

Several points emerge strongly from Morgan's analysis. One is that concreteness and abstractness are important, and are relative rather than absolute. Indeed, War (or at least Combat) and Predation may be more concrete even than Team Sports (which involve a great many abstract rules), and all of these seem more concrete than Elections or Business Competition or Argument. And indeed this is probably part of the reason why we don't understand Combat in terms of Elections, or (at least typically) as Business Competition, even though the reverse mappings are common.

Another emergent point is the importance of the shared Competition frame which enables all these varied mappings; such shared inheritance of frame structure can apparently enable mappings even in the absence of correlational motivation from a primary scene. It is highly unlikely that small children have a daily experiential correlation between Business Competition and War, or between Team Sports and Predation. But even without such experiential correlation, shared generic frame structure can license mappings between the domains. Table 3.4 gives some of these mappings for some of these domains: we have not mapped

Combat separately from War, or Races separately from Team Sports. Note that the exclusivity of the Purpose in each domain – only one participant can be the "winner" – is common to all of the domains, and defines the generic Competition frame.

A third emergent point is that, despite the shared Competition frame, the differences between these domains are just as important in determining mappings as the similarities. The WAR IS ARGUMENT *border squabble* example showed this; it trivializes the armed conflict referred to and de-emphasizes its deadliness. Warfare, unlike an individual fistfight, involves strong cooperation within each armed force, as well as extreme competition between them, which could map well onto organized groups of team members or business employees. However, also unlike a fistfight, warfare generally involves both combatant and even noncombatant fatalities and added collateral damage to the surroundings. It may therefore be an overly strong metaphor to use for Business Competition, or Elections, unless you want inferences such as that the business competitors don't care what happens to the communities in which they operate, or that candidates are willing to ruin the reputations not just of the opposing candidates but of their ("noncombatant") spouses or children as well. Football might be a safer metaphor to use if you want to suggest that the businesses are still "obeying the rules" or that the candidates are competing vigorously but "playing fair."

Although inheritance relationships are involved both in metaphor families and in metaphor subcases (discussed in Section 3.3 above), they are involved in very different ways. The subcase examples involve more general metaphoric mappings being inherited by more specific ones (sometimes with more than one general mapping being inherited by a specific metaphor, as in *glass ceiling*). The frames involved are not necessarily similar: one would not say ideas are "like" objects or that they share basic frame structure with them, nor that one is a subcase of the other. Rather, a very generic mapping IDEAS ARE OBJECTS is shared between construals such as COMMUNICATION IS OBJECT EXCHANGE and INTELLECTUAL ASSIMILATION IS DIGESTION. In the case of metaphor families, a set of *frames* shares generic structure inherited from a more general frame, like Competition. Then, if metaphoric mappings are built up between these somewhat similar frames, it is sometimes possible to build metaphors in many different directions (BUSINESS IS WAR, COMPETITIVE SPORTS ARE WAR, WAR IS A COMPETITIVE SPORT, BUSINESS IS A COMPETITIVE SPORT, and so on). Such a group of mappings constitutes a *metaphor family*.

3.6   Conclusions: concrete and abstract, generic and specific

An important strand of our story starts with experiential correlations (*primary scenes*), which underlie Primary Metaphors and motivate an asymmetric correlation between abstract and concrete experiences. This makes a great deal of our cognition metaphoric, and explains why crosslinguistically we find vocabulary for Quantity taken from the domain of Verticality or height, or vocabulary for Time taken from the domain of Space, but not vice versa. And interestingly, these Primary Metaphors often seem to be developed at a very *schematic* or generic (sometimes *image-schematic*) level. Despite the fact that children never directly experience generic schemas of Up/Down or of Quantity, but only individual specific instances of spatial relations and quantities, nonetheless they do generalize, and the correlation and the metaphor develop at the level of MORE IS UP. So Primary Metaphors are both highly schematic and also concrete to abstract in directionality.

It is normal for these very schematic mappings to also be manifested in more elaborated specific *subcases*: uses such as *prices skyrocketed, supplies were low* involve more specific mappings than MORE IS UP, but inherit all of MORE IS UP. In fact, everyday metaphoric linguistic usages are typically at the more basic imageable level, much richer in information than the schematic primary mappings which they instantiate. We mentioned earlier that these richer images can also be inferentially rich: the cat being let out of the bag has an inference of irreversibility which is not present in a schematic understanding of reversal of physical concealment, and which is highly relevant to the irreversibility of information revelation in the target domain of SECRECY IS CONCEALMENT. We call the relationships between more schematic and more elaborated metaphoric mappings *cascades*, since the structures of more schematic mappings are inherited by and fully present in the more specific ones.

Metaphoric mappings also arise, however, in cases where there is *shared frame structure* between two domains, even when there is not a primary experiential correlation – for example, where all the domains involve a Competition frame as one of their components, that shared structure allows mappings between them. Such a group of metaphors, whose relationships are motivated not by shared mappings but by shared structure of the input frames, is called a *metaphor family*. Thus it is possible for Predation to be construed as either War or Sports Competition – and for War to be construed as Predation, or Sports Competition. Although there still seems to be some preference for seeing more abstract domains in terms of more concrete ones (ELECTORAL POLITICS IS WAR, not the other way round), shared frame structure can allow mappings without this asymmetry.

Complex mappings arise when *more than one* set of higher-level (more schematic) metaphoric mappings are inherited by a more specific mapping: for example, the metaphor of the *glass ceiling* inherits LIFE IS A JOURNEY, AUTHORITY IS UP, and KNOWING IS SEEING, while the THEORIES ARE BUILDINGS mappings inherit PERSISTENCE IS REMAINING ERECT, DEPENDENCE IS PHYSICAL SUPPORT, and ABSTRACT ORGANIZATION IS COMPLEX PHYSICAL STRUCTURE. Metaphors may thus be related to each other by subordinate vs. superordinate category relations: one can be a subcase of the other. But this relationship is a complex one, since a given lower-level (more specific) metaphor can be a subcase of *more than one* higher-level mapping.

The general wisdom that metaphors map from concrete to abstract is thus partially right. But it is certainly not the whole story: if Football can be mapped onto War, and War onto Football, it is clear that differences in concreteness are not absolutely controlling mappings between domains. Shared frame structure of the right kinds (to be discussed further in Chapter 4) seems to license mappings at the same level of concreteness. Later, in our discussion of metaphors in scientific discourse, we'll discuss metaphors like THE ATOM IS A SOLAR SYSTEM, which are another case of mapping one concrete domain onto another. Image metaphors like *hourglass waist* also seem to map one concrete image onto another – one way in which image metaphors are very different from conceptual metaphors.

We do see strong tendencies for mappings to go from concrete frames to abstract frames in large classes of metaphors, but even there the motivations may be quite different in different classes of cases. Primary Metaphors naturally go from concrete to abstract because of the direction of experiential correlations (Height is a cue for Quantity, not the other way round). But ontological metaphors are used to "make" the abstract concrete – they are making things "human scale," for example by seeing a nation or an abstract quality as a person.

And, for relationships *between* metaphors, the key relationships are not between more concrete and more abstract frames (as is often the case *within* a metaphor). Inheritance relationships between metaphors have to do with the level of *schematicity* or *specificity* of the frames involved: LIFE IS A JOURNEY inherits the mappings of the more generic PURPOSIVE ACTION IS MOTION, and bequeaths structure in its turn to more specific cases such as *glass ceiling* (which also inherits from other schematic metaphors such as KNOWING IS SEEING).

3.7   Summary

This chapter has shown how connections between domains emerge in metaphoric mappings. The main point of the discussion was that mappings do not emerge on one level only, but with complex relationships between levels. For example, expressions describing goal-oriented activities in terms of some aspects of directional motion should be considered at many levels. Also, we argued that mappings should not be automatically described at the highest level of specificity, as important generalizations are lost that way. A frame of a Journey seems to be a natural source domain choice when salient details are fleshed out, but we need to consider all the more abstract and general levels of mappable structure which it inherits.

We have shown how various mappings are related – through shared schemas, Primary Metaphors, cascade effects, or metaphor family relations. We argued that metaphors do not exist independently, but as part of a network of other metaphors. Metaphoric language depends on numerous connections across different mappings, which calls for a full analysis of such connections – for example, many metaphoric mappings depend on ontological metaphors, as well as personification and objectification patterns. Also, engaging in metaphor analysis requires decisions with respect to the desirable level of schematicity for a particular analysis, and should further be enhanced through a discussion of cross-metaphor links. Connections across mappings are systematic; we should be uncovering networks of metaphors, rather than individual mappings. And we have emphasized that, within this framework, it is unhelpful to refer to a linguistic expression as a *metaphor*, although it may often be an unavoidable shorthand. In this complex network of inheritance between levels, a single linguistic form may instantiate quite a complex group of metaphoric mappings, and labeling it *a metaphor* may lead us to neglect that complexity.

We also fleshed out our understanding of the expectation that source domains are typically concrete and target domains are usually abstract. We presented a number of examples to show that such considerations may be helpful in many cases, but not in all. *Concrete* and *abstract* are fuzzy and complex terms. And while concrete-to-abstract patterns are often clearly there, specific choices of metaphoric expressions are more clearly explained through inheritance patterns across different mappings and the specificity of the frames required. And it is often more helpful to think about asymmetries in intersubjective accessibility than asymmetries in concreteness, in comparing source and target-domain frames.

4 Mental spaces and blending

In this chapter, we will start looking beyond metaphor. While metaphor is probably the most-discussed class of mappings in recent literature, we want to show how the general nature of figurative language can be analyzed in broader conceptual terms. We will start with a discussion of multidomain mappings (some of them metaphoric), but we will also be trying to clarify the nature of lower-level concepts (such as analogy and similarity) which underlie mappings of many kinds.

One of the concepts we will introduce here is a type of multidomain mapping known as **blending** (Fauconnier and Turner 2002). In much of the literature on figurative language, no distinction is maintained between metaphor and blending, so we want to make it clear where our analysis stands. In many traditional discussions of metaphor, any example where a lexical expression is used in a meaning considered "not literal" is referred to as "metaphor" – and more detailed discussions of metaphor are clearer, but often focus only on predicative constructions such as *Achilles is a lion* or *My job is a jail*. For in-depth linguistic analysis of figurative usage, we need to look systematically at a range of constructions and of figurative meanings. On the one hand, figurative sources of lexical polysemy fall into a number of categories, including metonymy and blending as well as metaphor. On the other hand, constructional forms such as simile and nominal modification play an important role in evoking figurative mappings, and so the focus on predicative constructions distorts many linguistic facts. Finally, broader discourse contexts yield interpretations such as irony, where nonliteral meanings emerge on the basis of conceptual domains and viewpoint.[1] We will gradually be introducing these figurative thought patterns throughout the rest of the book.

4.1 Why we need to talk about more structure than two domains: metaphor as blending

Metaphor is a reconceptualization of one domain (the target) in terms of another (the source). But looking at a depiction of a metaphor as a mapping

---

[1] We should also note here that we do not rely on the Metaphor Identification Procedure proposed by the Pragglejaz Group (2007) and developed in Steen et al. (2010). While useful in many ways, it is intended primarily to identify a broad range of metaphoric usages in corpora, including cases where more complex types of mappings are involved (occasionally, the word *hybrid* is used to represent combinations of lexical and visual prompts).

between two domains, one might wonder where in the representation to find that conceptualization or construal. There's a place for source-domain structure and frames, and a place for target-domain structure and frames – and a specification of mappings between particular substructures and frames in those two domains. But the metaphoric cognitive structure which emerges from those mappings – the understanding of Anger as Heat/Pressure of a Liquid rather than as a Wild Beast, or of Argument as Combat – is presumably different from either the source or the target considered alone. But it doesn't seem to have a representation of its own. In a diagram, the arrows (between Anger and Heat/Pressure, between Degree of Anger and Degree of Heat/Pressure) would represent the mappings; but what represents the metaphoric construal of Anger as Heat and Pressure?

Nor is there any place in a two-domain table or diagram where we are representing the generic structure shared between source and target domains which guides those mappings. As we have said, things like aspectual, causal, and scalar structure not only are generally shared by source and target domains, but seem to *constrain* the mappings between the two domains. The Heat/Pressure model of Anger exemplifies all three of these kinds of pairings. We map the scale of increase or decrease in heat and pressure onto a scale of degree of anger. Just as we know that liquid which is steaming or simmering is not on the verge of violently blowing off the top of the container, so we know that a person who's *simmering* is not as furious as someone ready to *blow her top* or *explode*. Similarly, speakers can identify the shared aspectual structure involved; a liquid has to first start being heated by some heat source, and has to go through the whole intermediate scale of heats and pressures before it reaches the final result of explosion. This maps onto the idea that an angry person doesn't typically instantly "blow her top," but rather, her anger develops over time before that happens. And we could not map it the other way: it would simply be incoherent to have *explode* refer to a lower level of overt anger-manifestation than *simmer*.

The Invariance Principle (Lakoff 1993) has suggested that scalar, causal, and aspectual structure must be preserved in metaphoric mappings. Thus not only is it impossible to map sudden rage onto *simmering*, it is impossible to map the *causal source* of the rage (perhaps bad behavior on the part of the person at whom the anger is directed) onto the *result* of the heat/pressure (the explosion) – result must be mapped onto result, not onto cause. There may be very exceptional cases where this constraint is violated (see Fauconnier and Turner 2002), but overall Invariance seems to hold. Therefore it would be useful to have a way to represent the shared content between source and target, because that shared content could well indicate the constraints on mappings. But so far, we haven't talked about representing shared structure on its own.

So we think it is helpful to expand our analytic structures. There are times when it is quite sufficient just to notice the systematic structure of mappings between source and target, and other times when it seems crucial to be explicit about the shared structure which constrains a mapping, or about the new cognitive structure which emerges as we reconstrue the target domain. Conceptual Integration Theory

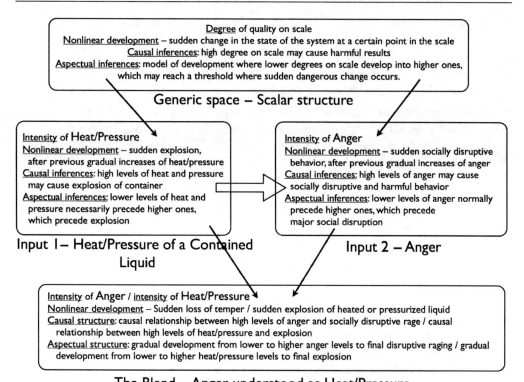

Figure 4.1. *The "Anger/Heat" blend*

(or Blending Theory), developed by Fauconnier and Turner (1994, 1996, 1998a, 1998b, 2002) gives us formal mechanisms to describe all these things. It does so by treating the source and target domains as *input spaces*, reserving an independent construct for the shared structure (the *generic space*) and postulating an explicit construct where the emergent structure of the metaphoric construal of the target concept is represented (the *blend*).[2]

Let's therefore imagine a diagram which includes not only a target and a source, but also the shared generic structure and the new metaphoric construal produced by the metaphor. We will represent it as four spaces, with four lists of corresponding entities which are mapped onto each other, rather than two. This will be a four-space structure – that is, four different structures will be involved instead of two. In the case of ANGER IS HEAT/PRESSURE OF LIQUID, we now have Figure 4.1.

---

[2] We are introducing Blending Theory here in contrast not with metaphor but with many two-domain mapping treatments of metaphor. As we will show in the remainder of the chapter (and the book), it is a general theory of meaning emergence, of which metaphor is a subcase. Blending Theory has been fruitfully applied to the analysis of a number of linguistic concepts, but also to narrative texts, theater, mathematics, art, etc. In this book, we will focus on examples which demonstrate avenues for the emergence of figurative meaning.

The structure described as "the blend" can be described as follows:

> Blend: an emergent conceptual construct, resulting from integration of other (often already complex) constructs and serving new meaning-construction needs.

Much of this structure was discussed in Chapters 2 and 3; the new thing is that we now have separate descriptions of the generic structure (the generic space) which guides mappings between the source and the target (the two input spaces), and of the blend, the new structure which emerges from those mappings and constitutes a new construal of the target domain. In the remainder of this chapter, we will describe various types of blends and the ways in which these mental constructs emerge. First, however, we will situate the concept of blending with respect to the larger context of Mental Spaces Theory, and the analysis of frames proposed in Chapter 2.

The next question which obviously arises is: what are these very different kinds of structures which we have just mapped? The generic structure for the "Anger/Heat" blend is a rather skeletal, un-filled-out structure involving just a schematic scalar structure (i.e. no particular scale) and a schematic causal and aspectual profile. The source and target structures are more filled out in the case of *blow one's top*: we can have a source-domain *image* of a boiler or a pressure cooker about to blow up, and a target-domain image of a person about to fly into a rage, but it is hard to picture an image of the generic structure. It seems clear that cognitive structures of very different levels of specificity are mapped onto each other within this one metaphor, and so it is useful at this point to stop and think about what kinds of different structures these mental spaces are, and how to categorize them and their behavior.

4.2   The relationship of mental spaces to frames

Blending Theory is a development of Mental Spaces Theory. Mental Spaces Theory was originally introduced by Fauconnier (1994 [1985]), primarily to solve problems of reference,[3] and was further developed in Fauconnier 1997 and elsewhere. The essential idea is that mental spaces are *cognitive* structures, prompted by language; human cognition and language don't have access to anything beyond human experience and thought. So in using mental spaces to

---

[3] Many readers are likely familiar with the mental spaces analysis of examples such as *In the picture, the girl with blonde hair is a redhead*. The mental spaces analysis allows us to identify that presence of two spaces in this construal (the "reality" space, or base space, and the representation space, or "picture" space). The cross-mapping linking the actual (perhaps blonde) girl and the (redheaded) representation allows us to resolve the issue of the same referent being described as having two different hair colors at the same time.

analyze linguistic structure, we're using a representation which is explicitly not connected to any extralinguistic reality. Mental Space analysts agree that there is a world out there (and that it would still be there if we weren't), but people's experience of it lies in their perception of it and their interaction with it, and we can never access it independently of that. The world that a human knows is the world she conceptualizes. The role of language, in this view, is to guide conceptualization by prompting cognitive spaces and frames, rather than simply to represent it.

As well as being mental constructs, mental spaces are *partial* cognitive representations. Unlike Possible Worlds, Mental Spaces are not built up on the assumption that humans are accessing their entire coherent cognitive systems or looking for coherence in every corner of them. It is well recognized that humans are much better at local coherence than global coherence. So at any given time we are taking partial, local cognitive structures and integrating them with other such structures. The concept of a *mental space* allows us to discuss these spontaneous processes of meaning construction, and turns out to permit clear and accurate semantic descriptions of a range of grammatical phenomena including pronoun use, conditional constructions, temporal and causal constructions, and constructions of intersubjectivity (see Fauconnier and Sweetser 1996, Dancygier and Sweetser 2005, Verhagen 2005).

Particular linguistic structures appear to exist precisely to help language users track the location of referents within mental spaces: for example *when* marks the fact that the speaker is identifying the contents of the clause as taking place in an actual situation, while *if* situates the clause contents only in a conditional space. *In the movie, Eliza marries Professor Higgins* situates the described event as taking place in the movie, as opposed to in Shaw's play or in reality. It is useful to keep these spaces separate: in the real world, no Eliza Doolittle existed, while in Shaw's play she existed but did not marry Professor Higgins. So we can talk about representation spaces (such as fiction and art), imaginary spaces, conditional or counterfactual spaces, etc.

But other cognitive structures evoked by language do not necessarily profile such broader structures which locate events with respect to a Base Space: instead, they describe entities and situations. Words such as *run* or *dog* don't tell us whether they are being used to talk about reality, fiction, or possibility. Also, linguistic forms provide the degree of specificity appropriate to the intended content, which is why we can describe the same animal as a *vertebrate*, a *mammal*, a *dog*, or a *golden retriever* – and nothing about any of those four descriptions tells us whether the animal is part of a past, present, conditional, or fictional space. This is equally true in inputs to metaphoric blends. If we describe the pricing practices of a store metaphorically by saying *This is highway robbery*, we are not necessarily construing the overpricing in terms of some specific instance of robbery, complete with location, time, or robbers of specific height and hair color, carrying specific weapons. Nor, in the overpricing frame, are we even necessarily thinking of an evil employee of the store deliberately overpricing the goods. A rather schematic source frame of coercing people to part with money may be mapped onto a rather schematic target frame of overpricing.

The specific content of spaces evoked may of course differ depending on the reader or listener and the context. In some cases, the structure evoked by the *highway robbery* example may be quite simple, essentially frame-based; in other cases, someone may think of a specific person's specific behavior at a specific time, or recall a story read in her childhood about evil robbers and travelers in peril. The analyst's job cannot be to try and uncover the details of the actual conceptualization evoked in the language user's mind. But we can describe the minimal components of such a blend (the "robber" and the "victim," the use of force, etc.): what enables this blend to be understood (as it surely is) by speakers of English in general? Using the blending framework, we can say that there is a generic image of coercion being used to obtain wealth, we can describe the two inputs (the overpricing and the robbery), and we can identify how these yield a blend in which the pricing practices are considered hurtful to the customer (so we would map, for example, the robber onto the store, and the victim onto the customer). Note also that this blend, like many metaphoric mappings, takes one participant's viewpoint – the *highway robbery* description clearly represents the viewpoint of the customer feeling forced to pay too much, and not that of a store manager scheming to get more profit and using ruthless methods.

Regardless of how much specific structure may actually be evoked in the mind of any given person processing them, we will typically refer to the structures involved in blending as *spaces* – even in specific instances where the space is exclusively *frame-based*, and thus relatively skeletal.[4] For example, a purely frame-based input space will typically have enough structure to distinguish the type of event, but may not profile specific participants, deictic features, etc. In other words, frames have the potential to be conceptually elaborated and become less skeletal spaces, but they may also remain simple.

4.3   Spaces and frames: types and relations

When discussing blending and metaphor, it is important to distinguish differing levels of specificity or schematicity. Below, we will outline the major types of input structures and some types of relations between input structures.

---

[4] Blending theorists are not always consistent in their choices between the terms *frame* and *space*. The term *frame* is commonly used in analyses of modification constructions or compounds (Coulson [2001, 2006] uses *frame*; Sweetser [1999, 2000] uses *space*), while the term *space* prevails in the standard Fauconnier and Turner presentations of blending. We believe that most theorists use the term *space* as a default term, when making a clear distinction between frame structure and space structure is not of importance; we also follow that practice.

Possibly the simplest type of structure is exemplified by Primary Metaphors, where the primary content of the input frames is image-schematic structure. A mapping like STATES ARE LOCATIONS, or TIME PERIODS ARE BOUNDED REGIONS (*on Monday, in the coming month*), does not give a lot of detail to either side of the mapping: States, Time Periods, Bounded Regions, and Locations are all very schematic. Similarly, MORE IS UP, LESS IS DOWN evokes the highly schematic structures of Quantity and Verticality. Of course, Primary Metaphors actually emerge from an individual's full sensory experiences of specific inputs such as heights and quantities (the height and quantity of liquid in the child's sippy cup at a given time), or of specific experienced states and locations. But their power lies precisely in the fact that they are abstracted away from those specific cases to form the basis for conceptualizing the correlated general parameters.

On the other hand, many complex metaphoric mappings are more fleshed out than MORE IS UP. In saying that someone *missed the boat* or *reached a dead-end in her career*, we surely evoke more complex and more specific imagery of boats or dead-end streets, even though the very schematic Location ESM (ACTION IS MOTION, PURPOSIVE ACTION IS GOAL-DIRECTED MOTION) and its subcase LIFE IS A JOURNEY are still present as a major component of that more specific complex structure. So the metaphoric expressions *miss the boat* and *reach a dead-end* are specific *subcases* of both the (very general) Location ESM and its (still quite general) subcase LIFE IS A JOURNEY. We need to keep in mind that all expressions and mappings participate in hierarchies defined by levels of schematicity, and also that more specific instances activate the more schematic ones as part of their structure.

The level of specificity of mappings depends of course on the levels of specificity of the frames mapped. We will use the term *superordinate frame* or *schematic frame* to talk about frames which do not have visual and motor imagery (see Rosch 1977, Mervis and Rosch 1981 for more discussion of the special basic level of categories, involving visual and motor imagery). The frames of Sinking and Soaring are specific cases of the superordinate Up and Down schemas. There is no motor imagery, and only minimal schematic visual imagery, in the abstract Up and Down frames, but there is a specific type of motion and much richer visual imagery in, say, the expressions *Prices sank* and *Prices soared*, which combine the Up/Down schema with CHANGE IS MOTION, with specific manners of motion and moving objects. An input space which is essentially structured by a single highly schematic frame will be referred to as a *superordinate* or *schematic space*, while a *basic-level* space or frame evokes visual and motor imagery.

At the other end of the schematicity spectrum, an extremely specific and detailed space, with links to some particular set of participants, time, and place – let's say we're talking about having coffee with a specific colleague between classes yesterday – will usually include many different frames. Some of them might include general knowledge about collegial relations in academia, friendship, coffee shops, and gossip. Others might include (for both speaker and hearer, if they both know the participants in the coffee date) the specific appearances of the two participants, their voices, their likely styles of clothing, and so on. This is definitely at the *subordinate* level of categorization (as described by Rosch) and it is highly complex and multiframed as well. We would like to give the label *fully embodied space* to a space structured by this level of detailed frame structure. The level of detail a space can achieve in a specific situation may depend on various aspects of our cognitive functioning. In the case of the "coffee-shop chat" space, we may be filling in much of the information from memory (of the participants, the coffee shop's location, etc.), but we also use "generic" memories to fill in the structure of an imaginary or fictional space. In fact, we also do a lot of similar "filling in" to embody spaces in fictional narratives, which is how some people end up with the idea that Colin Firth in the movie based on *Pride and Prejudice* does or does not "look like" Mr. Darcy. Thus it is not only descriptions or memories of actual events which are filled out in this way. On the contrary, our hopes, wishes, and fictional plots are structured by borrowing from our embodied experience of real events.

In a story or in an extended discourse, mental spaces form networks of spaces linked in terms of temporal sequences and/or causality chains. Thus *temporal and causal relations* among spaces constitute another dimension of analysis. Importantly, this is a property of frames and spaces that holds whether or not linguistic expressions themselves refer to a sequence of events. We discussed above the metaphoric construal of an extreme expression of anger as an explosion, suggesting that the frame of an overheating and exploding boiler is "a frame" structuring "an input space" – and this now makes another important point, namely that frames are dynamic, with aspectual and causal structure, as we have seen. And the spaces that they structure are dynamic too: we can, as Fauconnier and Turner (2002) say, "run" them and see what the next stage or the result will be – so a boiler overheating can eventually explode, just as an angry person can eventually be unable to repress expression of their anger; this frame is thus inherently open to a causal, sequential interpretation. Nonetheless, we will need to treat causal and temporal sequences *between* spaces as a unique kind of relationship. Let us call this the *succession relation*: if one space is the *successor* or *predecessor* of another, they cannot be simultaneous, and they have to be fitted into slots of cause–result or result–cause, and their sequencing related to the broader aspectual structure of the events involved.

Fortunately or unfortunately, the segmentation issue (what counts as "a" frame or "an" event in such a dynamic sequence) is a well-identified though as-yet-unsolved problem. We know that there is no such thing as an *event* in the world: segmenting the structure of our experience into events is something we do as cognizers. And we're capable of different-sized chunkings: a vacation could be an event, if the chunking is coarser-grained, or the particular moment when you got stung by a bee during that vacation could be an event.

Another important relation is that of paired networks of spaces, as in cases where we need to simultaneously construe two causal chains – one real and the other one negated or counterfactual. For example, if one says either *He could have gotten that job* or *He didn't get that job*, it prompts two scenarios: one the scenario of the protagonist getting the job, and the other (the real one) wherein he did not get it. Counterfactuality and negation both involve a special relation, namely *alternativity*. The positive and negative spaces can't both hold in the same space–time slot, nor can the factual and the counterfactual spaces; they are *alternatives* (Dancygier 1998, 2010, 2012b, Dancygier and Sweetser 2005). Alternative thinking is often expressed by specific grammatical construc-tions, and these constructions crucially depend on frames, spaces, and blending processes.

Another crucial dimension of spatial categorization is that of conventionality vs. novelty. Frames rely on shared cultural knowledge, though they may be shared by groups of various sizes – from an entire community to a group as small as a family. They are part of our "prefab" knowledge about the world. Not being new-born babies, we are able to recognize a scene of medical consultation, or of ordering food in a restaurant, as such without conscious work. Other animals do this kind of thing too: a cat may associate being put into the car with a visit to the vet, on the basis of past experience. And frames, along with established object-categories, help us structure our experience. These cognitive structures reside in long-term brain patterns, and remain accessible to our abilities or memories without being constantly activated. On the other hand, the specific dynamic situation which we're imagining when we're told the story of yesterday's coffee date is not being pulled from long-term memory. It is being constructed on the fly, though using (as we said) aspects of familiar frames and categories such as Coffee and Coffee Shop. This we might call an *online space* – to refer to the original formulation in Mental Spaces Theory, where mental spaces were talked about as cognitive structures that emerge "online" as discourse progresses.

If the criteria we have proposed are combined, the "coffee-shop-chat" space can be described as an *online, subordinate, fully embodied space*. It has been prompted in ongoing discourse, so it is *online*; it relies on a number of complex, interrelated frames, so it is *subordinate*; and it is filled with specific details regarding the time, the location, the participants, the relationships between the participants, etc., so it is *fully embodied*. Furthermore, if the speaker then said, *And then I had to go teach*, she would add a *successor* space along a temporal and causal dimension, but if she said, *If the weather had been nicer, we could have sat outside*, she would be prompting the construction of an *alternative* space, wherein different weather conditions on that given day would have resulted in a somewhat different location for the encounter.

Crucially, as we will show, all of these kinds of spaces can be mapped in the ways that we have been talking about throughout this book: metaphoric mappings and other kinds of blending can involve these very different kinds of structures, all of which are frame-based in content. Generic or schematic structures may be mapped onto each other in primary or other high-level mappings, but they also often *guide* mappings between more specific structures, as we saw in ANGER IS HEAT/PRESSURE OF A LIQUID.

4.4   Blending processes and types of blends

The processes which transform (or *integrate*) two or more independent input spaces into one blended space are critical in producing the effects of blending. Our minds do not necessarily go through these processes in every case; however, identifying how a blend emerges is useful in considering different examples.

4.4.1   How to build a blend

Let us consider several expressions used in the early days of the Occupy Wall Street movement (the end of 2011) to describe the effects of long-term exposure to a certain view of the world and the need to reverse those effects: *mental resuscitation, pollution of our minds, infotoxins, mental detox.* All of these expressions rely on the same organizing frame of an organism affected by unhealthy influences and in need of healing. Together, they map the input space of a living organism onto the input space of the mind (where by *mind* we do *not* mean the physical brain, but cognitive structures and processes). To understand the structure of the blend, we need to look at various aspects of how it emerges. First of all, it is important to identify how various elements are connected across the inputs: here, we want to analyze the way various substances which can negatively affect an organism (polluting factors, toxins) are cross-mapped with the standard vision of the world presented by the media and other representatives of the establishment. The body of an organism can be poisoned by substances which bring about illness; in the same way, in the blend, human minds can be "poisoned" by information provided through official channels. The cross-mappings determine how the organizing frame of a poisoned organism will be used to restructure the understanding of the mind.

The inputs cannot be projected into the blend as wholes; rather, the structure needed for the blend is selected and then projected into the blended space (thus we talk about *selective projection*). In this case, most of the space topology comes from the organism input rather than from the mind input – this is why we would call the blend *metaphoric*, since it involves conceptualizing one space in terms of another. But the projection is selective, since the blend does not focus on other possible aspects of organisms (reproduction, habitat, etc.) but primarily on biological health and interaction with toxic substances. The structure projected into the blend forms a coherent whole, the *emergent structure* – the mind equipped with metaphoric states of health and illness, and the factors affecting those states (the content of the news, propaganda, etc.). Having put that structure together, we can *run the blend* – that is, understand the inferences it yields in terms of various aspects of the setup: the kinds of infotoxins our minds are exposed to, how one would clear people's minds of the effects of the poison, the sources of the "poisoning" (which need to be identified so they can be prevented from

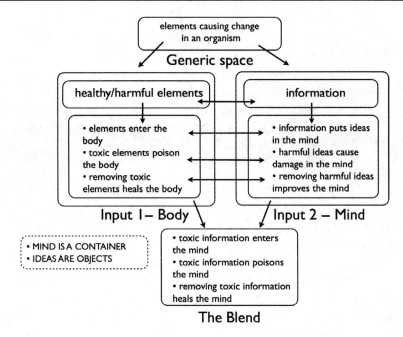

Figure 4.2. *The "toxic info" blend*

continuing to poison the mind). The impact and power of the blend is not in its structure alone, but in the inferences it yields. At the same time, the blend allows us to reason differently about the inputs (this process is referred to as *backward projection*). In this case, the blend yields a new, emotionally loaded view of the types of information we are exposed to and the effects it has on the clarity of our thoughts.

The processes responsible for the range of expressions treating information as toxic are represented in Figure 4.2. The inputs link the Body and the Mind, and, specifically substance intake and (mis)information, as factors affecting the functioning of complex organisms. Importantly, the blend does not represent any of the specific expressions we discussed, but provides a conceptual structure against which both existing and potential expressions can be explained. Additionally, it relies on metaphors which frame many mental processes in terms of bodily processes (motion, digestion, manipulation of objects, etc.). Note that Figure 4.2 shows the general structure of the two inputs, and some of the structure of the blend; it does not fully specify the mapping relations between the inputs. It does show, as must be true for the blend to be as specified, that toxic substances do not map onto ideas in the mind generally, but only onto harmful ideas that cause negative mental states; similarly, healing would map onto positive changes in informational state, not onto general changes.

Blends have very general structural properties. Fauconnier and Turner (2002) pointed out that – as we have also observed for other metaphoric blends – mapping (or *projection*) is selective. We saw that not all of the biological organism frame was projected onto the information-absorbing mind frame – the organism's reproductive cycle, for example, seems irrelevant. Aspects which will not map may simply be omitted: for example, in COMMUNICATION IS OBJECT EXCHANGE, it would be impossible to map the fact that when you give an object to someone, you no longer have the object. We know that when you tell someone something, you don't forget it as a result. So that is simply not mapped. Also, sometimes blending results in backward projection, that is even though we think of blending as projection from two input spaces into the blend, structure may also project "backward" from the blend into the input spaces. This may result in new structure in one or both of the input spaces. For example, Mark Turner's (1987) analysis of the metaphoric *Vanity is the quicksand of reason* notes that a listener or reader may not have had a role in the Reason frame which corresponded to the role of Quicksand in the Travel frame. But being asked to map Vanity onto Quicksand demands that such a role be constructed for the Reason frame, and thus that the Vanity frame include vulnerability.

We have also mentioned that blends are normally dynamic, as frames are. Part of how literal and metaphoric blends work is by simulation or "running" the blend, and simulating the resulting spaces. These spaces are structured by what Fauconnier and Turner (2002) term *vital relations*. The vital relation of *Identity* allows us to understand Mark at age ten as "the same person" as Mark at age forty, or real-world Mark as "the same person" as the Mark I am remembering meeting last year. Vital relations such as *Change* and *Cause–Effect* allow us to connect events and situations in systematic ways, and *Intentionality* allows us to judge the relationships of participants to those Cause and Effect sequences. These are closely related to vital relations of *Time* and *Space*; very different situations may prevail at different times in the same location, or in different locations at the same time, but contradictory situations cannot occur in the same space and time. *Categorization* and *Similarity* judgments allow us to decide whether some entity is part of the same category or frame as another. *Frame–Role* Structure allows us to integrate roles and fillers into frame structures, and *Part–Whole* Structure allows us to do the same with whole objects and their parts (these will become relevant in the next chapter on metonymy). *Representation* allows us to connect some mental spaces (books, paintings) with others as being representations of those other spaces: this relation can be embedded – imagine a true-crime novel which represents some past real-world events, and a movie based on the novel.

Another of the vital relations is *Analogy*. Fauconnier and Turner point out that analogical mappings operate on every level of cognitive structure, from assessing literal similarity or categorization of objects, to highly abstract analogies between complex frames – e.g. comparing the decline of US power to the decline (and eventual fall) of Rome. We constantly reason about situations based on analogy with situations we have previously experienced. For example, someone who has previously had a negative experience of an oral examination in some institution or country may have negative expectations about similarly structured situations in a different university or nation. This would be an analogical blend, since inferences would be transferred from one situation to the other. Crucially, however, analogy is an extremely general human cognitive process. When scientists prefer to use the term *analogy* for scientific models (even simple ones such as the Atom as Solar System metaphor [Gentner 1983, Gentner and Bowdle 2001]), they are avoiding the term *metaphor*. But the "atom as solar system" blend – to be discussed in Chapter 8 – clearly has the characteristics of metaphor as we have set them out. It is a blend involving two input domains, one of which (the Solar System) provides the organizing structure for the blend. And to build up the blend, identification of analogical parallels in structure was needed, in order to establish a generic space and *align* the structures for role-to-role mappings between the two frames.

All of these vital relations are part of the structures of inter-space mappings: for example, in a blended space, the two inputs may have corresponding Cause–Effect structures, which would then also be represented in the generic space. The harmful causal effect of some earlier situation on the individual's future well-being is part of the shared structure between the inputs in the "toxic info" blend.

Considering all the structural aspects of how the blends emerge (vital relations, selective projection, running the blend, backward projection) gives us a more accurate view of two processes. On the one hand, uncovering the structure of the inputs and the partial nature of the projections allows us to better understand the nature of the conceptual structures involved in the blending processes. On the other hand, understanding the results of the process (new conceptualizations, new inferences, reconstrual of the inputs) allows us to capture the nature of meaning emergence and of the processes responsible for linguistic creativity.

It is also important to identify how the spaces which are inputs to the "toxic info" blend involve the kinds of space structures we talked about above. The blend establishes new causal chains (media influence causes an unhealthy state of mind; the Occupy movement can reverse that) and succession chains (first poisoning, then treatment and healing, then possibly prevention). This blend also involves superordinate schemas, such as the Container schema (MIND IS A CONTAINER, toxins cross boundaries), but also subordinate frames, such as Pollution and Detoxification Treatment. And once again, viewpoint is important in this blend: it is because the state of being poisoned or polluted is not desirable that the need to change the situation is obvious. One could argue that the difference between poisoning and pollution (as well as the difference between the body and, perhaps, the environment) requires that we talk about two blends here, not one. This is, of course, possible, but we argue that the expressions analyzed here as part of one blending structure uniformly represent the viewpoint of a person who is forced to ingest toxic substances (whether they are pollutants or poisonous substances in food). This viewpoint gives added coherence to the inferential patterns that emerge.

This blend motivates a broader range of linguistic patterns. We have looked at some of the attested expressions motivated by the blend, but it would be easy to think of further expressions (e.g. *a toxin-free press*, *mental environmentalism*, *antimedia medication*, or *innoculation*). The blend is set up by the expressions originally used, but once its structure is clear it can yield further creative linguistic forms. Moreover, the blend does not have to be associated with a single formal pattern (though formal patterns can certainly be conventionally tied to particular blends, as we will see in our discussion of constructions in Chapter 6). No one word or construction is responsible for prompting this complex structure, and we have seen different morphological and modification patterns even within the limited range of expressions considered here. And in relation to other conceptual structures, note that this blend is part of the broad range of MIND IS BODY mappings discussed in preceding chapters (the mappings that give us, for example, *nutrition for the mind*, *a fit mind*, or *a mental workout*). We have looked at these patterns as instances of metaphor; we can now see those metaphors as instances of broad patterns of cross-domain blends.

One important process we have not mentioned yet which characterizes every blend is the process of *compression*. In our minds, the concept of toxins and the concept of information (or, specifically, media-distributed information) are very distant from each other and not closely related. But in the emergent structure of the blend, they are fused – so that inside the blend information can be characterized in terms of toxicity. The distance has been compressed. Also, we can talk about a different dimension of compression; that is, temporal compression of the processes that are fused in the blend: the effects of (dis)information, like the effects of slow but constant exposure to toxins, are often not highly perceptible, and are very diffuse over time. Likewise, the idea of physical "detox" compresses a lengthy process of returning to health, and this is also the case in the imagined reeducation process, where one is subjected to a long-lasting regime leading to improvement.

Compression can work along various dimensions of the blend (as we will show in more detail below), including time, space, identity, analogy, disanalogy, causation, and role-value mappings. Vital relations such as the ones mentioned above provide dimensions for compression: individuals and temporally local events, with close temporal proximity of cause and effect, are conceptually "human scale." Thus if someone accuses the media of *murder* for their informational *toxification* of our minds, the complex long-term scenarios of cognitive damage from misinformation, and of long-term gradual physical poisoning, are compressed into a single unified event with clear boundaries and causal structure. The diffuse set of agents involved in the media are also compressed into a single individual, now accused of being a poisoner.

Some blends also involve the process of *decompression* – wherein concepts that are unified in the inputs are split or "decompressed" for the purposes of the blend. Many of the mechanisms of blending are illustrated in example (1).

(1)   When I look back on this now, I'm quite touched by my younger self. I would like to be him again, perhaps just for a day.[5]

---

[5] Paul Kingsnorth, "Confessions of a recovering environmentalist," *Orion Magazine*, Jan/Feb 2012.

The writer, an adult man, is thinking about his *younger self* – an identity he now considers different from his current understanding of himself. This decompression along the vital relation of identity yields a situation in which the-writer-now and the-writer-then are construed as different people. The two mental spaces created by the decompression have different temporal features, and one is a successor of the other. For the writer, they are both fully embodied spaces, furnished (respectively) with memories and his current sense of self. The past space in which the writer was younger and the current space in which he is older are treated as independent inputs, inhabited by the two identities. The idea of *being him* (being the younger self), then, blends the two spaces in such a way that the Present space is inhabited not by the older man, but by the younger identity – even though we can assume that the writer desires to keep his current perceptions, to better appreciate his younger self. This blend relies crucially on both compression and decompression, along the common vital relations of time and identity. First, the writer's identity is decompressed along the dimension of time, but it assumes more than the age difference; rather, the younger persona probably had different thoughts and ideas. The current persona of the writer is also decompressed along the same lines. In the "being him" blend, the dispositions of the younger self are blended with the age and experience of the older self – in effect, the idea of *being him* means compressing the previously decompressed aspects of identity onto a new identity, consisting of the physically older person with the younger mind of the same person. One can argue further that the dual personality in the blend (being him, but also being me) is set up along the relation of *Role and Value*, so that the current role of an older man is temporarily filled by the younger value.

4.4.2   Types of blends

In discussing the Occupy Wall Street examples in Section 4.2.1, we noted that one of the two inputs, the living organism, is the one providing the organizing frame for the blend. In earlier chapters we talked about metaphor as involving structure unidirectionally projected from the source to the target, but, as we argued above, there are some benefits in explicitly describing the emerging construct itself. We now rephrase our description of metaphor as a blend where one of the two inputs provides the primary organizing frame for the blend, and thus determines the basic blend structure. This kind of blend has been referred to as a *single-scope* blend, since the projections it makes are primarily controlled by the structure of one input space (the source). In the case of the Anger examples discussed earlier in the chapter, the source input gives most of the structure to the blended concept of anger as fluid in a heated container, while the target input is present but not controlling the topological structure (the causal and aspectual structure and other vital relation structures) of the blended space. One could instead imagine thinking of Anger in terms of righteous indignation, and resulting in appropriate retribution and restoration of moral balance, after which the world is a better place. But this conceptualization of Anger would not be compatible with the topology of the Pressurized Liquid explosion input; we need a model of Anger in which the expression of anger has negative or damaging results for the Pressurized Liquid input to map onto. Similarly, in the "mental detox" blend, someone might think of media-provided information as (on balance, at least) useful rather than harmful: but that framing of media information would not fit into a blend structured by the Detox source frame.

The question of whether single-scope blends are all metaphoric is a complicated one. Let us consider example (2).

(2)   I was not alone. I was bringing up the rear of a long queue of certifiable
           obsessives ... John MacGregor stood at the head of the line.[6]

Jonathan Raban is talking about a long lineage of people who have explored the world in small seagoing vessels and written about it (MacGregor, who lived in the nineteenth century, was known for designing canoes and sailing them along the coast of the British Isles; Raban travels in a small sailboat). Having lived in different times and places, these men have never shared the same spatial or temporal location (much less been arrayed in a physical queue), but because their travels and their accounts of those travels can be arranged in a temporal succession, they can be imagined to be together in a single location, forming a line. In the blend, the image of people standing in line provides the organizing frame, while the vital relation of time (temporal succession) becomes the vital relation of space (spatial order). This is a single-scope blend, and the imagined physical gathering of these individuals sounds rather like the *Great America II–Northern Light* "race" – and similarly would not be described as metaphoric, in the sense we discussed in Chapters 2 and 3. It is a novel construal of a situation, and the matching of the domains relies on the reader's understanding of the target as a whole cluster of spaces, rather than as a single domain to be structured in a new way. The blend gives a new organization to the "sailors" input (treating them as a co-present group), but does not construe the sailors in a metaphoric way. Partly because of that, the reader needs to know a bit about the "sailor writers" input to really understand what is being talked about. This is often not the case in metaphor.

However, the "queue" itself has structure which seems reasonably construed as metaphoric; as we will discuss in more detail in Chapter 7, one metaphoric model of time involves seeing earlier times as being "in front of" (ahead of) later times. Examples like *If winter comes, can spring be far behind?* are pervasive in English. And indeed, Raban's forbears are arranged in a queue where the spatial front of the queue corresponds to the earliest times, and the rear of the queue (Raban himself) to the most recent time slot. And further, if we think of each character in the queue as representing a specific space (temporal at least), then many different spaces are drawn on to create this blend, with its single structuring frame of the Queue.

[6] Jonathan Raban, *Coasting*, New York: Vintage Books, 2003[1987], p. 22.

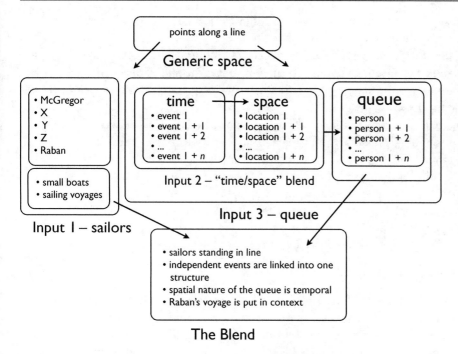

Figure 4.3. *The "queue" blend*

Example (2) is represented in a diagrammatic form in Figure 4.3. The *queue* input combines a number of concepts, including the understanding of time in terms of space. All the inputs are linked through the image of points organized along a line, and this connects events in time, people in a line, and a sequence of voyages. The example illustrates the salience of one organizing frame in a single-scope blend.

Examples (1) and (2) bring us back to the question of how to define figurative language (and thought), which we have so far addressed only partially. These examples do not "feel" figurative in the same way as saying that someone is *about to explode* with anger. Metaphors for Emotions take as inputs things like the sense of anger felt by most humans in a similar way, while examples (1) and (2) represent the writers' sense of their own situation at the moment of writing. Some of these expressions sound more conventional (including, in our view, the anger metaphors), while other expressions feel coined to suit the purposes of the current communicative intent. But it is also the case that the more creative expressions rely crucially on their conventional roots. The "queue" blend does draw on conventional time metaphors, by arranging the ancestors in succession spatially *ahead* of Raban, corresponding metaphorically to their temporally *earlier* status. And the "looking back at the past self" blend draws on conventional models of the Divided Self (found in expressions like *Just look at yourself!* and *I hate myself* – see Lakoff [1996]). This is to be expected: as observed by Lakoff and Turner (1989), creative usages generally build on conventional ones. We can argue, then, that patterns of figurative language and thought are not necessarily less conventional or more obviously creative than literal ones; rather, the nature of a "figurative" construct is in its partial use of concepts, in patterns of selection and projection from one conceptual domain to another, and in the ability to construe one situation in terms of another. We will follow these issues throughout the remainder of the book.

Returning to the typology of blends, a single-scope blend is one of four types, the others being simplex, mirror, and double-scope blends. A *simplex* blend involves a space which provides an input frame, and another space which provides fillers for the roles in that frame. Role-value mappings are important and very common. They rely on frames which profile specific roles (within, e.g. a family, a government, or an organizational structure) and map these roles onto the specific individuals or objects that fill the roles in particular instances. For example, the frame of the US Presidency is used in the simplex blend in example (3).

(3)   Hillary was Bill Clinton's First Lady.

In this frame, which is one of the inputs, the presidency also includes a special position for the current US President's wife. The name of the role is First Lady, and it involves specific privileges and obligations. Examples like (3) evoke the Presidency frame, with the role of First Lady, and also profile a second input – an embodied mental space (in the sense introduced above) for the man and the woman who fill the roles. These roles also participate in the Family frame, in which the President can be profiled as a Husband, and the First Lady as his Wife. However, example (3) only refers to the marriage status as a subcomponent of the Presidency frame, while a sentence like *Hillary is Bill Clinton's wife* only concerns the Wife role in the Family frame. Both sentences are simplex blends, where the roles in a frame are filled by the values of the actual people. But they are different simplex blends because they involve different frames. Note that our analysis of example (3) treats as blending (conceptual integration) the very basic process of fitting values into frame roles – and far from being figurative, this is the very bread-and-butter of literal meaning.

Figure 4.4. shows the functioning of the simplex blend. One of the inputs profiles the roles (President and First Lady, who are also framed as Husband and Wife), the other provides the values – actual people playing the roles. Such blends are very productive, as they yield a number of specific role/value pairs over time.

Examples like (3) have been described in terms of constructions; the term used by Fauconnier and Turner (2002) is XYZ Constructions, based on the related format *X is the Y of Z* (*Hillary is the wife of Bill*). (XYZ Constructions will be discussed further in Chapter 6.) While example (3) is a basic case of connecting a value and a role, such constructions can often be more elaborate, depending on the complexity of the input frames. For example, Elizabeth Taylor reportedly described her husband, the actor Richard Burton, as *the Frank Sinatra of Shakespeare*. The surface construction is very similar to the one describing

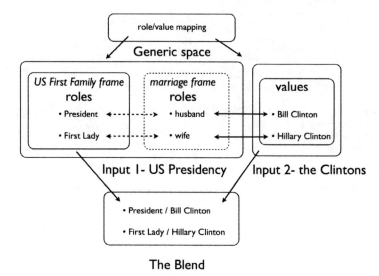

Figure 4.4. *The "First Lady" blend*

Hillary Clinton as Bill Clinton's wife. But the role *Frank Sinatra* is not exactly as conventional and fixed as the role *wife*: reference to Frank Sinatra evokes a complex set of frames, and we need to choose one. But if we assume that Frank Sinatra evokes the role Top Performer in the frame of Popular Music, and that Sinatra was in fact considered one of the best, we can map that role onto Burton's similarly high position in his area of performance (the directly specified frame of Shakespearean acting). For some, an additional aspect of both frames might be the unusual popularity (the "rock-star" crowd appeal) both performers enjoyed (unusual as it was for a Shakespearean actor). Like all XYZ Constructions, this one requires an understanding of the frame evoked and the type of relation between the role and the value. And note that we would not say that this example is literal; literally, Sinatra and Burton are two different individuals, and bring with them two different frames which need to be integrated here. Hence this example is not a simplex blend, with individuals being fitted into the roles in a single frame, but a single-scope blend, where great popular success in Shakespearean acting is understood as "rock-star"-type crowd appeal.

There are also instances where the two inputs are structured by the same organizing frame; these are known as *mirror blends*. In example (4), an example of a "mirror" blend, Raban describes his experience of sailing through the western waters of the British Isles.

(4)   As islands nearly always do, the Isle of Man came up unexpectedly, in the wrong place. It was steaming straight past my bows like a rusty ship.[7]

---

[7] *Coasting*, p. 53.

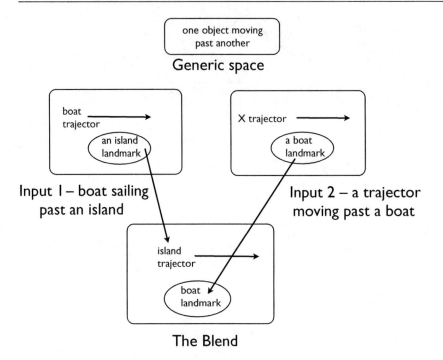

Figure 4.5. *The "boat/island" blend*

The organizing frame evoked is that of moving past various islands in a seagoing vessel. The pattern is quite clear – the boat is moving, while the islands remain stationary, and so the boat is moving past them. This is true regardless whether one is on the island or on the boat. But when one is actually on a moving boat, the viewpoint experienced by the traveler is often that of feeling stationary, while the islands seen along the way are moving past his bows. This illusion is described here. It is an interesting blend, in which the two inputs are distinguished solely by viewpoint. In one input, the viewer is on the boat, moving past islands which remain stationary. The perception of motion is thus prompted by the boat (the trajector) moving past the landmark (the island). This input is a fully embodied space, including the writer as the participant, and a specific landscape the boat is moving through. The second input includes the experience of something passing the boat – a frequent actual experience while sailing, since other boats do go past. This space is not fully embodied (the traveler is not actually seeing something go past), but it is naturally evoked from previous experience – though it does not necessarily have to evoke a specific time and place. It is thus either a memory space or a rather general frame which the writer/traveler is aligning himself with.

As we show in Figure 4.5, both inputs are very similar, as they profile trajectors moving past landmarks. But in the reality space (Input 1), the boat is moving past an island, while in the blended construal the island is moving past the boat. The reversal maintains the frame represented in both inputs and in the blend, but the trajector and landmark roles are reversed between the two frames: the boat is the trajector in the actual space of passing the island, and in the blend, the island is the "trajector" going past the boat, preserving the trajector–landmark relations in the other input. The mirror network such as this one does not really change the frame evoked, but changes the way in which its roles and relations are filled.

Crucially, both inputs focus not on the actual spatial location, but on the visual experience associated with the situations. The visual experience in the two cases may in fact be very similar, since our brains process relative motion all the time, but it is normally filtered through general factual knowledge – i.e. one knows where one is and judges the situation accordingly. In the blend, the traveler is on the moving boat, but feels like the boat is stationary while the islands are moving past. The visual experience is thus the crucial concept holding the blend together, since the actual trajector/landmark relations are disrupted. The actual location of the traveler (on the boat) is projected from one input, while the perception of the trajector and the landmark is projected from the second input (the sense of being positioned at a stationary landmark, watching trajectors in motion). In the blend, the viewpoint of one situation is applied to the actual fully embodied space in the other. This viewpoint blend not only profiles the traveler's situation, but also his subjective sense of the embodiment – the sense of motion and location which does not depend solely on the rational analysis of the coordinates. Importantly, this viewpoint is crucial to how the writer is representing the story – not from the perspective of objectively occurring events but from the fully embodied perceptual viewpoint of the traveler. If the text had said that the writer *felt as if the island was steaming past his bows* it would have had a different effect. The construal would be similar, but the perceptual viewpoint of the traveler would be profiled as a part of an imaginary space, not the actual travel space – and this would change the effect of the narrative significantly.

The final type of blend we will describe here is the *double-scope* blend, where the inputs are structured by different organizing frames, but one single frame does not provide the organizing structure for the blend. Instead, both frames contribute to the blended organizing structure. An often-discussed example of this type of blend is the "debate with Kant" blend (Grady et al. 1999, Fauconnier and Turner 2002, Pascual 2008). In this example, a philosopher lecturing on Kant might use expressions such as *What I say to Kant is X* or *Kant disagrees with me on that*. There are two inputs, each with its own organizing frame: one is the Lecture frame, with the living philosopher as the only speaking participant, and the other is a collection of writings by a philosopher who is no longer living, but for whom there is an obvious frame of Opinion-expressing, evoked by his known writings. In the emergent structure, the interaction between the two philosophers is framed as a Debate, and so the lecturer and Kant are both presented as alive and actually exchanging views. There are important differences between the inputs – the participants in the lecture room do not share time, space, language, or the mode of expression with the input of Kant's writings. And yet in the emergent structure, through the filling out of the roles brought in by the Debate frame, Kant becomes a participant in the conversation, and is aware of the contemporary philosopher and his views. All of the blending processes are exemplified here, and both inputs are thus informed by the structure of the blend (we learn not just about Kant's views, but also about a possible response to them and the potential response to the response). Crucially, unlike a single-scope blend, neither input is reconstrued in terms of the other; both Kant and his views and the modern philosopher and his views are present, and it is not the case that either is understood as the other.

Double-scope blends are extremely varied, and thus it is difficult to find principles which govern this particular type of emergent structure. In talking about simplex, single-scope, and mirror networks, we have identified distinguishing features of those classes of blends. This cannot quite be done in the case of double-scope blends, since the nature of the inputs and the ways in which they might be combined into a coherent emergent structure are hard to predict. This raises an important question: what limits can analysts identify on the processes of blending? Fauconnier and Turner (2002) propose optimality principles based on the vital relations mentioned above, which govern the meaning-construction process. For example, it is optimal that the blend constructs a tightly integrated scene – e.g. a boat race or a face-to-face debate – as opposed to constructing a relationship between temporally distant scenes. The blend has to be cognitively manipulable as an integrated whole, but can also be subjected to *unpacking* – an understanding of what the inputs contribute and how. We will not discuss these optimality principles in detail here, as they are not clearly linguistic in nature, but we will at least mention the claim that, optimally, a blend gives global insight into a situation (rather than focusing on multiple details) and that it compresses complex concepts to a *human scale* – so that the emergent concept can be grasped and manipulated as a meaningful whole, understandable in terms close to human experience.

4.4.3   A complex multiscope example

In the following example, we will show how multiple inputs can yield a coherent, manageable, but also communicatively useful construal. In his speech at Rice University announcing the plan for American astronauts to land on the moon, John F. Kennedy used the sentence in example (5).

(5)   Those who came before us made certain that this country rode the first waves of the industrial revolutions, the first waves of modern invention, and the first wave of nuclear power, and this generation does not intend to founder in the backwash of the coming age of space.

Kennedy's combination of expressions and images prompts a complex megablend. The most obvious input is that of Surfing, where a person can use the power of ocean waves to steer a surfboard along the length of the wave.

This input contributes the idea of smooth and seemingly effortless motion, using energy produced not by the person moving but by the motion of the water. At the same time, Kennedy sets up the input of temporal succession by mentioning the *first* wave – this implies being ahead of others in doing something important, in this case constructing crucial inventions and harnessing nuclear power. Based on that, Kennedy describes Americans as being leaders in innovation of all kinds (Forward Position in the sequence is mapped onto Technological Leadership, on the basis of the relative positions of the "waves" described). He first talks about those who *came before us*, looking at past achievements; then, when he returns to *this generation*, he refers to the present, and the future. He is thus setting up a temporal succession of a different kind, focusing on the progress his country has made over generations (as opposed to its leading role in technological advancement). Finally, he returns to the Wave frame (*backwash*), to declare that his countrymen will continue to be in the forefront of change, rather than allowing others to take over and suffering the side effects of other participants' activities. Catching the first wave leads to Forward Position ahead of those on later waves; it also avoids getting caught in the backwash of earlier waves and other surfers. International competition to be a technological leader now maps onto inter-surfer competition to catch that first crucial wave.

There are at least three inputs then, each contributing different frames. The Surfing input (prompted by the expression *riding the wave*) contributes the frame elements of Waves approaching the shore (and then retreating, leaving the *backwash* behind) and Surfers using the power of moving water to glide along the edge of the wave; importantly, while the waves move towards the shore and back, the surfer does not, as a true long ride for a surfer has her moving along the shore. As a result, this input is in itself complex: it structures two directions of motion, the waves moving towards the shore and back, and a surfer moving along the wave. The longer the surfer rides the wave, the more successful he or she is; but it is also important to *catch the wave*, rather than being left behind when it retreats. The Surfing input is then cross-mapped with the second frame of Technological Progress. It allows Kennedy to describe various stages of innovation and present Americans as successful "surfers" (inventors, engineers, etc.) who excel at using newly emerging technologies. The Surfing frame structures the input of the changes in technology.

Additionally, the succession of waves/technological breakthroughs is cross-mapped with a third input: the History of American Technology frame, with its temporal sequence of events. The temporal dimension is first prompted by the expression *those who came before us*, which uses motion through space to represent the flow of time. This is a rather standard usage (which we will be discussing in detail in Chapter 7). Time is typically seen as Motion through Space, but the moving entity may be an experiencer (as in *We are approaching the end of term*) or an event (*The end of term is approaching*). In example (5), Kennedy talks about generations of Americans as moving through space/time in a succession, but in the final expression (*the coming age of space*) he presents the future technological changes as approaching the current generation. Unlike a simple construal of individual experience of time, this input has numerous participants – generations of innovators and engineers, and thus the current generation is expected to measure up against the past ones. Kennedy's contemporaries are facing a new challenge inevitably approaching, and are expected to *catch the next wave* in order to live up to the expectations set up by earlier generations.

This segment of the speech creates a rather complex construal. It depends, first, on the metaphor/single-scope blend structuring Time as Space. This structure is combined with the History of American Technology frame, so that temporal events are now stages in technological progress, measured in terms of generations, rather than just a span of one person's life. This construct is blended with the Surfing input, so that stages in technological progress are also targets of human activity. Achieving new technological breakthroughs requires skill and determination, and is marked by specific stages or goals (catching individual waves/attempting to achieve technological advances), but also by sustained periods of development which require skill and attention (riding the wave); rather than portraying progress as a steady course of change accomplished by anonymous contributors, Kennedy focuses on the idea of progress as a series of major challenges undertaken by generations.

One sentence thus evokes a number of frames and spaces, structuring two types of sequential relations (from past to future and from the most innovative to the least innovative) and two directions of motion (along the wave, developing the technology, and forward through time to reach further innovations), summing up the past and outlining the future, while clearly delineating the area of competition in which Kennedy wants America to participate. Each of the inputs contributes something to this complex construal, but none of them provides the overriding organizing frame.

Several vital relations are involved in the compressions that the blend achieves. First of all, the time period of the generations of innovation is compressed into a frame involving several Waves that a surfer attempts. Also, past generations of millions of people are compressed into the much smaller and cognitively manageable sequence of individual surfers.

The meaning-structuring power of blending is clear in Kennedy's prose. Blending can be a multilayered process, and blended meanings can be built on the basis of other blended meanings. In the paragraphs above we tried to unpack the full structure and impact of the network Kennedy's sentence constructs, and we could probably add more to that discussion. But the example is not only an illustration of the conceptual and linguistic complexity of discourse, it is also an illustration of the concepts of human scale and global insight. The structuring of complex challenges through the concept of Surfing allows hearers to simulate the embodied sense of what that activity involves and provides access to the concept of facing repeated challenges and having to harness enormous power through skill and commitment. Hearers did not need to unpack this blend the way we did to "get it," and they understood at the lowest level of bodily activity what the challenge Kennedy was presenting to them required. This is a brilliant example of blending producing global insight about a complex situation, by compressing it to human scale. At the same time, the network can be mentally manipulated as a whole – it is easy to imagine someone in the audience responding by saying, *Yes, we need to catch that wave*, or *Yes, but the trick is to recognize the wave that will carry us there*, or even *I'm in the humanities; I'll be watching you guys get wet*. Such responses would be manipulating the blend as a whole, elaborating further details in the network and taking a specific viewpoint (of the surfer/inventor, the coach, or the viewer sitting safe and dry on the beach).

Such examples are the best illustration of blending as a flexible and powerful mechanism of meaning emergence. Not every aspect of Kennedy's text might feel overtly "figurative" to every listener or reader – but the structures evoked would naturally be recognized as figurative in a literary text. Throughout the remainder of the book, we will consider other examples of blends, to gradually clarify the varieties and processes of blending.

4.5   Conclusions

As we have shown, blending is a type of projection which varies widely from case to case. It involves inputs of varying complexity, and may profile just two inputs or may profile many more. What is crucial about blending is the way in which it creates new construals of situations by relying on preexisting frames. The complexity of the actual construct a blending analyst might be interested in could be extremely varied. Recent work on narrative fiction (Dancygier 2012a) argues that entire novels can be viewed as linguistic artifacts whose meaning is constructed based on processes of blending. Above, we have seen examples ranging from modified nouns and compounds all the way to stretches of continuous text. What is important for all of these cases is the way in which blending combines and recombines concepts by structuring words and larger expressions and yielding new conceptualizations.

Importantly, blending may involve a series of figurative operations, one working on the effect of the other. The Watergate Hotel in Washington, DC, has become known worldwide as the site of a break-in which led to a famous political scandal, which was known as the *Watergate scandal*, or simply *Watergate*. The name of the hotel thus came to evoke the entire frame which resulted from the initial break-in. Ever since, the US media have formed convenient names for political scandals by using the ending -*gate* (some, like the Monica Lewinsky scandal, were given several -*gate* names, such as *Monicagate*, *Lewinskygate*, *Tailgate*, and *Sexgate*).[8] The emergent form, now given the status of a suffix in the Oxford English Dictionary, is a result of several stages of metonymic and blending

---

[8] The Wikipedia page for names of scandals which include -*gate* is several screens long.

processes – from the location of the initial event to the whole scandal, and from that to other scandals. The projections are selective, in terms of both meaning (the original role of a *hotel*, the Watergate, which gave its name to the original scandal, has long been lost from the meaning) and form (-*gate* now stands for the entire Scandal frame). The emergent structure now profiles the kinds of scandals which are quickly picked up by the media and explored until the readers' and viewers' interest wanes. The suffix can now be attached to any expression which is sufficiently evocative to then provide a distinct name for the current pet scandal of the press.

It seems clear that such emergent forms rely on blending preexisting frames and spaces (like the Watergate scandal) with new frames and spaces, retaining necessary parts of the topology and finding a form which can be recombined with markers of each specific new input. But none of this would work without a mechanism which allows a whole situation to be evoked through one crucial linguistic form. This type of projection, where one aspect of a frame is selected and used to represent the whole frame, will be described in the next chapter as *metonymy*.

4.6   Summary

In this chapter we have moved away from metaphoric mappings to explore other ways in which language prompts construals and re-construals of situations. We started with an overview of the difference between a frame and a mental space, and we also distinguished types of mental spaces. The distinctions drawn added some categories to the standard discussions of mental spaces, and were intended to clarify the nature of conceptual domains evoked in processes other than the types of metaphoric mappings discussed in Chapters 2 and 3. The overall goal of the discussion was to show that a rigorous explanation of what mental spaces are and what they do lies not in a definition of what a mental space is or is not, but in an explanation of the role such constructs play in the emergence of complex meanings. A simplistic view of mental spaces, we argued, would yield a simplistic explanation of how individual speakers evoke complex meanings and use them in prompting further meanings.

Specifically, we introduced the concept of a blend – a multi-space construction which involves a greater variety of projections than those described as metaphoric. We discussed the nature of blending, also introducing common types of blends (simplex, single-scope, mirror, and double scope). We also discussed a more complex megablend in detail, showing the varied avenues of meaning construction in blending and the complexity of emergent meanings. The goal of this discussion was to demonstrate that blends range from very simple to extremely complex, and that the complexity of emergent meanings depends both on the nature of the frames evoked and on the layering of projections.

   As in earlier chapters, our discussion focused on the processes of meaning construction made available by the constructs discussed. Given that the meaning-construction processes exemplified in this book rely either on frames or on mental spaces, which are more elaborate and complex, our focus in this chapter remained on the types of processes which yield complex figurative meanings.

5   Metonymy

In traditional discussions of figurative language, metonymy comes up almost as often as metaphor – and, as we shall see, it has even deeper cognitive roots. The development of Conceptual Metaphor Theory has made metaphor a hotter topic for linguists in recent decades, but metonymy also takes a major place in any treatment of cognition or language. It has been discussed in a number of collections of papers (Barcelona 2000, Dirven and Pörings 2003, Kosecki 2007, Panther et al. 2009) and in a special issue of *Cognitive Linguistics* (17 (3), 2006); it is also treated in some detail in Croft and Cruse (2004); finally, a recent monograph provides a useful overview of the issues (Bierwiaczonek 2013). In what follows, we will not directly engage in the ongoing discussion of the nature of metonymic domains; rather, we will focus on proposing categories that can best be deployed in the actual linguistic analyses, including the role of metonymy in the emergence of polysemy, metonymic usages of form, and the roles of categorization and framing. Finally, we will discuss a visual example to highlight the role of metonymy in the emergence of new meanings.

Traditional grammars described metonymy as being about part–whole relationships; however, these grammars often distinguished between *metonymy* and *synecdoche*, though not always in the same way. *Synecdoche* is sometimes seen as specifically referring to part-for-whole (e.g. *hands* for 'workers') while *metonymy* covers either whole-for-part or some larger range of relations; others see metonymy as basically associational (e.g. *suits* for 'business people') and synecdoche as referring to all part-for-whole and whole-for-part relations. Guides for English students seem to mix these up in other ways; *Crown* for 'monarch' is not infrequently cited as a part–whole relationship. And the current definition of *synecdoche* on Wikipedia brings up part-for-whole relationships between categories as well as between parts and wholes of objects. The cognitive linguistics work on metonymy has found it useful both to group many of these phenomena together and to subdivide them rather differently than earlier analysts, so we will start by giving current cognitive linguistic definitions of metonymic phenomena. One clear division among the phenomena is between *categorial metonymy* and *frame metonymy*; this distinction will be the starting point of our exposition.

> Metonymy: the use of some entity A to stand for another entity B with which A is *correlated*.

Categorial metonymy is based on a relationship between a larger category and a smaller subcategory which is part of the larger category. The metonymic relationship consists of the smaller category standing for the larger one, or the larger category taking on the label of the (salient) subcategory – or vice versa. This is indeed a relationship of correlation, since membership in the smaller category presumably correlates entirely with membership in the larger one, and membership in the larger category saliently or frequently correlates with membership in this particular smaller category. It is well known that linguistic polysemy and linguistic change reflect these kinds of relationships, in that the same label may be used to refer to superordinate and subordinate categories. For example, the English word *dog* once referred to a particular kind of dog but became more general; on the other hand, the word *girl* once meant 'young person' but became restricted to girls.

In **frame metonymy**, on the other hand, the metonymic relationship is between parts of the same frame. Again, presence of a frame correlates with presence of parts of the frame, and vice versa. One important kind of frame metonymy is **part–whole metonymy** (also called *meronymy* or *partonymy*) which involves mentioning a part as a way of referring to the whole of which it is a part. This is the kind of usage involved in *deck hands* or *field hands*, both of which refer to whole working people who may well be using their hands in their work. Similarly, the expression *two heads are better than one* refers to two people. Part–whole metonymy does not, however, involve a random part being used to refer to the whole, any more than categorial metonymy is equally possible with every subcategory. Notice that it is precisely the association of hands with another frame, that of Physical Labor, which makes *hand* a metonymy for a physical laborer, while *two heads are better than one* refers to people gathering for cognitive rather than physical activity.

The more general concept of the term frame metonymy refers to all usages where one reference to an element of a frame is used to refer to either the frame as a whole or to other associated elements of the frame. Classic examples include *the White House*, used in English to refer not only to the relevant building, but to the entire executive branch of the US government, because it is the residence of the President who heads that branch; *the Crown* refers to the British monarchy, the physical crown being a symbolic object worn by the monarch; and *Hollywood* means the mainstream US movie industry, since many major studios are (still) located there. In other words, places, buildings, and objects which are tightly linked parts of cultural or other frames can be used to name those frames as a whole, or to name aspects of them.

All these classes of metonymic cognitive links are pervasive; like metaphor, every human language provides prolific evidence of them. Although animals probably don't have complex social frames of the kinds humans have – they could not understand *democracy*, *marriage*, or *driver's license* as concepts – they do clearly link associated frames. Animals that only travel in a car to visit a veterinarian may develop a fear of cars, and, as Pavlov showed, an association with food can be transferred from the food itself to an associated stimulus. All animals form categories based on experienced correlations in the world. And of course they link parts with wholes: it is crucial for an animal to be able to identify prey or predator when only seeing some part of a mostly hidden whole animal. *Pattern completion* from partial visual data is a basic part of perception. So the cognitive basis for metonymy is extremely deep in brain patterns – but of course, only in humans do we have linguistic patterns resulting from metonymic cognitive relationships.

5.1   Part–whole frame metonymy, framing, and objectification

Although metonymy has often been thought of as primarily a reference device, it already seems clear from the discussion above that – like metaphor – it adds crucial meaning beyond just reference to an object. In the case of part–whole metonymy, some of this added meaning emerges because part–whole metonymy interacts with larger kinds of frame metonymy. *Two heads are better than one* does not just refer to people (the whole Body frame of which a head is a part), it refers specifically to people participating in cognitive tasks (a frame evoked by *heads*); *many hands make light work* refers to people engaged in more physical work, where hands are an essential part of the frame of a Working Body.

This brings us to the process which Chen (2012) has called *objectification*. Many unpleasant sexual epithets in particular refer to parts of the whole body of a woman. Calling a woman *a cunt*, *a piece of ass*, or *a pair of boobs* is apparently referring to her by referring to parts of her body – and in particular, parts of her body which are understood to be saliently indicative of her female sex. One could start by saying that such a reference sounds as if the only important part of the woman is the relevant section of her sexual anatomy – her whole self does not matter. That might be demeaning enough. But consider the vast difference between those expressions and the idea of referring to a woman as *a vagina*, *buttocks*, or *breasts*. These latter words are relatively neutral in their framing – *vagina* is even medical, while *buttocks* and *breasts* are usable in a wider range of contexts. In contrast, *cunt*, *boobs*, and *ass* evoke not only female anatomy, but in a frame of assessment by a male as a potential sexual partner. Note that other body parts, more explicitly part of female reproductive anatomy, would never be recruited as metonymic labels in this frame: male sexual partners do not see, or interact with, ovaries or wombs, and so don't assess them in considering a female as sexually attractive. So these epithets, in sum, assume that not only are a woman's sexual parts all that matters, but they are significant primarily in this male viewer's or user's framing. She is reduced not only to an object, but to an object in a particular frame.

To anticipate our discussion of constructions in Chapter 6, we might note here that the particular expression *a piece of ass* adds extra meaning to *ass*. *Ass* is normally a countable noun – that is, each individual human has a pair of buttocks so labeled, *an ass*. But here, female sexual parts are seen as some undifferentiated transindividual substance "ass" from which portions can be allocated (perhaps for male use); and when a woman is only a piece of some undifferentiated substance, she is not even an object. We could compare these uses with references to males via body-part metonymies: *asshole* or *prick* is a negative comment on a man's character, but it is not a reduction of a man to a sexual object because it is not framed exclusively in terms of sexual evaluation, certainly not by a female viewer.

Moving to a different domain, we might compare these sexual body-part metonymic usages with the standard hospital parlance that might refer to *the appendix in room 2013* or *the broken leg in 514*, and be understood as speaking of the patient who has had an appendix extracted or the one who has suffered a broken leg. Such uses do sound impersonal and possibly objectifying, since they make it clear that some particular part of the patient's anatomy (rather than the patient as a person) is what matters to the medical staff. However, since the framing they evoke is not an entirely negative one (hospitals are there to heal, and the patients actually do want some extra attention to the parts of their body needing the most medical care), these usages are not hostile or contemptuous, even though they may be off-putting.

Someone being (perhaps only temporarily) classified specifically with reference to their ability to do some particular kind of manual work – work that perhaps they themselves value – may well not mind being referred to as *another pair of hands*. They would be likely to object to that being the *sole* metonymy used to refer to them. But the framing is not in itself negative, and therefore not necessarily derogatory. Clearly, then, part–whole frame metonymy, and the choice of part–whole labels, is understood crucially in interaction with larger frame-based construals.

5.2   Metonymy and metaphor

Frame metonymy is closely tied to the kind of correlations which are involved in experientially based metaphors, in particular Primary Metaphors (as discussed in Chapter 2). It is precisely the development of a complex frame out of correlated simpler frames which makes a primary scene so powerful. For example, the frame of Judging Height is part – a crucial part – of the child's usual single frame of judging quantity of liquid in a container. And it is this correlation which motivates the metaphoric mappings between those domains. Of course, as we have noted, once the metaphoric mappings are in place, the usage goes beyond the original correlation between frames, so that we can say things like

Prices soared, where only abstract quantity is involved and no literal height. So we cannot at all say that these metaphors are instances of metonymy – but they have their roots in the same kind of correlation which is involved in frame metonymy, the difference being that when children separate the two correlated frames, the correlation becomes a between-frame correlation, and becomes the basis for metaphor.

This is an old idea in Conceptual Metaphor Theory; Lakoff and Johnson (1980) stressed the experiential–correlational base for conceptual metaphor, as have many authors since. But correlation between domains is only the basis for metaphor – we cannot predict exactly when a correlation will be so conceptually basic that it will give rise to metaphoric mappings which go far beyond references to the situations where the two domains are correlated. And while correlations in primary scenes may underlie Primary Metaphors, such correlations are much harder to find in metaphors relying on more elaborate and culturally salient frames. Kövecses (2013) explicitly argues that all conceptual metaphors are based in metonymy; however, correlation is not metonymy but the *basis* for metonymic uses of one thing to stand for something correlated with it. And we come back to Lakoff and Johnson's original statement that conceptual metaphors have some basis in correlation – though not every conceptual metaphor is based on correlation at the level of the mappings; theories are not correlated with buildings. And metonymy is definitely based on correlation.

We have described both metaphor and metonymy in terms of frames – metaphorical domains rely on frames (though they are not identical to them) and metaphorical mappings project structure from frame to frame, while metonymic patterns focus on parts of frames but give access to the frames as wholes. In other words, our overall approach to figurative language relies fundamentally on the concept of a frame – but our discussion has made it clear that frames have structures of differing complexity and cultural salience. What we believe to be crucial is the *nature* of the mapping, and we have noted repeatedly that specific mappings are determined, among other things, by the level of schematicity. In other words, a situation may be described through a basic Event Structure Metaphor mapping such as PURPOSES ARE DESTINATIONS or through a more fleshed-out subcase such as LIFE IS A JOURNEY, and this is a choice of the level and complexity of the frames involved. In a similar way, recognizing the correlational basis of some metaphors does not change our argument about the nature of metaphoric or metonymic mappings, but it highlights a level of schematic interaction which offers a clearer view of how frames participate in such mappings.

It is important to note further that some expressions combine metaphoric and metonymic roots. There is much literature analyzing human construals of time, which are generally based on the conceptualization of space (we will discuss the data and the implications in Chapter 7). So when we say that *The end of term is approaching*, we use the spatial sense of the verb *approach* to represent the fact that there is not much time between the speaker's present and the future event. However, when measuring space or time, we often use metonymic patterns in ways which provide access to specific frames needed to understand the events. Consider the following examples:

(1)   The gas station is *two blocks away.*

(2)   The gas station is *two minutes away.*

(3)   The director's office is *three doors down.*

(4)   *Three meetings down the line* we still didn't know what to do.

In the italicized expressions, various different countable concepts serve as units of measurement. In example (1), the concept of a city block (by no means a precise measure) metonymically evokes the frame of a North American city structure to estimate spatial distance: the distance between two intersections in a street-grid correlates loosely with some particular physical measurement of distance, and is used to refer to it. In example (2), a standard measure of time is instead used to evoke spatial distance, so that one needs to estimate the distance one can cover driving (or cycling, or running) for a minute. Note that this metonymic example structures space in terms of time, rather than what we usually see in time-related metaphors. The expression in example (3), *three doors down*, is based on evoking a frame of access to rooms – *doors* in this case signals rooms (though when said in the context of a street, it would signal buildings). Finally, example (4) constructs a measure of time spent in terms of events (number of meetings). It uses a spatial construal (*down the line*) and metonymic reference to events to signal that the amount of time spent making the decisions in question was long. Even if we do not know how much time elapsed between meetings, or how long the meetings were, we still understand that the process was not efficient.

All of these examples are essentially frame-metonymic. They rely on accessible frames involving the structure of buildings or cities, but also on frames which associate time spent moving with the amount of distance covered (which seems to underlie all mappings between the domains of Time and Space) and on the frame of Events as Landmarks which help measure the amount of time elapsed. Each example focuses on a different aspect of the frames involved, and the unidirectionality characteristic of Time as Space metaphors is not preserved in metonymy, yet the motivation for these metonymies is very similar to the motivations discussed in connection with time metaphors (see Chapter 7) and the role of events in one's sense of time passing (Fauconnier and Turner 2008). These examples suggest that, because of the potential complexity of the frames evoked, metonymy can be extended over both conventional and innovative usages which are based in frame *correlation*, and do not maintain the directionality of projections we see in the case of metaphor. Note that these really are correlations. Examples (1)–(3) all involve motion, with both time and space present as part of the scenarios. Example (4) is different, since it piggy-backs metonymy on the Time as Motion metaphor, and uses specific times as metonymic for the intervals between them; once again, both the intervals and the meetings are actually there as part of the frame. This is not the case in the Time as Motion metaphor itself, where physical motion (the metaphoric source domain) need not happen at all in order for us to end up *five days further into the month*.

Another example of the synergy between metaphor and metonymy in American English is the relatively recently coined verb *to astroturf*, meaning 'to engineer a campaign which looks as if it is originating naturally from the general population, though actually it is instigated and organized by large corporations or political parties.' This may have originated in the compound *astroturf campaign*, and in any case clearly depends on another phrase, *grassroots campaign*, where the word *grassroots* metonymically evokes a whole frame of very everyday plants springing up out of soil naturally, which in turn metaphorically refers to political action which emerges naturally from people's everyday desires. *AstroTurf* is the name of a successful brand of manufactured plastic fake grass; it would not be used for an everyday lawn, and is unnaturally bright green and would be difficult to mistake for real grass, but it does uniquely evoke the frame of imitating natural grass. Metaphorically, the manufacturing of AstroTurf from unnatural materials corresponds to the "unnatural" fabrication of a political campaign by authorities, and the (implausible) grasslike appearance of AstroTurf corresponds to the (perhaps unsuccessful) attempt to make the campaign look as if it was originating from citizens and not funded from above. Without these metonymic catchwords, the metaphoric mappings involved in *grassroots campaign* and *astroturf campaign* would be much more complicated to evoke.

As these examples suggest, there are excellent reasons to maintain the distinction between metonymy and metaphor as different kinds of relationships, but it is also important to note that in actual discourse they are in constant interaction, often working side-by-side in the emergence of new expressions.

5.3   Metonymic polysemy and meaning change

We noted in Chapters 1 and 2 that metaphor can motivate multiple meanings (polysemy) for a single word, and can thus motivate directions of meaning change as well. Metonymy does this too: both category-metonymic and frame-metonymic cognitive relationships help to structure the patterns of lexical meaning and the directions of historical meaning change.

Category-metonymic polysemy relationships are extremely common, and are normally between a higher-level category and the most prototypical or central subclass of that higher category. Berlin et al. (1973, 1974) documented this relationship in folk botanical and zoological classification systems, wherein the name for a particularly common or salient species may be inherited from the larger genus. One example is that of the European oak, which Linnaeus named *Quercus quercus*, the 'oak oak,' because unlike other species of oak (*black oak* or *white oak*), folk nomenclature just called it *oak*, the same as the folk name of the genus as a whole. Similarly, a particularly salient genus, seen as typical of the larger life-form group, may give its name to the super-ordinate class: thus, in many Native American languages of the southwestern United States, the word for 'cottonwood tree' is the same as the word for 'tree.' It seems as if, in folk classification systems, the names start at the genus level and are extended upwards (from a prototypical genus to a life-form) or downwards (from a genus to a prototypical species). It has been argued (Rosch 1977, Mervis and Rosch 1981) that for nonurban societies where people are interacting with plants and animals more frequently and directly than modern big-city dwellers do, the genus level is approximately the *basic level* of categorization, i.e. a cog-nitively basic level involving a shared image and interactional structure. They suggest that this could be why (as Berlin et al. note) the genus is generally named first, crosslinguistically, while other levels of categorization may not be named at all.

In ongoing meaning changes in English and other languages, we can see related phenomena happening with brand names. A brand name that becomes salient and prototypical for the relevant product (even though there may be other competing brands) can come to refer to the product in general. Thus *kleenex* is popularly used in American English to mean 'paper tissue' in general, and not just Kleenex-brand tissues; *xerox* became in the 1970s and 80s a common verb meaning 'photocopy', not just 'photocopy using a Xerox machine'; and *hoover*, originally referring to the Hoover brand of vacuum cleaners, is now a common word in British English for that appliance. Similar stories can be told about the K-Way windbreaker jacket, whose brand name became the French word for windbreakers in general, and Havaianas, a brand of plastic beach sandals which won a huge market share in Brazil, with the result that *havaiana* now means 'flip-flop' in Brazilian Portuguese. In the initial stages of such a development, companies are torn between pleasure at seeing their brand name win out so dramatically over competitors (which proves the centrality of their product to the larger category, and provides free publicity) and concern over the infringement of their registered trademark name. But *hoover* in English, and *K-way* in French, are now common words in everyday use.

Having noted that such category–metonymic relationships normally involve a link between a category and a very central subcategory, we can also note locutions which help us to confirm that relationship. For example, *I didn't want a dipping pen, I wanted a **pen pen*** tells us that, for the speaker, a calligraphy pen dipped in ink is not a central member of the category *pen*. The word *pen* itself carries a history based in Latin *pinna* 'feather,' since early European pens were made from large feathers with slant-cut ends; as technology changed, the word came to refer to metal-tipped pens dipped in ink, then fountain pens, ballpoint pens, and so on. The center of the category changed, and now we would definitely need to say *quill pen* to refer to the original feathers, while unmodified *pen* most likely means a ballpoint or a marker.

An interesting feature of categorial metonymy is that it apparently motivates both *broadening* and *narrowing* of a word's meaning. That is, central subcategories give their name to larger categories (as with the brand names, or the word for 'cottonwood' coming to mean 'tree'), and higher level categories also give their names to central subcategories (as apparently happened with the 'Quercus quercus' species sense of the word *oak*). This kind of bidirectionality is very different from what we see in metaphor – or even in some other kinds of metonymy.

Part–whole metonymy is also extremely common in word-meaning relations. Many languages have the same word for 'hand' and 'arm' (cf. Irish *lamh*) or for 'foot' and 'leg,' not to mention usages like *wheels* to mean 'vehicle.' It has also been observed (Wilkins 1996) that part-for-whole metonymy is a normal direction for historical meaning change, while whole-for-part is not. For example, words for 'hand' come to mean 'arm,' or words for 'eye' come to mean 'face,' but change in the other direction does not occur. This is in contrast with the apparent bidirectionality of categorial metonymy, which is frequently observed to move both up and down from some basic level. The generalization about part-for-whole metonymy appears to be that the *active zone* of the whole (in the sense used in Langacker 1987, 1990, 1991) stands for the whole – that is, the part centrally or directly involved in an activity stands for the whole. The hand, for example, is the part of the arm used for holding, touching, etc.; hence it is the active zone of the arm for many purposes. There is a cognitive asymmetry between parts and wholes which may help to account for this active-zone phenomenon: to think of something as a part, it must be a part *of* a whole, so it entails the presence and activities of the whole, but a whole can be thought of holistically without reference to its parts.

General frame metonymy is perhaps the most pervasive of all kinds of metonymy in its linguistic effects. We have mentioned some metonymic uses of the names of buildings, locations, and objects closely associated with frames. Of course, the name of an entity with multiple close frame associations could have multiple frame-metonymic uses. For example, *Paris* could refer to the French national government seated there (*Paris and Berlin agree on European Union budget revisions*), or to the fashion industry centered there (*Paris brings out new longer skirt lengths*). Since cities naturally have spatial limits and city governments, of course Paris can also refer to the physical space within the Paris city limits (*Paris is on both banks of the Seine*), or to the city government of Paris (*Paris puts more street cleaners to work*), and so on.

Although large collections of these metonymic links have been noted and named (see Panther and Radden 1999, Radden and Kövecses 1999, Panther 2006, Benczes et al. 2011), it seems hard to predict exactly what the conventionalized metonymic meanings of a given word will be. For example, *the Crown* refers to the institution of the British monarchy, not to the reigning monarch who wears the physical object. One would say that *the Queen*, not *the Crown*, had paid a visit to a hospital or hosted a party. But locutions such as *skirts* (meaning 'women') or *suits* (for prosperous business people) do not refer to general institutions but to classes of individuals likely to wear such clothing. One thing that does seem clear is that many of these frame associations are two-way, as are the developed patterns of word meaning. *The White House* can refer to the executive branch of the US government, or to a spokesperson for that branch of government, as well as to (its original primary sense) the building housing that branch. But the reverse direction is equally possible: *The New York Times* could certainly refer to the building housing the offices of the *New York Times* journalistic enterprise, as well as, of course, to the organization producing the newspaper, the spokespeople writing the editorial opinions, the contents of the paper, or physical copies of the newspaper.

In given languages, some patterns are very salient while some are less so; for example, BUILDING FOR ENTERPRISE is less productive in English than ENTER-PRISE FOR BUILDING. Almost any business's name can be used to refer to the main offices of that business, but referring to a named building does not necessarily as easily identify the business housed there. What seems to be required is some degree of salience which guarantees that listeners and readers can clearly asso-ciate the term used with the frame intended. Importantly, the salience may rely on general cultural salience – so it seems to be internationally known that *the White House* is the residence of the US President, but only a Canadian probably knows that Rideau Hall is the official residence of the Governor General of Canada. What is more, even accessibility of the frame-based connection may not suffice. Metonymy analysts often mention examples like *a Picasso*, where the name of the artist stands for the artistic product – such examples are assumed to represent salient patterns. But it is not likely that the expression *a Dickens* would evoke a similar framing, even though Dickens is the unique author of *Great Expecta-tions* just as much as Picasso is the unique author of *Guernica* (and both creative pieces are clearly associated with the authors). The crucial difference is that there is only one authentic *Guernica*, while there are probably zillions of copies of *Great Expectations* in existence, and none has a status different from that of the remaining ones. This difference clearly arises from aspects of the frames of authorship for paintings and for novels, and the details of those frames determine the availability of a pattern which otherwise seems highly available (Radden and Kövecses 1999). But the nature of frame evocation may be even more complex. To refer to the type or genre of a specific text, one can say that one *is reading an old Dorothy Sayers*, or ask *Which is your favorite Dorothy Sayers?* Furthermore, this can also be done using the name of a recurring character, so one can ask either *Which is your favorite Agatha Christie?* or *Which is your favorite Poirot?* These examples show clearly that the subtleties of the frames evoked may alter-nately allow or disallow the type of metonymy which is generally recognized as a productive pattern.

Generally, the patterns of metonymy are so varied that it does not seem helpful just to catalogue them; it seems clear that speakers are quite creative in making connections between frame elements and exploiting forms metonymically. Even in cases where the pattern is indeed clear, the actual discourse purpose for which a given expression is used may yield an interpretation which uses the frames in much more complex ways than these conventional metonymic links. We will consider such examples in Chapter 8, on discourse.

5.4   Linguistic-form metonymies

Perhaps following general principles of economy of effort, speakers pervasively use a smaller part of a form to frame-metonymically evoke the larger form, and thus the *meaning* of the larger form, in addressees' minds. Many proverbs are standardly expressed only in partial form; that is, the partial form has become the canonical or conventional representation of the whole meaning. For example, English speakers never actually say, *A word to the wise is sufficient*, as a preface to advice, they just say, *A word to the wise*; but this is not taken by a listener to mean just 'this is a word to the wise,' which would certainly be a compliment. Rather, the listener understands something more like 'I assume this word will be sufficient since it is addressed to someone wise,' or possibly 'This word will be sufficient *if* it is addressed to someone wise.' Similar partial uses representing whole proverbs include *Don't count your chickens (before they hatch)*, *A bird in the hand (is worth two in the bush)*, *Birds of a feather (flock together)*, and *A rose by any other name (would smell as sweet)*. The usually quoted portion only has the relevant proverbial meaning because it evokes the whole form, and thus the whole meaning.

Abbreviations of all sorts, in fact, are examples of part-for-whole frame metonymy. Nicknames and diminutives are very often shortenings of full longer names. *Elizabeth* is shortened in English to *Eliza, Liza, Lizzy, Liz, Beth, Betty*, and *Betsy*; although the final *-y* (or *-ie* or *-i*, depending on the version) is a general diminutive marker, all of these forms otherwise consist of pieces of the longer full name. Many of them are now full names in their own right, though metonymic in origin; meeting someone named Beth, one does not know whether her full name is Elizabeth or Beth. Common-noun abbreviations which have become full words include *bus* (shortened from *omnibus*), *taxi* (shortened from *taxicab*), and *zipper* (originally *zip fastener*). Speakers of different languages, or dialects, often make different conventional abbreviations: *brolly* for *umbrella* is British but not American, and Americans have adopted McDonald's own abbreviation in referring to a particular hamburger as a *Big Mac*, but they don't abbreviate the name of the company to *MacDo* as the French do.

Acronyms are another example of metonymic abbreviations, and like nicknames, they take on a life of their own. Most people know that *UN* stands for *United Nations*, but it is far more common to use the abbreviation. And many users of acronyms such as *NAFTA (North American Free Trade Agreement)* or *NATO (North Atlantic Treaty Organization)*, *OPEC*, or *AIDS* could not instantly call to mind the words constituting the full names of the relevant institutions or entities. Two- and three-letter acronyms are frequently highly ambiguous, since there are a great many different phrases they could represent. A friend who has digestive health problems, and whose husband has sugar-level problems, complained recently that she could not determine without context – more context than some e-mailers gave her – whether *GI* meant *gastrointestinal, glycemic index,* or for that matter *Geophysical Institute* or (the most common use on the Internet) a US soldier "GI." This last is a particularly interesting story, since it originally stood for *Government Issue* – that is, *GI* was a label for food rations and equipment items which were not sold on the general market but produced for and distributed by the US Army to its soldiers. By further frame metonymy, this label came to refer to the soldier who used those items ("GI Joe") and they are now called *GIs*; the US law giving veterans scholarships to college is normally referred to as the *GI Bill.* Of course, contextually it is usually (despite the complaint mentioned above) quite obvious which meaning of an acronym is intended – that is, these abbreviations are effective in communicating, as well as being labor-saving and (in the case of print) paper-saving for the communicators.

A particularly fascinating formal-metonymic connection is the one which allows part of a word's form to evoke the whole, even when that part is part of *another* word. Thus rhyming words evoke each other, particularly in the context of rhymed verse: Sweetser (2004) has discussed authors' use of a semantically unrelated but rhyming word to "prime" readers or listeners for a following rhyme word. A neat example is the folk song "The cruel war," in which a female character repeatedly begs her male lover to take her along as he leaves for war, and he repeatedly refuses. In each verse, her request rhymes with *no,* the answer which she duly receives from her lover: *I'll dress as your comrade, no one will ever **know** / Won't you let me go with you? **No**, my love, **no**.* But finally, in the last verse, her plea rhymes with *yes,* and the audience can guess before hearing it that the lover's response will be different: *I love you far better than words can e'er express / Won't you let me go with you? Yes, my love, yes.*

But this artistic use of rhyme to evoke semantics is simple compared to the patterns in Rhyming Cockney. In this traditional British dialect, which may have originated as a thieves' cant, speakers use conventional phrases which are semantically unconnected with the intended meaning, but which rhyme with the standard-language form for that meaning. Thus *apples and pears* means 'stairs,' *bread and honey* means 'money,' *trouble and strife* 'wife,' and *Barnet Fair* 'hair.' But to make matters even more interesting, the standard metonymy of part of a form for the entire form applies on top of the rhyming structure: *barnet,* an abbreviation of *Barnet Fair,* can be used to mean 'hair.' Certain such forms have spread to the wider British-speaking population; a wide range of British speakers say or understand *take a butcher's* to mean 'take a look,' where *butcher* is an abbreviated version of *butcher's hook,* the conventional Cockney rhyming phrase which means 'look.'

We will prepare the way for the discussion of constructions in Chapter 6 by noting here that parts of grammatical construction forms are similarly used to evoke the whole construction's form and meaning. It is quite common to use just an *if* or *when* clause to refer to an entire conditional or temporal construction. This is true both of conventional formulaic uses (*When in Rome* for *When in Rome, do as the Romans do*) and for more innovative or productive ones: any speaker could say *If you even touch that cake!* to mean that unexpressed but possibly dire consequences will ensue if the addressee touches or consumes any of the cake in question (Dancygier and Sweetser 2005 discuss this case at more length). More productive uses are of course more interesting in many ways. In the conditional just mentioned, the *identity* of the consequences is not part of the construction evoked, since *if* only conventionally evokes some consequent clause. The speaker may find this useful, since it may be more rhetorically effective to leave the punishment for cake theft to the addressee's imagination.

Forms emerging through metonymy are also common at the level of grammar, as we shall discuss in more detail in Chapter 6. But languages vary in their strategies for incorporating metonymic meaning relationships into grammars. English happens to be a language with extremely productive zero-derivation processes, so that deverbal nouns and denominal verbs are created with great freedom. A verb such as *cut* has frame-associated nouns that refer to the discontinuity created by the event of cutting (*There is a cut in the edge of the paper*), specifically to a wound created by cutting (*The cut bled*), and to the shape of a garment, which is attributable to the initial act of cutting the cloth (*The cut of that jacket is very fashionable*). This list does not even include the various metonymic compounds, such as *haircut*, nor metaphoric nouns like *a cut*, meaning 'a portion of profits' (*get your cut of the money*). The deverbal noun *hit* includes a type of baseball play among its senses. And going in the opposite direction, from nouns to verbs, English speakers can *bridge a river*, *rope a steer*, *paper a wall*, and more. They can literally *cut a bandage*, and metonymically *bandage a cut*. Not all languages have such freedom, and many instead have complex morphology to transform words between word classes – like English gerunds (*cutting* from *cut*) or other derivational processes (*happiness* from *happy*). But these processes too depend on the understanding that there are normal frames whose different aspects or parts can be named: there is some state named by the noun *happiness*, which is independent of predicating the adjective *happy* of some particular entity. Nikiforidou (1999) offers a general treatment of semantic patterns of nominalization in English in terms of frame metonymy; this kind of treatment could readily be extended to other languages.

Frame metonymy is the most important factor in many crucial aspects of pragmatics – for example, one might guess that a fellow student had a job interview just from seeing that she was wearing a suit. This is no less true in linguistic pragmatics: what analysts call *indirect speech acts*, for example, generally depend on metonymic relations to speech-act frames for their interpretation. Suppose that an evening lecture on campus has just ended, and you see a colleague who you hope might give you a ride home. As Searle's (1969, 1975, 1990) work on speech acts makes clear, it is a general *precondition* of a request that the addressee is understood to be able to do what is requested. (You could not reasonably ask a six-year-old for a ride home, since she would be unable to drive.) So before requesting a lift, you might ask your colleague, *Did you bring your car this evening?* However, since your colleague is just as aware of this frame as you are, he might well be able to construct the full Request frame from the question about a precondition – and going one step further, he might allow the precondition-checking phase to count as performance of the full Request speech act. Thus, assuming the car is there, he might respond not with just *Yes*, but with an offer or a check on the request, such as *Would you like a ride home?* By this kind of indirectness, he has also helped you avoid the awkward and potentially imposing phase of directly requesting a ride.

In general, one would expect linguistic part-for-whole frame metonymies to be subject to the same cognitive restrictions as other kinds of metonymic usages – can addressees successfully recognize the intended whole, so that the speaker succeeds in conveying more meaning with less form? This does not seem to be particular to metonymy or metaphor, but is a general communication constraint.

5.5   Frame metonymy and asymmetry in language and cognition

Frame-based reasoning has been shown to be very normal for humans; we will not here discuss the general effect, since most of the relevant cognitive science research is not specifically about *frame metonymy*. But since frames are gestalts, frame-metonymic recognition of a whole frame is also a very basic consequence of cognitive structure. And crucially, *characteristic* parts of frames are particularly powerful in evoking the whole frame. For example, the word *table* or the sight of a table in a film scene does not necessarily bring up any specific frame, since tables are used in a great many situations. But the word *waiter* or *menu* much more clearly evokes the Restaurant frame – and in a movie, seeing a character examining a menu, or talking to someone dressed like a waiter, makes it clear that the setting is a restaurant. Even *plate* is more likely to evoke Eating, in contrast with the broad range of activities in which a table might take part.

Frame-based categorial recognition is therefore not equally likely to be prompted by every frame element, but rather by the ones which are *valid cues* for the whole frame. Tables are certainly a normal part of the Restaurant frame, but a table is not a valid cue for the Restaurant frame in the way a menu is, since a menu occurs *only* in the Restaurant frame. This presumably explains why *skirt* can frame-metonymically mean 'woman.' It is not that women necessarily, or even usually, wear skirts; it is that canonically – or prescriptively, at least – in the relevant usage community, *only* women wear skirts. So *jeans* would be of no use to signify 'woman,' or 'man' for that matter, because there is no unique association between jeans and men or women. Similarly, those who use *suit* to mean 'conventional business-community member' assume that suits are pretty much only worn by members of that community – at least on a regular daily basis.

Linguistic markers are also metonymic in crucial ways for social-group membership. This is how sociolinguistics works. Mention of the *IPA* (International Phonetic Alphabet) marks the user as someone who knows what the IPA is, and hence has probably taken at least one linguistics course; use of the term *valid cue* marks us as having at least some limited familiarity with psychology literature. Reference to a *sub*, a *hero*, or a *grinder* (all names for the same kind of sandwich) will locate a speaker on the US dialect map. A listener might successfully place someone who used the words *apartment* and *truck* as American, and someone who used *flat* and *lorry* (for the same referents) as British. And a Californian knows that someone who uses *the 101* (a metonymic expression) to mean 'Highway 101' is from southern California, as someone from northern California would just use *101* (a different metonymic expression). Spellings (and pronunciations, which will not be discussed here) are equally sociolinguistic markers: *honor* and *center* are American spellings, *honour* and *centre* British ones. In all cases, choice of a form may end up meaning something about personal identity, not just about the form itself: the broader frame of linguistics, or British culture, is evoked by forms associated (again, more or less uniquely) with those frames.

We will save for Chapter 8 a full discussion of the ways in which linguistic usages can evoke genre or guide discourse structure; and visual frame metonymy will come up again in the chapter on multimodality. But a final point we want to make in this section on the patterns and uses of frame metonymy is that the choice of the particular term in each specific case depends on which frame the speaker/writer wants to evoke. For most speakers, the choice of *fetus* rather than *baby* in particular contexts may suffice to let a listener know a great deal about the speaker's position on abortion – even if nothing else in the utterance indicates that position. Words or linguistic forms can be unique to particular rhetorical or discourse framings, and thus evoke a full discourse frame.

This is equally true of images, where the metonymic effects of text and image are often best discussed as prompting blends. For example, there are antiabortion billboards in the US that show a cute blond baby old enough to sit up; the ad says something like *I can feel pain at twenty weeks*. The visual image of the baby is thus one of the inputs, while the text (*at twenty weeks*) suggests the second input, that of the fetus. Compression is crucial here – the temporal distance between the fetus and the baby is reduced, and the natural boundary event of the baby's birth is also compressed out of the picture. The newly constructed compressed identity (fetus-as-baby) helps get the message across. Visually, the ads never show a twenty-week fetus, because the intended frame is that of a fetus's development into an eventual baby. The focus then is on the well-being of a baby – a strategy that brings more supporters to the campaign. What is notable here is that, in artifacts like these, the visual form and the text often trigger different inputs, by evoking their frames and prompting the blended construct.

5.6   Cognitive bases for categorial metonymy

Categorial metonymy has been particularly closely investigated in cognitive science. As early as Rips (1975), it was shown that the centrality of a subcategory in a larger category affects similarity judgments and reasoning patterns. For example, in Rips's experiments, urban American subjects over-whelmingly judged robins to be more central members of the category *bird* than ducks: they listed *robins* sooner than *ducks* on lists of birds, identified pictures of robins as birds faster than pictures of ducks, and drew a picture of a bird which looked more like a robin than a duck. Subjects were told that there were robins and ducks on an imagined island, and were either (1) told that the robins on the island had a disease and asked how likely it was the ducks would catch it, or (2) told that the ducks had a disease and asked how likely it was that the robins would catch it. Subjects consistently found it more likely that the ducks would catch the robins' disease than the other direction. In this and other parallel experiments, speakers consistently reasoned from central to peripheral category members – in this case, from robins to ducks, where robins are a more central subcategory of *bird* than ducks.

If this seems a surprising result, it should not, given that the same speakers actually judged ducks to be more *similar to* robins than vice versa: so if similarity is a good metric of whether animals will catch the same disease, then obviously ducks will catch robin diseases more easily than the other way round. But similarity is something we normally think of as symmetric, so that if A resembles B, B resembles A, and presumably to the same extent (since the characteristics A shares with B are also the ones B shares with A).

However, as we have pointed out in our discussion of polysemy and meaning change earlier in this chapter, it is precisely the asymmetric nature of category structure which makes some subcategories "better" representatives of a larger category than others. Nobody would or could have a category of *chair* centered on beanbag chairs. And yes, category membership is often based on similarity – but it is based specifically on deciding whether peripheral members, or potential members, are similar enough to the central case, and not on judging how similar the central case is to the peripheral members. People do not spend time figuring out how much like a beanbag chair a straight-back chair is; but yes, they have decided that beanbag chairs (which share at least the sitting routine with other chairs) are similar enough to prototypical chairs to be called *chairs*. The center of the category is the *standard of comparison* for membership judgments.

It also seems that research subjects use their own country as a standard of comparison, naturally enough: what country do they know better, or want to make comparisons to so often? US subjects thus (in separate questions from Rips) rated the similarity of Canada to the US higher than the similarity of the US to Canada. Before we attribute such asymmetric judgments solely to the egotism of the subjects cited above, consider practical real-world policy examples. In the 1990s, one of the authors was somewhat surprised to discover that German phone cards worked in the Netherlands but Dutch phone cards did not work in Germany. But she would have been more surprised if the asymmetry had been the other way, since Germany is larger, more powerful, and more "central" to the structure of the European Union.

More policy-making examples of category-based reasoning abound. To give just one instance: between 1977 and 1993, coincidentally during a particularly productive period of new pharmaceutical development, female subjects were entirely banned from general drug trials conducted by American pharmaceutical companies. And yet the drugs being developed in those trials were, of course, intended for use by women as well as men. Historical reasons for the male-only pools ranged from concern about women becoming pregnant during trials, to trial sites being at US military hospitals (with almost all male patients), to the more interesting claims that women's hormonal cycles and sex-specific medications (such as birth-control pills) might be "confounds" in the studies. Of course, these "confounds" were exactly the reasons why a drug might have different results in a female population, and therefore exactly the reasons why including women in the trials was important. This was eventually realized, and in 1993 (due in part to the establishment of the Women's Health Initiative in 1991) the national Food and Drug Administration policy barring women from trials was reversed. But it seems obvious that the medical establishment could never have imagined, even briefly, that they could automatically extend treatments to men which had been developed based on an entirely female subject pool. Rips would, however, have predicted this reasoning, assuming many of the reasoners to have men at the center of their category of *humans*.

These kinds of reasoning patterns seem relevant to evaluating the controversial use of category-metonymic "inclusive" masculine language, such as the use of *he* to mean 'he or she' and the use of *man* to mean 'person.' Plenty of linguistic evidence suggests that these cognitive and linguistic metonymies are based on asymmetric categorization, and that the category *person* is still (for some purposes at least) centered on the minority of white straight male people. This comes as no surprise to linguists who have noted that when a larger category shares a name with a subcategory, it is usually because that subcategory is prototypical: the two different senses of a word like *man* already cause us to suspect that some members of the higher level "inclusive" usage are more closely included than others. Novelists writing for a Euro-American audience do not have to mention, in introducing a cellist or a bus driver into the cast of a detective novel, that this person is white, or male; they would have to mention that the person is female, or nonwhite. (The African-American novelists Toni Morrison and Terry McMillan have broken with that in making African American the default for a new character.) We might refer to that white, blond baby on the antiabortion billboard to make the same point. We might also elaborate to saying that the center of the category *human* is also hearing, sighted, neurotypical people; linguists discussing "child language acquisition" don't have to say so explicitly when they are referring to neurotypical hearing children acquiring a spoken language, while they would have to specifically say that they were talking about deaf children and sign language acquisition, or about autistic children's language acquisition.

5.7   The contribution of metonymy to Mental Space building and blending

In building complex blended spaces of the kind discussed in the preceding chapter, metonymy plays at least as central a role as metaphor. A classic example where metonymy helps build a metaphoric blend is Fauconnier and Turner's (2002) analysis of the Grim Reaper blend. The Grim Reaper, a character in Western European folklore, is a skeleton wearing a hooded monk's robe and carrying a scythe; dying is metaphorically *meeting the Grim Reaper.* Note that it is precisely metonymic connections which inform us of the two input spaces to this blend: the scythe is metonymic for the source-domain frame of Reaping, while the skeleton is metonymic for the target-domain frame of Death (as is, they argue, the monk's robe, since monks were understood in medieval Europe to have been the normal professional performers of prayers for the souls of the dead). For an audience who failed to make these metonymic connections, it would be very hard to build the metaphoric mappings between the Human Life Cycle and the Plant/Crop Life Cycle which constitute the Grim Reaper blend. In the blend, dying is *being reaped.* But note that, crucially, even nonviolent deaths are *meeting the Grim Reaper.* So in fact the source-frame-evoking scythe does not necessarily map onto any implement in the target domain; there is no murder and no murder weapon in most of the relevant deaths. Further, a stalk of wheat leaves no skeleton behind, and is not mourned by anyone. So the skeleton and the monk's robe which metonymically evoke the target-domain Death frame are also not mapped onto anything in the source domain. The Grim Reaper blend, laid out in Table 5.1, is now considered a classic example of the ways in which a blend can be partially metaphoric but not entirely so – the metonymies are equally important, and indeed are necessary to the metaphoric mappings.

As we noted, the Grim Reaper blend relies on several inputs, but because of its highly compressed form, it is co-opted into many images which need a simple visual representation of Death. One can see the Grim Reaper feeding bear cubs in a park poster discouraging the feeding of wildlife, or other activities in humorous

Table 5.1 *The Grim Reaper blend*

Generic: Life cycle	*Source:* Plant life cycle	*Target:* Human life cycle	*Blend:* Human life cycle as plant life cycle
Living being	Plant	Human being	Human as plant
Life cycle	Plant life cycle	Human life cycle	Human life cycle as plant life cycle
Death	Death of plant	Death of human	Death of human as death of plant
–	Act of reaping	–	(Act of reaping as cause of death)
–	Sickle	–	Sickle
–	–	Skeleton	Skeleton
–	–	Monk's robe	Monk's robe

cartoons. Additionally, the Grim Reaper image is typically used in construals where someone or something causes death, so that the figure offering food to a bear cub *is* death, but also *causes* death – an example of what Fauconnier and Turner (2002) refer to as causal tautology. In some traditional European cultures, the Grim Reaper figure has very human attributes, so that folk tales are told about people who were not afraid of death and so could give the Grim Reaper a good beating and survive an "encounter with death."

The Grim Reaper is thus used in multiple blends (blends consisting of multiple layers of blends are often called *megablends*), where, in combination with other frame-evoking visual forms, it participates in constructs involving many levels of blending. One such example is a print drawn by Banksy (a well-known British graffiti artist), which circulates under the name of *Grin Reaper* (see Figure 5.1). The image consists of three components: the Grim Reaper, wearing his cowl and holding the scythe, is sitting on the face of a clock; the clock shows that the time is just a few minutes to midnight.[1] The most important addition, however, is that instead of showing his usual skull face, the Grin Reaper has the yellow face of a Smiley symbol. This megablend thus plays on a number of frame components, relying entirely on visual-frame metonymy – for there is no language accompanying this image.

The actual content of the input frames evoked will depend to some degree on the background of the viewer, but most viewers will probably agree that the Grim Reaper stands for Death, while the clock stands for the passage of time; for some viewers, its similarity to Big Ben might evoke British culture. Additionally, the time shown on the clock reminds us of suspense movies, but perhaps equally of the

---

[1] To some, the clock strikingly resembles the London clock Big Ben, but it is in fact not identical to it (e.g. Big Ben has no weights attached, and the hands are slightly different). Overall, the "identity" of the clock may be of little consequence, but if indeed it is considered to represent the UK icon, then the frame evoked may participate in the interpretation.

Figure 5.1. *Grin Reaper, Banksy 2005*

Cinderella story or New Year's Eve celebrations – situations where people count the minutes to midnight, knowing that something new and important will happen at the salient boundary between the days or between day and night (ghosts appear after midnight, and then disappear at dawn, etc.).[2] The Smiley face is a much more unspecified icon. It is ubiquitous, mostly signifying an overall "feel-good" mood and disposition. But more specifically, it might be associated with the culture of the seventies, especially in America, and all the artifacts of popular culture which feature similar Smileys (tee-shirts, buttons, mugs, toys, etc.). More recently, the Smiley face is perhaps the most common emoticon in Internet communication.

The most striking disanalogy in the emergent blend is the contrast between the grim nature of the Reaper and the happy nature of the Smiley – and yet the two are attributed to the same figure in the image. But perhaps all viewers need is to

[2] In fact, some languages, like Polish and Dutch, have expressions which are roughly equivalent to *five minutes to midnight* which are used in contexts suggesting a need for urgent action.

consider the potential victim of the Grin Reaper – in most instances, such blends prompt the viewer to align herself with the victim. In spite of the jocular collage in the image, then, the emergent structure profiles the viewer as under some kind of threat, and the threat is also portrayed as imminent – in five minutes the clock will strike midnight and all will be over.

The image clearly shows how frame metonymy and blending work. Frames are evoked (visually, in this case), but the emergent blend is determined by what the viewer considers to be the most salient aspect of each of the frames, and what coherent emergent structure the combination of the frames can yield. Some viewers may assume that popular culture is a threat to their British identity, while others might believe that the print warns them against assuming that all "feel-good" objects are harmless when in fact their effects are imminent and frightening. Still others might read the image as saying that we should laugh at all discussion of cultural decay, or that the world as we know it is about to end while we are smiling happily through the destruction (in this case, the viewer would be aligned with the Grin Reaper, rather than being his victim).

In other words, though similar frames are evoked by the visual prompts, the emerging blends will differ across viewers, and there are typically several levels of blending involved. For example, consider a case where the viewer (or another person) is understood as happily causing a disaster. First, we have to combine the two inputs, the Grim Reaper and Smiley. The Grim Reaper input is itself a blend, but in the "Grin Reaper" blend it is refocused to suit the needs of the emergent structure. Primarily, it has to be framed as a generic image of a human body. The Grin Reaper is seated (actually dangling his skeletal feet) in a posture not typically associated with the Grim Reaper. The blend also relies on the importance of the human face in our understanding of the body as representing a person. The face is central to our recognition of the individual we are interacting with, and it is also the site of the primary expression of emotion. While the Grim Reaper is grim primarily because of what he does, his face, which is simply a skull, is not understood to have any expression. In fact, most representations of the Grim Reaper hide his skull in a cowl, thus perhaps adding to the idea that Death does not really interact with the victims – we do not know what he feels, if he even sees us; we cannot maintain eye contact with him, etc. At the generic-space level, then, the human body and face provide an image against which other inputs are viewed.

The Smiley input, for comparison, is nothing but a face – a cartoonish happy face of no particular human at all. This input does not imply that there are any particular reasons for happiness; it also does not suggest any succession wherein the mood might change from happy to sad or vice versa. Interestingly, the Smiley emoticon evolved into a range of images expressing all kinds of feelings – sadness, surprise, disappointment, anger, etc. But the original Smiley is just a token of unspecified good mood. Also, the Smiley, in spite of the varieties, is never more than a face, so it does not have limbs which could be responsible for motion or action. Unlike the Grim Reaper, Smiley resists attribution of agency.

In the "Grin Reaper" blend, the figure created has the body of the Grim Reaper and the face of the Smiley. Because the face (still based on the schematic body-image space) is taken to give outward expression to thoughts and feelings emerging in the brain, the blended figure of the Grin Reaper is perpetually frozen in the expression of happiness, even though the rest of the figure suggests the opposite; on the other hand, the Grim Reaper in this image has a rather relaxed body posture, in spite of the grim attire. But the 'death' meaning of the Grim Reaper requires that he uses his body in the ways that humans do – so he walks towards the victim and uses his scythe to "reap" the human life. Consequently, the blend (in this meaning at least) creates a figure which does this deadly job while being perpetually (and thoughtlessly) happy – it is only a face, not a head with a brain and a mind in it. This element of the emergent structure yields the aspect of meaning wherein whoever is aligned with the Grin Reaper is someone causing damage while being blissfully unaware of or at least unmoved by the harm done.

The "Grin Reaper" blend is then combined with a third input – the clock, metonymically evoking the passage of time. Evoking the image of the face of a clock has been discussed in blending literature (Williams 2004) as a material anchor (Hutchins 2005) to a very complex blend which we rely on in measuring time. Furthermore, the face of the clock is here using the position of the hands of the clock to signal some imminent dramatic change. In the final input, the Grin Reaper is sitting on the clock, as if waiting for midnight, whereupon he will start his grim harvest. The meaning of *midnight* is, in the Cinderella input sense, only that of a time where things will change dramatically – but the nature of the "things" that will change is what the viewer will read into the emergent blend (whether her primary fear is that of climate change, terrorism, financial crisis, or something else).

The nature of the interpretation we are analyzing here is further limited by the ways in which the viewer aligns herself with the frames. She may be the one with the happy face, blind to the grim effects of her actions, or she may be a participant in activities which are in effect deadly, or she may be threatened by external events which are inevitably approaching. More specifically, she can further imagine the viewpoint she is taking to be representing an individual, a social group, or a nation. These alignments use the nature of the frames in ways which profile a specific viewpoint. The viewpointed nature of the construals is what governs the remaining choices of just which elements of the inputs are projected into the blend, and just which kinds of vital relations are assumed to hold the blend together. It can mean (dis)analogy between the viewer and a construct in the frame (we are the reaper or we aren't, we are wearing a smiley face or we aren't), or it can mean being in a different part of the causation schema – as a destructive agent or a hapless victim. We can assume that the Grin Reaper is a new, blended cultural identity, or that the disanalogy is what will destroy us. Time can also be understood differently here – the minutes until midnight can be short or long, since a minute on this particular clock might count as a millennium or a decade (though the sense of inevitability of destruction is still part of the meaning).

To conclude, we point out that there is an important difference between rich ambiguity and indeterminacy. We would not claim that the reading of the *Grim Reaper* in any given case is radically unpredictable. It is only as broad as the frames evoked allow, and the mechanisms of blending make sure that the emergent structure is coherent and optimal (as coherent and optimal as the viewer can make it), and relies clearly on selective projection from the frames. But we also have to note that examples like these are the ultimate expression of what figurative thought is like – evocation of frames prompts the emergence of conceptual structures in ways which are guided by the viewer's participation in some participant's viewpoint. These principles apply to textual blending and visual blending, and to combinations of the two. But it should be clear from this discussion that metonymic projection is a basic foundation of figurative thought. In the final section of the chapter, we will look at how it helps to construct and maintain important cultural icons.

5.8   Metonymy in visual blending

As with the Grim Reaper, many other metaphoric blends depend on metonymy for access. We have mentioned that Greco-Roman gods were in large measure metaphoric personifications of human qualities and states. But since statues and paintings of Greco-Roman gods were never portraits, but were idealized depictions of (very beautiful) humans, traditional iconography depended largely on the frame-metonymic association of individual gods or saints with symbols of their identity. For example, Athene was depicted with an owl, another personification of wisdom, and typically with her chariot and wearing a helmet – masculine accoutrements, since she represented the not-very-feminine characteristic of rationality. Venus was often depicted with doves, Hermes with winged sandals, and so on. Without the frame-metonymic markers, who could have recognized these metaphoric personifications of rationality, love, and trickery? The same is true with Christian saints, who are often depicted accompanied by aspects of the frames of their stories – sometimes gory elements of their martyrdom frames. St. Peter, keeper of the keys of Heaven, holds a key, but St. Catherine of Alexandria is recognizable by her wheel (she died on a wheel), and St. Barbara is depicted with her tower (she was immured). Further fascinating metonymic developments have associated these symbols with professions; St. Apollonia, whose martyrdom torture included her teeth being pulled out, is depicted carrying her teeth – and therefore became thought of as the patron saint of dentists.

As a result of such associations, readers are cued by frame elements to expect or construct aspects of text worlds. For example, in medieval Iceland, someone going out to avenge a relative's death conventionally was supposed to don blue-black clothing. This would have been well known to the readers or listeners of the sagas; hence, reading that a character *put on his blue-black clothing* would make the reader say *Oh, no!* – nothing more is needed to uniquely cue a scene of violent revenge to follow. In medieval Irish literature, if a King met a woman sitting on a green hill, or riding on a horse, the readers knew that this was a land-goddess whom the King needed to marry to validate his kingship. This was politically useful to redactors of such tales during the later Christian medieval period, since the redactor (probably Christian, perhaps a monk) did not need to mention explicitly pagan elements such as land-goddesses for the frame to be evoked. In modern romance novels, when an attractive male character (often tall and dark) clashes dramatically with the heroine, those conflicts indicate to readers that he is the one destined to be the heroine's ultimate romantic fate.

And finally, we will bring in another example from our 2005 book, and mention Manet's painting *Olympia*. This painting, now in the Musée du Quai d'Orsay in Paris, depicts a beautiful woman, coiffed and wearing jewelry but otherwise nude. She is reclining on a couch, and her servant is handing her a bouquet of flowers. Somewhat to the surprise of twenty-first-century art lovers, what made this painting scandalous in Manet's day was not its depiction of a nude woman – sophisticated Parisian art patrons accepted nudes as a legitimate artistic genre. Rather, it was the bouquet, which to them clearly indicated that there was a gentleman caller coming to visit this lady, who was apparently preparing to receive him nude. That is, it was the imagined, *nondepicted* gentleman in the "picture" world, evoked only by the *frame* of flower-offerings from gentlemen to ladies, who scandalized the viewers – not the actual gentlemen viewers at the exhibit, looking at the painting. (Of course, Manet also made far more overtly sexual depictions such as *Déjeuner sur l'herbe* – which shows clothed gentlemen with nude women – and twenty-first-century viewers need less help to see what was shocking about those.)

5.9   Conclusions

Metonymy is, like metaphor, pervasive in language because it is pervasive in perception and cognition. Both categorial metonymy and frame metonymy are recognized cognitive modes, evidenced in innovative usages, polysemy patterns, known historical-change patterns, and form abbreviations. The correlational basis of metonymy is also, as has long been recognized, a crucial basis for metaphor. Conceptual metaphors which have experiential bases are normally based in frame association, although of course they go beyond that association to metaphoric mappings between the two frames. Metonymy is more cognitively basic than metaphor – frame evocation by elements (as well as category judgments, of course) characterize many species, while only humans engage in metaphoric conceptualization. Metonymy is also the central organizing principle of pragmatics, the contextual use and interpretation of meaning; contextual interpretation is essentially grounded in the use of frame-indicating cues and categorial judgments.

Another crucial point is that metonymy is, like metaphor, *viewpointed*. When Toni Morrison and Terry McMillan challenge white category-metonymic patterns of reference in fiction writing, they are doing more than just reversing a biased usage; they are expressing a cultural and social viewpoint which is not expressed by those established patterns, most obviously because those patterns are not the ones used in the African-American community. What is the central example of a category, and therefore how to choose a metonymic label or reason about that category, depends on who you are and what your understanding of the category is.

Frame metonymy likewise depends on shared frame structure, which is often culture specific; our discussion of menus and restaurants assumed that such a frame is accessible to the addressees and viewers who use the sight of the menu (or the word *menu*) as a cue. Metonymic patterns depend on the structure of the cognitive, and often cultural, world of the speaker and thinker. This is why Manet knew he could shock his contemporaries with the bouquet in *Olympia*, while twenty-first-century viewers may not catch his reference to the frame in question. And further, one could say that the bouquet frame-metonymically intrudes not only male presence, but a male viewer and *viewpoint*, into a space which is still private and feminine at the moment depicted: only the female servant and Olympia's little black cat are actually able to see her in the "picture" world.

The most crucial point of all should now be clear. Metonymy has often been wrongly categorized as primarily "about" achieving reference, while metaphor is understood to reconstrue one thing as another. According to this view, we only say *hands* to mean 'workers' or *White House* to mean 'executive branch of the US government' as a convenient way to evoke the entire referent entity; but we say, *Our relationship is a dead-end street*, to develop a new understanding of the relationship. However, first of all, metaphor certainly does not always involve *active* reconstrual: when we say, *Taxes rose*, we are not creatively developing some new understanding of tax increases as upwards motion, but evoking an already-conventional metaphoric construal. And indeed, my primary intention may be referential – this metaphoric usage is the easiest conventional way to express my referential meaning in the target domain.

Langacker (1987, 1990, 1991), who coined the term *active zone*, would surely disagree with a "pure-reference" summary of metonymy as well: although he points out that there are indeed referential patterns based on relationships between wholes and active zones, his entire linguistic model is premised on the further understanding that linguistic choices are choices of *construal*. It is certainly true that *The dog bit me* is a convenient referential expression to describe an event wherein the dog's active zone (jaw and teeth) bit an active zone of the speaker (perhaps a portion of the calf). But it is also true that in choosing this linguistic form rather than *The dog's teeth went into the skin of my calf*, the speaker is profiling the responsible agent and the affected patient, not merely their body parts. The speaker, as a whole person, is the one who suffered pain; the dog, as a whole dog, is responsible for it. The speaker cannot punish the dog's teeth. Similarly, *Put the pencil in the pencil sharpener* does indeed mean that the hearer should put the sharpenable lead end of the pencil into the hole in the pencil sharpener – but it is precisely the entire pencil which is the functional object that needs improvement (one can't just use the tip), and the entire pencil sharpener mechanism which can bring about that improvement (not the hole alone). And, as we have seen above, this kind of active-zone metonymy applied to people leads to objectification, and hence to possible derogation. Pencils, of course, don't care whether we refer to all or part of them, but people do – particularly if the part is involved in a negative frame-metonymic construal.

So it seems best to think of both metaphor and metonymy as having both central construal functions and basic referential functions. Metaphor systematically construes one frame as another; metonymy construes a category in relation to a sub- or supercategory, or an entity with respect to some particular aspect of a frame rather than another. Once either of these construal functions is in place, it can be used referentially. One can now talk about (or visually evoke) the source frame via the target frame, or the frame via the frame element.

5.10   Summary

In this chapter we discussed another major type of mapping – metonymy. The important point we made throughout the chapter is that metonymy is possibly more common than metaphor and plays a role in lexical usage patterns across a wide range of uses. We distinguished a specific pattern of categorial metonymy, where a subcategory is used to stand for the entire category, or vice versa. In this case, we have also referred to findings from cognitive science which strongly support the distinction. But we devoted most attention to frame metonymy, where an aspect of a frame is used to evoke the frame as a whole or its major part. Also, we accounted for the traditional definition of metonymy as a part–whole relation in terms of frame metonymy.

We have further shown that metaphor and metonymy work together, rather than in isolated ways. More complex expressions can combine metaphoric and metonymic mappings. We have also shown that metonymy, like metaphor, motivates numerous polysemy patterns. At the same time, metonymy relies on correlations which are not always predictable across the lexicon, which sometimes makes even common varieties of metonymy seem less systematic than the most widespread metaphoric mappings such as KNOWING IS SEEING. We have further noted that metonymy is present between forms of linguistic expressions – a shorter form is often used to stand for the longer version.

Finally, metonymy was shown to participate importantly in blends, including visual blends. We have also noted numerous ways in which metonymy helps construct cultural icons. Most importantly, though, all the examples discussed suggest that metonymy is much more than a particular pattern of reference. It plays numerous meaning-construction roles and is crucial in the emergence and maintenance of cultural categories.

This chapter also concludes the overview of primary mappings. We have considered metaphor, metonymy, and blending, and we have shown that they rely on many similar mechanisms of meaning construction. They project partial conceptual structures from frames and construe new frame-like configurations. They often participate jointly in the emergent meaning or rely on shared motivations. They constitute various ways in which meanings are figuratively constructed.

6 Grammatical constructions and figurative meaning

6.1 Introduction

So far in this book, we have discussed the ways in which everyday cognition and language pervasively use metaphoric and metonymic structures, as well as nonmetaphoric Mental Space blends. We have mostly been talking about the role of words, or images, in cuing figurative cognitive structures. But in fact, grammatical constructions can be used figuratively, and some are also systematically involved in cuing figurative meaning. It is therefore now time to turn to the role of grammar.

We have shown in Chapter 5 that metonymy is a constant and crucial aspect of grammatical usage. We discussed several kinds of frame-metonymic structures exploited by grammar, one example being the relation of deverbal nouns to their source verbs by frame metonymy: the English noun *cut* can mean an act of cutting, a division left by that act, and so on. We noted some of the ways in which *partial* expression of a form – a word, a fixed phrase, or a grammatical construction – can convey the complete meaning associated with the whole form. And we argued that contextual meaning interpretation – pragmatics – relies essentially on frame-metonymic and category-metonymic relationships.

But for many people, it may be easier to accept these metonymic aspects of grammar than to think of grammar as having metaphoric functions. Partly this is because we may have been taught to think of syntax as a system for combining meanings of words, rather than thinking of syntactic constructions as having independent meanings – sometimes quite rich ones. And of course, for a grammatical construction to have metaphoric meaning, it is first necessary for the construction to have *meaning* – i.e. a literal source-domain meaning which can be mapped onto the meaning of some target domain. Not every grammatical theory would see this as possible, but more and more researchers are willing to acknowledge that grammatical constructions themselves are meaningful.

Consider a literal caused-motion sentence such as *They dragged Joe out of the hole*. Here we could potentially lay the primary responsibility for the caused-motion meaning on the verb *drag*, which is a verb of force exertion which normally involves intent to cause something to move. But how about an example like *We laughed Joe out of his depression*? *Laugh* is not a verb of physical force exertion, nor is it ordinarily associated with causing any intended result; it just refers to the single-participant activity of laughing. One way of thinking about this would be to say that there is a Caused-Motion Construction in English: Subject Verb Theme-NP Path (in a very oversimplified description), where Path will be either a prepositional phrase or an adverbial constituent (Goldberg 1995). The construction *means* that the subject caused the theme to move along the specified path – meaning which integrates easily with a verb such as *drag* (easily interpreted as specifying the means of causing motion) and a path description such as *out of the hole*. In this case, the prepositional phrase mentions the starting point of the path, but in other cases the path can be determined with reference to its end point, as in *The mother dragged the son into the doctor's office*. Evidence that this meaning is attached to the construction comes from cases of literal caused motion such as *She walked him out of the room* or *They laughed her off the stage*. In these examples, we understand that the subject literally caused the theme to move physically along a path out of the room or off the stage, but the verb does not supply such a meaning – *walk* and *laugh* don't mean 'cause to move by walking' or 'cause to move by laughing.' So it is the construction itself which contributes the meaning that the subject caused the theme to move.

But we are already well aware, from the preceding chapters, that metaphorically CHANGE IS MOTION and PURPOSIVE ACTION IS GOAL-DIRECTED MOTION. Another related mapping involved in the Location ESM is CAUSED CHANGE IS CAUSED MOTION. Words signifying physical causes of motion regularly refer to abstract causes of change and action: *We **pushed** her into applying for the fellowship*, or *Sue gently **nudged** Kara out of her naïve prejudices*. Goldberg argued that the Caused-Motion Construction itself, which literally refers to caused motion, is used metaphorically to refer to caused changes of state in examples like *We **laughed** Joe out of his depression, Cindy **coaxed** Kim through the admission process*, or *They **threatened** the captives into submission*. As we shall see, there are many such examples: once we understand that larger grammatical constructions are meaningful, we can easily see that their meanings are mapped metaphorically onto other domains.

We will also consider in this chapter ways in which grammatical constructions are systematically involved in the expression of metaphor: for example, why is it the case that *bloodstained wealth* necessarily refers to literal wealth (acquired by violent means), while *spiritual wealth* necessarily refers to abstract metaphoric "wealth" (moral principles, for example), and cannot refer to morally acquired literal wealth? Sullivan (2009, 2013) has argued that a better understanding of grammatical constructions – in this case, different English adjective–noun modification constructions – can offer explanations for how they can be used to express metaphoric meaning. In particular, *bloodstained wealth* is an example of an Attributive-Adjective Construction (like the literal *bloodstained shirt*), while *spiritual wealth* is an example of a Domain-Adjective Construction (like the literal *spiritual advisor*). As we shall see, these two constructions interact with processes of metaphoric construal differently.

In general, grammar can be thought of as a range of conventional ways of prompting the construction of particular kinds of Mental Space structures. Since grammatical structure is present at every level of grammar, it is available to shape different levels of meaning structure, in figurative as well as literal construal. So we will see different configurations of inputs prompted at the level of phrase structure (as in Sullivan's examples mentioned above), including more complex networks of spaces in the case of constructions such as conditionals or predicative constructions. But we will also see that certain grammatical patterns (such as copula constructions) are specifically useful in setting up correlations between spaces which are then used for the purpose of figurative construals. And we will show that other extremely frequent and multipurpose constructions such as *like*-comparison and genitive morphology (like copula constructions, these are not in themselves figurative) function to help construct particular figurative meaning patterns in larger units of form. Overall, we will show how grammatical form may be used to carry figurative meaning, even where its primary meaning is not figurative. And returning to metonymy, we will in the last section of this chapter examine how constructions which are basically frame-metonymic in function can be used with reference to more than one frame, thus prompting metaphoric mappings between the evoked frames.

6.2   Grammar and meaning

Before we go further, we should explain why cognitive linguists have come to the strong conclusion that grammatical constructions themselves can express meaning, rather than simply "tying together" the meanings of words used in the constructions. Construction Grammar (Fillmore et al. 1988, Fillmore and Kay 1991, Goldberg 1995, 2006, Croft 2001)[1] and Cognitive Grammar (Langacker 1987, 1990, 1991) in particular specifically hold that linguistic structure consists of constructions, which are *form–meaning mappings* at every level of the grammar. Thus, the form *cat* with its meaning 'cat' is a lexical construction, the English regular plural is a morphological construction (consisting of a slot for a noun form and meaning plus a suffix -*s* form whose meaning is 'plural'), and so is the English Subject–Predicate Construction (which semantically links the meanings of subject and predicate in a relation of semantic *predication*).

---

[1] For more recent developments in Construction Grammar, the John Benjamins series *Constructional Approaches to Language* is a good source; see in particular Fried and Östman (2004b), Östman and Fried (2005), or Fried and Boas (2005). Some of these volumes include the theory of embodied Construction Grammar, a more recent simulation-semantics approach; for example, see Bergen and Chang (2005); see also the discussion of Embodied Construction Grammar in Gibbs (2005).

In the process of developing Mental Spaces Theory, Fauconnier (1994[1985], Fauconnier and Sweetser 1996) uncovered a repertoire of space-building *meanings* marked by constructions: for example, conditionals bring up complex groups of mental spaces, so a listener will assume that *If it rains, they'll cancel the game* also means that they will not cancel it if it doesn't rain. Dancygier and Sweetser (2005) have labeled these Mental Space networks *alternative* spaces. The definite article (in one central use) is an instruction to bring up an already-accessible entity from some active space, while the indefinite article (in one central use) is an instruction to set up a new entity in some space. So in general, cognitive linguists working within Mental Spaces Theory and Blending Theory have paid close attention to the semantics of grammatical constructions.

But what about syntactic argument-structure constructions such as *Transitive* or *Ditransitive Constructions*, which are usually thought of more as instructions to assemble word meanings into sentence meaning, than as having semantics of their own? Goldberg (1995, 2006) has argued convincingly that certain argument-structure constructions in English, such as the Ditransitive (i.e. the Double-Object Construction), not only have semantics, but have semantics rather similar to some word meanings. The sentence *Sandy baked Sue a cake* does not express in words a crucial part of its conventional meaning, which is that Sue is the intended *recipient* of the cake. That aspect of meaning is expressed by the argument structure – that is, by the Ditransitive Construction, in which a verb is followed by two objects, the first of which is understood to express a recipient and the second a theme to be transferred to the recipient. We would not want to put the responsibility for the 'giving' or 'transfer' sense of this sentence on the words – *bake* is not a verb of transfer or even intended transfer. And, as Goldberg argues, putting 'transfer' into the lexical meaning would require us not only to create a second meaning of *bake* (e.g. BAKE$_1$ means 'bake' and BAKE$_2$ means 'bake in order to give to someone'), but also similar second meanings for a great many other creation and preparation verbs of English. And strikingly, these second meanings would occur precisely when the verb was used in this grammatical construction. *Kim **knitted** Jan a sweater*, *Zoe **painted** Andy a picture*, and *Joe **boiled** Marie an egg* would require special intended-giving senses for *knit*, *paint*, and *boil* which would be absent in other uses such as *Kim knitted a sweater*.

Goldberg proposed instead that the Ditransitive Construction itself carries a meaning of transferring a theme to a recipient, so these sentences are actually integrating (blending) the meanings of the words used with the meaning of the Ditransitive Construction. The meanings of the individual words are still fully present (a full instance of *baking* or *knitting* is involved), but we also have the frame of (in this case, possibly intended rather than necessarily actual) Transfer to a Recipient. With creation verbs in particular, it is easy to integrate these two frames by understanding the Creation event to be a causal and temporal predecessor to the transfer event: you have to bake the cake before there is a cake to give someone. These patterns are highly productive: invent a new creation verb *plick*, referring perhaps to a unique kind of crocheting, and a speaker need not ask whether it is possible to say, *I'm going to plick my mom a nice vest for her birthday.* Further note that of course it would be exceptionally easy to integrate this construction with the meaning of a verb such as *give*, whose lexical semantics is that of transfer to a recipient. In fact, the semantic contribution of the construction goes practically unnoticed (by grammarians as well as everyday speakers) in *I gave him a cake*, because it overlaps so much with that of the verb.

We outlined above Goldberg's case for the Caused-Motion Construction as having meaning of its own. Examples such as *They laughed her off the stage* involve actual caused motion; but *laugh* is not a verb of physical force exertion. And *off the stage* in itself does not mean motion: I could say *She's off the stage now*, just meaning location. So it seems that the construction itself must be responsible for the caused-motion meaning. Here again, it is exceptionally easy to integrate that constructional meaning with the constructional meaning of a caused-motion verb such as *carry*, or *push* – and under those circumstances, once again, an analyst might fail to notice the construction's semantic contribution.

In general, then, complex compositional linguistic forms involve not only combining the formal parts appropriately (putting nouns, verbs, and articles together into a grammatical syntactic form) but also combining the meanings of those forms in a coherent way. A very simple example discussed by Langacker (1987, 1991) and further examined by Fried and Östman (2004a) was the possibility in English of using so-called count nouns in Mass-Noun Constructions and vice versa. *Cat* is a count noun – it refers to a countable individual, a cat. Supposing there to be an assembly of cats snoozing on a sunny day, I could say *There are five cats sleeping on the driveway* or *There are a lot of cats on the driveway* but not *There's a lot of cat on the driveway.* *Water* is a mass noun – it refers to a substance which is not an individual and cannot be counted. Seeing the result of overwatering an adjacent flower-bed, I might say *There is water all over the driveway*, but not the plural *There are waters all over the driveway.* But if I say *I've got cat all over my skirt*, one is inspired to think of a mass associated with cats, rather than an individual or a group of individuals. One might therefore imagine, for example, large accretions of shed cat fur on my skirt – more than a few individual, countable hairs. Langacker's gorier example was *After I ran over Fluffy, there was cat all over the driveway.*

On the other hand, using a mass noun in a Count Construction will also alter the meaning. *Three waters* would have to mean something like 'three bottles of water,' 'three glasses of water,' or possibly 'three kinds of water' – I have to think of units which can be counted, not just of a mass of water. In short, the meaning expressed will be a combination of the meaning of the noun itself and the meaning of the construction in which it is placed – in this case, the Mass or Count Construction. This kind of resolution of apparent clashes between lexical and constructional meaning has sometimes been referred to as *coercion* of one meaning by the other (for extensive treatment of such cases, see Francis and Michaelis 2003). The count–mass grammatical distinction, incidentally, is often relevant to figurative construal. We noted in Chapter 3 that there is a rather dramatic semantic effect in mass construal of human beings, as when a woman is metonymically referred to as *a piece of ass* – where the woman is not even identified with her own individual body part, but is seen as part of an undifferentiated extent of *ass* metonymically representing undifferentiated femaleness.

6.3   Metaphoric uses of constructions

So not only do syntactic constructions have meanings, some of them even have meanings which are rather similar to the meanings that words can have – though of course syntactic constructions are always pretty general in meaning, so their meanings are more parallel to schematic lexical meanings. The Ditransitive Construction overlaps significantly in meaning with the rather schematic verb *give*; it would be much less likely for there to be a syntactic construction with a meaning such as *loan, sell,* or *bake. Give* of course can be used metaphorically: the noise level can *give* you a headache, or a discussion with a friend can *give* you a new idea. And like *give*, the Ditransitive Construction is used metaphorically to refer to cases where no literal physical object, or physical exchange, is involved at all, as in our earlier example where the Caused-Motion Construction was used in *laugh Joe out of his depression* to describe a situation involving no literal motion.

As we discussed in Chapter 2, Lakoff and Johnson (1980) pointed out a very basic metaphor of English, labeled by Reddy (1979) the Conduit Metaphor, and more generally labeled COMMUNICATION IS OBJECT EXCHANGE. This metaphor includes the mappings involved in IDEAS ARE OBJECTS: an idea can *be put into your head*, but it can also *go right out of your head*, even if it was not given to you; ideas can be *big* and *small*, and can *fit together* or not. You will recall from Chapter 3 that IDEAS ARE OBJECTS is a component in many metaphors, including the THEORIES ARE BUILDINGS and IDEAS ARE FOOD complexes of metaphors. But of course literal objects can also be exchanged: if I have an object, I can give it to you, and then you have it. Linguistic communication is metaphorically understood to be Exchange of such objects, and linguistic forms are metaphorically understood to be the Containers of the idea-objects. Not only can I *give you an idea*, which you then *get from me*, but as Reddy noted, I can also say that *I didn't **get** anything **out of** that sentence*, or that *you **packed** too many ideas **into** one paragraph*. The meaning of such expressions is thus based on many levels of constructional and metaphorical meanings.

In passing, we should note here that COMMUNICATION IS OBJECT EXCHANGE is a perfect example of how blending projections, metaphoric and otherwise, are selective (as discussed in Chapter 4). When I put an object into a container and give the container to someone, and they open it and extract the object, it is necessarily the same object which I put into the container; Reddy comments that, in the target domain (and in the blend, we would add), the inference is that the idea which an addressee will understand is going to be the same as the one which the speaker intended. This does not fully correspond to the actual experience of communication, but we could say that it is a pervasive folk model – "what was said" is in some sense supposed to be the same for speaker and addressee. However, some inferences are not mapped at all. It is also the case that when I give you an object, you have it and I do not have it any more. No folk model of communication could accommodate the inference that when I tell you something, I no longer know it myself; in other words, that inference is incoherent with the target domain.

Returning to constructional metaphor, Goldberg notes that the Ditransitive Construction is used very generally with verbs of linguistic communication in English: *she told me a story*, *he read me a poem*, and *he wrote me a letter* have been joined in more recent years by *she faxed me the letter*, *he e-mailed them the file*, and other verbs of electronic communication. *Tell*, *read*, and *e-mail* don't in themselves involve exchange of physical objects. But they do involve communication (even *read*, in the 'read-aloud' sense), and are thus construed metaphorically as Exchange. It is not a major surprise, then, that they occur in the Ditransitive Construction, whose primary function is to express literal exchange, and which is here used to express metaphoric communicative exchange.

This is parallel to the metaphoric use of the Caused-Motion Construction mentioned above: scenarios involving Caused Change of State, which is metaphorically understood as Caused Motion, are expressed with the Caused-Motion Construction (*laugh someone out of their depression*, *coax the two-year-old away from an incipient meltdown*). In some of these expressions, there is nothing which expresses either spatial motion or change of physical state, and thus no motion words which could be interpreted metaphorically to mean Caused Change of State. *Laugh* is not even a transitive verb, let alone a verb of force exertion or causation. And *out of* and *away from* literally express either location or path of motion – you can *be away from home* or *go away from home*; since STATES ARE LOCATIONS and CHANGE IS MOTION, they are thus compatible with a metaphoric reading about states or changes of state. But on their own, they don't even specify whether the source domain involves location or motion; they do not *motivate* a Change of State reading, let alone a Caused Change of State reading. The most plausible hypothesis is therefore that the Caused-Motion Construction itself is interpreted metaphorically in these cases, to mean Caused Change of State.

6.4   Grammatical asymmetry and source–target asymmetry

It has long been noted that some grammatical constructions are particularly suited to the expression of metaphoric meaning. Brooke-Rose (1958) noted the ambiguities of copula BE-Constructions, which can either identify entities (*Clark Kent is Superman*) or predicate qualities or roles of entities (*Joe is intelligent, Joe is Nancy's brother, Joe is a teacher*) – or express metaphoric mappings (*Life is a journey, Joe is my guiding star*). But, as Sullivan (2009, 2013) noted, even more interesting is the regularity with which particular grammatical slots prompt particular roles in metaphoric construal. It is now conventional to say TARGET IS SOURCE to express metaphoric mappings in linguistic analysis: thus, LIFE IS A JOURNEY. But indeed, the reverse sounds wrong as a statement of a metaphor: one could not just as well say A JOURNEY IS LIFE, or if one did, it would mean something different. Or consider the examples discussed in Chapter 2, A MIND IS A COMPUTER and A COMPUTER IS A MIND: it is clear that the first of these means that we are thinking of the Mind (target) as a Computer (source), while in the second, the target and source are reversed.

As the examples throughout this book suggest, it is not always the case that both source and target domain are expressed linguistically. And even when they are, it is not always unambiguous. Suppose that one reads *John kicked the can down the road*. *Kick the can down the road* is a metaphoric idiom in American English which means 'postpone dealing with a problem until a later date.' But a human being could either literally kick a can in such a way that it moves down a road (being a physical body with force), or metaphorically *kick the can down the road*, since he is a social and cognitive being who can postpone dealing with problems: so John could potentially fill either the source-domain role or the target-domain role. An automatic metaphor-extraction mechanism could have real trouble dealing with such an example, where no clear linguistic "domain clash" marks the involvement of separate source- and target-domain frames. But actual language users in everyday contexts generally have no problem choosing the right meaning.

However, Sullivan notes that there are very broad regularities about which grammatical slots are filled by source- and target-domain vocabulary, when both domains *are* expressed in language. For example, although it is not a one-hundred-percent rule, there are very strong tendencies for modifying adjectives to be source domain while the nouns they modify are target domain (*bitter sorrow, weighty problem*), and the same is true with adverbs and the verbs they modify (*weep bitterly, consider deeply*). (*Weeping* and *sorrow* are part of the target domain in a mapping between Emotions and physical Tastes, while *bitter* and *bitterly* are part of the source domain.) Particularly where there is no added context to push for different readings, this is a very pervasive pattern.

Langacker (1987, 1990, 1991) has argued that in (literal) modification constructions, there is an asymmetry of *conceptual dependency*: the head (Noun or Verb) is more semantically autonomous, while the modifier is more dependent. Thus, in interpreting *big elephant* and *big molecule*, the meaning of *big* seems quite significantly dependent on the meaning of the noun (in this case, the noun determines the size scale relative to which we interpret *big*), while the noun's meaning seems more independent of the adjective. The same is true in *walk fast* and *gallop fast*; the meaning of the modifying adverb *fast* is adapted to the verb's meaning, more than the other way around. This is not to say that in these constructions one word is *entirely* semantically independent, while the other is entirely dependent; a hearer might well also adapt his image of walking to accommodate whether the speaker had said *walk fast* or *walk slow*. Langacker's claim is rather that there is an *asymmetry* in semantic dependence.

For Predicate–Argument Constructions, Langacker would argue, the reverse holds true: the head is more semantically dependent and the arguments are more autonomous. The hearer simply does not know what kind of event the head verb *open* refers to without knowing what the arguments are in a given case. But the arguments themselves are not as dependent on the meaning of the verb. For example, *open a book*, *open your eyes*, and *open the bottle* describe quite different activities of opening. But it is not primarily the meanings of *book*, *eyes*, or *bottle* which are being adapted to the meaning of *open*; it is the meaning of *open* which is being adapted to the meanings of its arguments.

Sullivan (2013) demonstrates that the linguistic expression of metaphor has a strong tendency to put expressions of the target domain in *semantically autonomous syntactic positions*, and expressions of the source domain in *semantically dependent positions*. This makes intuitive sense, since ultimately the metaphoric mappings must express something about the target domain. Thus, the target domain is ultimately the constraining factor in the interpretation of these constructions, including the metaphoric aspects of the interpretation of dependent constituents. As we mentioned above, we simply cannot transfer to Communication from Object Exchange the inference that the giver no longer owns the thing given: the mappings have to conform to our basic knowledge of the target domain. Thus, in *bitter sorrow*, *sorrow* refers to the target domain, and therefore needs no reinterpretation to be taken as referring to the emotion 'sorrow.' But *bitter* is a source-domain word; we need mappings between Emotion and Flavor to decide what the corresponding meaning in the target domain of Emotion may be – as it will certainly not be literally 'bitter.'

And, Sullivan argues, the autonomy/dependency asymmetry explains the puzzle presented in the introduction to this chapter, namely why Domain-Adjective Modifying Constructions are different from Attributive-Adjective ones. In the Attributive-Adjective Construction, which we were just discussing above, the adjective is dependent and the noun autonomous – *large* does not mean the same thing in *large molecule* and *large planet*. But in Domain-Adjective Constructions, the reverse is true: literal uses like *academic job* or *religious leader* do not show adaptation of the domain-naming adjective to the noun, but rather adaptation of the idea of employment or leadership to the domain of academia or religion (rather than, say, politics or the military). And in metaphoric uses, we see exactly the patterns one would expect based on those different semantic dependency relations. *Bloodstained wealth* is an example of an Attributive-Adjective Construction (like the literal *bloodstained shirt*), and the dependent adjective is in the source domain while the autonomous noun is in the target domain. *Moral wealth*, on the other hand, is an example of a Domain-Adjective Construction (like the literal *moral advisor*), and the semantically autonomous domain adjective is in the target domain, while the dependent noun is in the source domain.[2]

Some of this may seem, at first glance, to go against the basic understanding of Conceptual Metaphor Theory. The analysis of metaphor which we have laid out is in part trying to explain how metaphoric mapping affects construal of the target domain. Our metaphoric blend will not be the same as our literal understanding of the target domain: we have pointed out that Anger is differently understood in different metaphoric construals. And in this example, understanding sorrow as bitter is *not* the only possible way to understand sorrow; it is a particular cognitive reframing of the literal emotion domain. So it would seem on the face of it that the target domain is the one being "changed" by the mappings. But crucial constraints on that reframing are set, Sullivan would argue, by our understanding of the target domain itself. This is again *not* to argue that either domain in a metaphor is fully autonomous or fully dependent, any more than syntactic heads are fully autonomous semantically with respect to modifiers. The metaphoric blend depends crucially on both the source and the target inputs.

Copula constructions are another important class of metaphor-evoking structures, as Brooke-Rose (1958) noted, and they have therefore been discussed by many cognitive linguistic metaphor and blending analysts (e.g. Fauconnier 1994[1985], 1997, Turner 1989, Sakahara 1996). Once again, we might ask why we find only certain metaphoric uses of copula constructions and not others; and as with modification constructions, we turn to the functions of the literal construction to motivate the metaphoric usages.

Among the classes of literal copula constructions identified in English (see Mikkelsen 2005 for a review) are the Specificational, Identificational, and Predicational constructions. Sullivan (2013) points out that these classes of constructions are in fact divergent in their dependency–autonomy relations. Specificational copula constructions specify role–value mappings. There is apparently little if any asymmetry of autonomy between role and value. Thus *The department chair is Linda* and *Linda is the department chair* are equally grammatical, though they may have different presuppositions about what is the topic of conversation. Similarly, Identificational copula constructions, which express identity between two entities, have little asymmetry and are apparently reversible: *The woman on the balcony is Linda* or *Linda is the woman on the balcony*. (We are not of course claiming that these two sentences are functionally interchangeable, but rather that the functional difference is one of information structure rather than of identificational function – they are good responses to different questions.) But Predicational copula sentences are not reversible: *Linda is an excellent teacher* could not be re-expressed as **An excellent teacher is Linda*. And this is exactly the class of copula constructions where Langacker (1991) argued that the subject

---

[2] Sullivan offers a parallel analysis of noun–noun compounds such as *rumor mill*, which is largely compatible with the earlier approach of Turner (1991); see also Sweetser (1999) on Noun–Adj Constructions as blends.

is semantically autonomous and the predicate dependent: if Linda is a four-year-old, I will have quite a different idea of what *excellent teacher* means than if Linda is a forty-year-old.

And, as Sullivan demonstrates in her analysis of corpus data (2009, 2013), metaphoric copula expressions in attested corpus data are predominantly TARGET IS SOURCE, though some are SOURCE IS TARGET (this tendency was pointed out by Turner [1991]). This is why TARGET IS SOURCE is the direction chosen by analysts for statements of mappings. However, metaphoric Predicational Copula Constructions are just like literal ones: we find *Last night had been a glorious voyage of discovery* and *International trade unionism was a difficult road* – but never *A difficult road was international trade unionism.* LIFE IS A JOURNEY falls into this class, which is why it is impossible to reverse syntactically. In other classes of metaphoric copula constructions, both orders are possible, however. For example, Specificational constructions show both orders in metaphoric uses as well as in literal ones: *Pace is the key to finding your stride* could express the same metaphor as *The key to finding your stride is pace.* But we still find a preference for TARGET IS SOURCE overall in corpus data – presumably due to the predominance of Predicational uses, where it is obligatory.

The claim, then, is that syntactic argument slots of source- and target-domain vocabulary are largely dependent on the semantic relationships of autonomy and dependence between the fillers of syntactic slots in constructions. Particular grammatical constructions involve asymmetry in the autonomy of semantic construal between head and modifier (where the head is more autonomous), between verbal head and arguments (where the arguments are more autonomous), and between subject and predicate in predicational sentences (where the subject is more autonomous). Metaphoric mappings themselves are constrained by the more autonomous target domain – hence the preference for target-domain expressions in more semantically autonomous syntactic positions. Therefore, we can have an expression like *a brilliant student* (source-domain modifier, target-domain head) based on the metaphor INTELLIGENCE IS LIGHT EMISSION, but the same metaphor could not produce **intelligent light* (target-domain modifier, source-domain head) to mean 'intelligent student' or 'intelligent mind.'

6.5   Simile as a mapping and a construction

Discussions of figurative tropes, whether focused on style, cognition, or linguistic form, often propose a distinction between metaphor and *simile*. To contrast the two concepts, analysts often classify them according to the predicative constructions used: *My job is a jail* is metaphor, while *My job is like a jail* is simile. Simile could then be considered a variety of metaphor that involves a more explicit expression of comparison. However, we need to note that the parallels between metaphor and simile identified in this way rely heavily on examples of

Predicational Copula Constructions – and in such cases, the presence of the word *like* seems to be solely responsible for whatever differences between metaphor and simile can be identified. We will argue that the meanings of similes do indeed depend on the contribution of *like*, but we will also show that, in spite of obvious similarities, metaphor and simile are different patterns of mapping.

Some analysts see metaphor and simile as essentially similar; this tradition goes as far back as Aristotle. Others draw important distinctions between these two classes of mappings. Gentner (1983) and Gentner and Bowdle (2001), among others, have argued that metaphor (like analogy) primarily maps relations (such as characteristic processes or functions), while simile primarily maps specific attributes (such as color or shape). So if one says, *This surgeon is a butcher*, the surgeon's manner of dealing with the bodies of patients is metaphorically mapped from the domain of butchery to the domain of medical treatment, but describing a person by saying that *Her lips are like red roses* evokes primarily the attribute of color. However, metaphors can certainly also map attributes (cf. *a bright student*, discussed above), while very general metaphors (including LIFE IS A JOURNEY) have often been said to resemble analogies, which are also said to map structural relations. (As we argued in Chapter 4, the dispute over the terms *analogy* and *metaphor* is a distraction: analogy is a kind of structural alignment, which goes on both in literal comparison and in metaphor.)

6.5.1   Characterization of simile

The analysis of simile proposed by Israel et al. (2004) has offered a different distinction, arguing that similes make explicit comparisons, while metaphors create similarities which could not be perceived independently of the metaphorical statements. Their proposal was that a simile such as *She's as sweet as sugar candy* (or a simile built with some other comparison construction) requires that two essentially dissimilar domains are evaluated with respect to potential similarity. Such examples do indeed select an attribute to guide the explicit comparison.

In a 2008 article, Gentner and Bowdle returned to the issue of attributes vs. relations, arguing that none of the constructions considered here so far specializes uniquely in attributes or relations. For example, the expressions in examples (1)–(3) represent a variety of types of metaphor.

(1)   Patience is bitter, but its fruit is sweet.

(2)   His eyes were deep pools of misery.

(3)   The voice of your eyes is deeper than all the roses.
              (e.e. cummings, *100 selected poems*, New York: Grove Press, 1923, p. 44)

Example (1) represents a relational mapping, example (2) is based on attributes only, and example (3) cannot really be described as either; all are examples of metaphor. Gentner and Bowdle thus conclude that the relations-vs.-attributes criterion does not reliably distinguish metaphor from simile.

Another recurring theme in these discussions is the distinction between categorization and comparison. It has been argued that metaphor is primarily concerned with categorizing one domain as another (Surgeon as Butcher), while simile is about comparisons (Glucksberg and Keysar 1993). Israel et al. (2004) affirmed that similes are primarily comparisons, but observed that the two tropes also have different formal features – because simile is an overt act of comparison, it relies heavily on comparative forms such as *like* or *as* (neither one of the two forms is actually privileged above the other in usage, even though standard examples of simile cited by researchers much more commonly use *like*). Conversely, as Moder (2008, 2010) showed using corpus data, *like* appears in comparison statements, such as *many of them, like myself*, but also in categorization statements, such as *media companies, like Time Warner*. The latter example clearly does not call for a comparison to be drawn, but exemplifies the category of media companies with Time Warner. These examples suggest that the comparison/categorization distinction may be helpful in distinguishing types of simile, but not in distinguishing *like*-similes from other tropes. And again, this is not unexpected. We know that the details of the source-domain meanings are essential in motivating possible metaphoric senses of forms – so we might predict that literal constructional senses would be crucial in motivating figurative ones.

Moder offers a categorization of similes by function, which we will rely on here. Using examples from a spoken corpus of radio programs, she shows that simile is in fact used in a variety of forms (even if most of them do rely on *like*) and that it has a variety of functions. She observed, among other things, that similes show a range of levels of conventionality. She also addressed the issue of relational vs. attributive mappings and distinguished two types of novel similes: *narrow-scope* and *broad-scope*. Narrow-scope similes seem to focus on specific aspects of the described entity – and indeed seem to be restricted to an attributive function. For example, when a man is described as standing at the door and *smiling like a proud father at a wedding reception*, the simile focuses on just one aspect of the man's behavior, and describes it in the form of a comparison. The second group, broad-scope similes, were much more common in the radio corpus, and appeared to typically be relational, like metaphors. They did not clearly specify the aspects of the described entity which were being compared; they were thus open to broader interpretation, and in all the cases analyzed they were followed by an explanation of the nature of the mapping evoked. One of the examples Moder quoted was a description of a town in Texas as *a reality which is like those 3-D pictures of Jesus. It changes depending on your perspective*. On its own, the comparison statement does not provide enough clues for the hearer to process the expression, and so the speaker provides an additional explanation. The conclusion Moder drew is that *like* prompts different mappings on the basis of discourse context – either the hearer is prompted to construe the similarity of attributes in some way without the contextual support, or the context elaborates the relational mapping in a specific way. As she put it, "one of the primary distinctions between similes and metaphors may lie in the cognitive cues provided to the hearer" (2010, p. 318). Cuenca and Romano (2013) also consider elaboration to be the central feature of simile.

These contrasting classes of similes may be parallel to classes of metaphoric mappings. Much of the research on analogy, metaphor, and simile relies on predicative constructions, rather than other (much more common) uses of metaphor. As we observed earlier in the chapter, the predicative constructions prompt various kinds of relations between the subject and the predicate, including identity statements, role-value statements, and also categorization. Predicative constructions used to express metaphors (*Achilles is a lion*, *My job is a jail*, or *That surgeon is a butcher*) function very differently from most common uses of conceptual metaphor (as in *We are not getting anywhere in this discussion*, *He was in a depression*, *They shot down all my arguments*). And this is no accident: Sullivan's account of the subject/predicate asymmetry in semantic autonomy would predict precisely this kind of usage of basic predicative constructions. The subject, being more autonomous, will be the target-domain element, while the more semantically dependent predicate will express the mapping to the source domain.

In discourse and conceptual terms, the processing of these two types of metaphor is different, and so they cannot be interpreted in the same way. The hearer cannot be expected to have the mapping between *Achilles* and *a lion* available as part of his lexicon, and so the mention of either expression cannot evoke the mapping. Talking about Achilles does not make most people think of lions, and lions are normally not associated with Achilles;[3] similarly, employment is not normally associated with imprisonment, and butchers are mostly talked about in connection to meat shops, not hospitals. The predicative constructions *establish* a mapping, rather than necessarily relying on one.

We should note that Moder's classes of narrow- and wide-scope similes correspond interestingly to Croft and Cruse's (2004) categories of *open* and *restricted* mappings: they say that similes are prototypically restricted in their mappings, while metaphors are prototypically open. A conceptual metaphor (perhaps the prototypical example of metaphor) engages in broad structural mapping, while a narrow-scope simile (again, perhaps a prototypical simile for analysts) does not. Croft and Cruse argue that some similes are more open, some metaphors more restricted; and we have noted that image metaphors (for example) do not involve broad structural mappings, while some similes can.

This brings us once again to the question of creativity and convention in metaphoric usages. We have in the preceding chapters discussed a wide range of metaphoric examples, more and less conventional. As we have pointed out,

---

[3] Incidentally, the *lion* description in the *Iliad* is used in connection with practically every incident of combat, whoever the participant is. So there is nothing special about "being Achilles" that triggers the connection – lionhood is a generalized *Iliad* metaphor for fierceness in battle.

metaphors which have a strong experiential basis (MORE IS UP, KNOWING IS SEEING) often result in new conventional meanings for words in the relevant semantic domains, resulting in lexical polysemy: one would certainly list the 'understand' sense of *see* in an English dictionary, and the 'increase in quantity' sense of *rise*. However, even in these cases, not every word in the domain is equally conventionally entrenched in its metaphoric sense. One can certainly say, *Prices hit the stratosphere*, and be understood as talking about an extreme increase in prices, but one might not want to list *stratosphere* in the dictionary with this sense.

For other examples, there is no such experiential correlation to serve as a basis. It is not the case that an audience hearing or reading *Achilles is a lion* necessarily needs to have associated Achilles with lions beforehand. However, as pointed out by Lakoff and Turner (1989), the audience does need to already have access to a culturally salient anthropomorphic metaphoric understanding of lions as brave (just as foxes are sly and doves peaceful). Without this conventional metaphor, the predicative usage would fail. Similarly, if we did not have a conventional cultural understanding of violence towards humans as slaughter of animals (with mass killings described as *the butchering of innocents*, for example), it might have been harder to understand the first description of a surgeon as a butcher – despite all the clear points of analogy between surgeons and butchers as users of sharp instruments on flesh (Fauconnier and Turner 2002).

Such predicative constructions can then become entrenched themselves. Casasanto (2013) argues that there is a category of mappings, which he refers to as *analogical*, which do not emerge from correlations in experience, but from correlations in entrenched linguistic usage. We have no experience of lawyers and sharks together, but once the description of lawyers as Sharks becomes established, the frames evoked in the context may allow one to refer to a lawyer as a *shark*. Of course, mentioning a shark when no Legal frames are evoked prompts no cognitive connections with the legal profession. Such examples are thus not representative of conceptual mappings in the proper sense of the word, as they depend crucially on the predicative construction attributing some features of sharks to lawyers, and then on a discourse context which may trigger the same connotation. One might add that a mapping like that probably starts out by mapping attributes (relentless and bloodthirsty pursuit of prey), and may develop some relational meanings (what causes the "feeding frenzy"), and eventually also inferences (the futility of resistance). Usage patterns can thus help in making an analogical metaphor entrenched, but at the initial stage the links between the source and target have to be established explicitly.

But returning to simile, let us consider the contributions of the literal meaning of the comparison construction *X BE like Y* to the figurative uses of that construction. As we discussed above, English copula constructions are multifunctional, and vary somewhat as to the semantic autonomy of *X* with respect to *Y*: this is why in some cases I can say both SOURCE IS TARGET and TARGET IS SOURCE (e.g. *The key to success in your exercise program is pace* and *Pace is the key to success in your exercise program*). However, comparison is an inherently asymmetric relationship between a compared entity and a standard of comparison. As a result, *X BE like Y* is an inherently semantically asymmetric construction. As mentioned in Chapter 2, since we normally attribute a parent–child resemblance to the parent's causal role in the child's genetic makeup, we would normally say, *Sue is like her father*, rather than, *Dave is like his daughter*. But if, for example, we were Sue's teachers, meeting her father for the first time at her college graduation, we could easily imagine saying, *I recognized Sue's dad immediately, he's so much like her*. This is because Sue is now our standard of comparison, since she is the familiar one. It is thus the case that *like* comparison constructions lend themselves well to the semantic asymmetry of metaphoric mappings, where the more dependent target domain is being construed as the relatively more autonomous source and not vice versa.

6.5.2   Narrow-scope similes

Much of the research comparing metaphor to simile (e.g. Gentner 1983, Gentner and Bowdle 2001) starts with the assumption that the linguistic forms to be compared are both predicative constructions (*My job is a jail/My job is like a jail*). These examples attribute the crucial distinction between metaphor and simile to the presence of the word *like*, and the meaning of 'comparison' that it brings with it. And indeed, the use of *like* in similes appears to be extended from its use in literal comparisons. As Sullivan and Sweetser (2009) point out, there appear to be fuzzy boundaries between literal and metaphoric predications, and this is true for similes as well. For example, *She is wriggling like her little sister* sounds like a comparison between two small girls' behavior (same domain, hence a literal comparison), while *She is wriggling like a kitten* could be understood as involving two domains (Little Girl and Kitten) or one (Cute Small Animals). And *She is wriggling like a snake* seems pretty clearly two domains, hence a clear case of simile rather than literal comparison.

However, it is not sufficient – though it is initially helpful – to treat simile as comparison. As Moder (2008, 2010) showed, *like* is used in a number of different constructions, each of which has a somewhat different meaning. We want to focus here on the mappings triggered by what Moder described as narrow-scope and broad-scope similes. The former seem indeed to evoke some similarity between the source and the target, as in examples (4)–(6).

(4)   The dancer twisted his body *like a snake*.

(5)   But when I saw her laid out *like a queen*, she was the happiest corpse I'd ever seen.

                                          (*Cabaret*, 1972, director Bob Fosse)

(6)   The classroom was buzzing *like a beehive*.

These very typical examples of the sort found in textbook descriptions of simile are important in that they all evoke quite specific *dimensions* of similarity between the frames evoked. In most cases, narrow-scope similes rely on evoking a vivid or extreme example of a perceptual pattern (*buzzing like a beehive* refers to sound, while *twisted his body like a snake* describes the perceived flexibility in the dancer's motion); in the *Cabaret* example, the frame evokes dignity and pomp. In other words, the similes evoke vivid, paradigm or exaggerated examples of the frames involved. The similarity is thus definitely there (e.g. beehives and classrooms can both be noisy in a similar way), but the source domain evokes a more salient or even exaggerated example representing the same attribute. In this respect, narrow-scope similes are very similar to image metaphors (discussed in Chapter 3), which map an image onto another image, as in *hourglass waist*.

All forms of simile seem to rely on a similar pattern of frame evocation, though there may be additional effects involved. In example (7) from Raymond Chandler, the *As X as Y* formula is used.

(7)   He looked about as inconspicuous as a tarantula on a slice of angel food.[4]

In this case, the frame is so extreme that it cannot be used to evoke similarity; instead, it evokes dissimilarity. The image described ironically relies on evoking the pattern of a vivid case of similarity to make the opposite point. Typically, examples of narrow-scope similes are acceptable in both *like* and *as* forms (as in *happy as a clam, happy like a hippo*), and irony seems possible in the *like* cases as well: *happy like a hockey fan whose team just lost the final Stanley Cup game*. Further investigation of various simile-evoking forms is beyond the scope of this discussion, but the pattern we propose for narrow-scope similes seems to work across at least these forms.

Overall, the introduction of a vivid and illustrative frame to get the message across characterizes many of the examples discussed in the literature. Moder's example where a man is described as *smiling like a proud father at a wedding reception* is a case in point, and the examples quoted by Israel et al. (2004) similarly show that tendency in narrow-scope similes. One can argue that narrow-scope similes are instances of frame evocation where a specific feature of the situation being described is given a more salient description by evoking a frame which involves that same feature, but to a more intense degree. The overall impact of the "proud father" simile is not the fatherhood, or the wedding, or even the reception, but the extreme happiness of the smile. If such similes are mappings, they do not make much of the domains used as "sources," but focus instead on one salient attribute of the situation evoked to apply it to a situation for which that attribute is normally much less salient or extreme.

This also applies to many conventional or idiomatic similes (*like a madman, like a bat out of hell, like an angel*, etc.). Somebody described as acting *like*

---

[4] Raymond Chandler, *Farewell, my lovely* (Vintage Crime), New York: Vintage Books, 1988 [1940], p. 4.

a madman could be laughing, running, dancing, or writing – what seems to be important is that the activity is performed with an intensity not found in everyday experience (the speaker clearly does not have to have specialized knowledge about the behavior of people considered mad). This confirms the requirement that the frame be vivid or even exaggerated.

Very unconventional similes, like the ones used in literary texts, seem to follow the same pattern.

(8)   The Duke's moustache was rising and falling *like seaweed on an ebb-tide.*[5]

(9)   My face looks *like a wedding-cake left out in the rain.*[6]

Example (8), from P. G. Wodehouse, is based on a vivid image of the motion created by flowing water, exaggerating the softness and impressiveness of the moustache – an image mapping which might in turn of course evoke other frame metonymies, such as inferences about the associated mental state of the person. Example (9), from W. H. Auden, also appeals to our imagination; we have to visualize the cake losing its smoothness and texture, and then project the image of shapelessness and deterioration onto a human face. The ruined-cake image was projected onto the look of the poet's face in his old age, but it was apparently also intended to describe the way in which prior experiences, even the most humiliating ones, affect one's features. In either sense, the image allows us to imagine the deep furrows left by both age and experience. (This is very much an image metaphor – and may well trigger a conceptual metaphor as well; for example, Auden could be understood to have been implying that his inner self was "weathered" by experience as well.) The literary simile is thus often more creative, but based on the same principle as the conventional one.

The apparent tenuousness of the source–target relation in certain examples of simile may stem from different causes. A sentence such as *Arguing with her was like dueling with hand grenades*, apart from conforming to the observed pattern of exaggeration, is also based on the familiar ARGUMENT IS COMBAT metaphor. In example (10) below, from a book by Anne Tyler, there is also no a priori connection between troubles and shoes; the point of the simile is only clear via a metaphor linking Difficulties and Burdens (consider expressions like *The responsibility weighed heavily on her shoulders*, *He was bent down by his responsibilities*, etc.).

(10)   When he lifted me up in his arms, I felt I had left all my troubles on the floor beneath me *like gigantic concrete shoes.*[7]

---

[5] P. G. Wodehouse, *Uncle Fred in the springtime*, London: Penguin Books, 2004, p. 155.
[6] W. H. Auden, as quoted by Humphrey Carpenter in *W. H. Auden: a biography*, London: Harper-Collins, 1981, p. 35.
[7] Anne Tyler, *Earthly possessions*, New York: Fawcett Books, 1971, p. 176.

This simile, again, exaggerates the "heaviness" of the burden (*gigantic concrete shoes*), to describe the emotional response of the character. Israel et al. (2004) also note this connection between metaphor and simile.

Overall, this observation suggests that, rather than being varieties of each other, metaphor and narrow-scope simile use frames in different ways. It would be difficult to argue that there is a structural mapping being prompted (let alone established) between classrooms and beehives or queens and corpses in the examples given above, and beyond the specific aspect of the frame evoked by the comparison, further inferences do not seem to be licensed. And yet there is a cross-mapping being established. We believe that simile is an example of a different kind of a single-scope blend, which we will refer to as a *limited-scope blend*. Its organizing frame is established as the simile is processed, and is a focused aspect of the source frame. In the target frame, an element of the frame structure is selected (noise is an aspect of the Classroom frame, though it is typically not the most salient one) and enhanced by being mapped onto its counterpart element in the source frame (the noisy Beehive). The relation between the inputs is such that, with respect to the selected element, the source is a vivid or extreme example. The target-domain input is thus enhanced through projection of this enhanced view of the shared aspect of topology. Importantly, the rest of the topology is not projected from the target – so it is a single-scope blend, but with strict limits on the material projected from the target to the source. The discussion of broad-scope similes below will further elaborate the contrast between these limited-scope blends and full single-scope blends.

6.5.3   Broad-scope similes

Broad-scope similes are different from narrow-scope ones in that the frames they evoke need not be salient at all with respect to the feature intended. This is why they necessarily require a further explanation of the nature of the connection. The primary feature of broad-scope similes is that the simile statement itself does not provide enough information to let the hearer/reader identify the selected aspect of the frame. The nature of the projection is typically explained in the following discourse. Also, broad-scope similes in English appear to be primarily realized through the Predicative Construction (unlike narrow-scope similes, which are instantiated in a variety of syntactic forms). One classic example is the simile repeatedly used in the movie *Forrest Gump*:

(11)   Life is like a box of chocolates. You never know what you're gonna get.
                                   (*Forrest Gump*, 1994, director Robert Zemeckis)

Such similes are different from the ones discussed above in that the source and the target are linked by aspects of topology which are not decipherable on the basis of obvious perceptual patterns extended into exaggerated forms. Unlike the already-accessible noise-making similarity between beehives and classrooms, the focus of the broad-scope mapping – the aspect of topology which links the inputs – is either revealed by the simile or outright created by it. The "chocolates" simile is further clarified if we compare it with a quote from Alan Bennett's *Beyond the fringe*:

(12)   You know life, life is rather like opening a tin of sardines. We're all of us looking for the key.[8]

The Chocolate Box simile and the Unopened Sardine Tin simile describe Life in terms of different aspects of our experience – the unpredictability of our lives vs. our difficulty in realizing the positive possibilities of Life. Notice that in this case, it is not an image metaphor but a broader conceptual metaphor that is triggered: Life is being understood as a Box of Chocolates, with varied and unlabeled contents which can only be identified by being tasted; or as a Container with a Key, whose desirable contents cannot be accessed without that key.

Importantly, we could not use these similes as metaphorical predicative constructions, without *like* (*Life is a box of chocolates* or *Living is opening a tin of sardines*). It appears that expressions such as *Life is a journey* (whether used as pseudopoetic wisecracks or sober descriptions of mappings) trigger the connections between the source and the target without much contextual support, but *Life is a box of chocolates* does not. Why? We argue that the difference is in two aspects of structure. One is the metaphorical grounding provided by the mappings at more schematic levels. In Chapter 3, we discussed the Object Event Structure Metaphor, where Situations are understood as Objects, and BEING IN A SITUATION IS HAVING AN OBJECT – and it is this metaphor which makes the "chocolates" simile ultimately understandable. KNOWING IS SEEING is also involved here: the construal depends on mapping things which are not visible (like the filling in a truffle or the variety of chocolates in a box) onto the inaccessibility of knowledge about future life situations. But this broader metaphoric construal becomes available after we hear the explanation (*You never know what you're gonna get*), rather than being prompted directly by the expression *Life is a box of chocolates*. In fact, one could argue that the explanation is what actually identifies the cross-mapping, rather than the initial juxtaposition of the frames of Chocolates and Life, which do not have a lot of prebuilt mapping structure between them. This would not generally be the case with the Journey frame, which comes with much more frame structure already premapped onto Life; however, we could defamiliarize the Journey metaphor by evoking an aspect of the source frame which is unexpected, as in *Life is like a journey; by the end of it you are so tired you just want to quit.*

Let us now return to the *like* Comparison Construction. The presence of the word *like* in similes serves the constructional role of announcing the need to find a pattern linking the source and the target, and to construe that linking in an asymmetric way: the target domain is "compared" to the source and construed in

[8] Alan Bennett, in the British stage revue *Beyond the fringe*.

terms of it, not the other way round. In narrow-scope similes, this process of cross-mapping can be done based on the inputs compared: we use the source-domain image (the paragon *buzzing beehive*) or the stated parameter (*inconspicuous*, in example (7)) to guide comparison with the target domain. But in broad-scope similes, these mappings need to be provided explicitly, as there is no image that guides the selection. It has to be guided verbally, often by overtly naming the qualities or relations to be mapped.

Broad-scope similes are often jokes, playing off the very idea that the two items are being juxtaposed without a clear reason – then that reason, once given, plays on the available frames, and often uses punning to shift the frame entirely (see Coulson 2001). For example, there is a whole series of jokes (widely disseminated on the Internet) comparing men to most unlikely concepts:

(13)   Men are *like government bonds*. They take so long to mature.

(14)   Men are *like mascara*. They usually run at the first sign of emotion.

(15)   Men are *like buses*. If you miss one, there's always another coming along.

In all such examples, *like* is necessary for the joke to work – as suggested above, it announces the blending process that has to start with finding a commonality between the inputs. The jokes also play off the fact that the source expressions are polysemous (*mature* can refer to human age, or to the time period from bond purchase to recovery of invested funds; *run* could refer to getting out of a stressful situation or to liquid streaming down one's face). Such jokes are extremely popular (and numerous), and they rely intrinsically on the central feature of broad-scope simile constructions: the need to find the conceptual link between the source and the target. The more unlikely, the more interesting the simile. Perhaps the most classic example is the Mad Hatter's riddle in the Mad Tea Party chapter of *Alice in Wonderland*: *Why is a raven like a writing desk?* The Hatter admits he has no answer to his own riddle, but readers have been proposing answers ever since the book was published.

This analysis would predict that if a simile became conventionalized, the relevant mappings would be conventionally available to speakers, and it would no longer be necessary to specify those mappings. At that point, a metaphoric usage with no *like* would become possible. And indeed, *The campus is a (buzzing) beehive today* is perfectly possible with the meaning that the campus is full of activity, even though there is no experiential correlation between campuses and beehives, any more than there is one between lawyers and sharks. Once the mappings between beehives and busy human activity are conventional, we no longer need *like* (or statements of parameters) to guide our identification of the mappings. And if the LIFE IS LIKE A BOX OF CHOCOLATES simile came up often enough in a stretch of discourse, so that mappings were conventionally established, one could imagine someone saying *I've just got a different box of chocolates than Suzie* to mean 'my life has a different range of unpredictable options from hers,' treating the mapping as a conceptual metaphor with no use of explicit comparison markers.

We will not discuss other comparison constructions here, but it seems clear that they can also have a role in building single-scope blends which result in construing the target domain in terms of the source. For example, *She's a snake* (meaning 'she's sly and unreliable') is a conventional metaphor. But one could also say things like *She's as slimy as a snake*, where *as . . . as* is an Equative Comparison Construction, once again asymmetrically comparing a target-domain comparee to a source-domain paragon of the relevant quality as the standard of comparison. The simile and the metaphor appear to establish very similar single-scope blends.

To sum up, we are claiming that simile (of any kind) is different from metaphor, for several reasons. Simile is evoked using different constructions, and the predicative constructions are just a subset (though by far the most analyzed subset) of the examples for simile as well as for metaphor. Whatever construction is used to express it, a simile prompts a blend which is similar to a metaphor blend (single-scope), but the cross-mapping is more focused and is usually not expected to yield rich inferences (we have used the term *limited-scope blend* to describe this). In extended discourse contexts, however, similes, like metaphors and analogies, can play more elaborate roles in construing concepts in new ways – but (as with metaphor and analogy) that depends on the discourse, rather than on the nature of the mapping itself. As we will show in Chapter 8, discourse often extends the scope of mappings and yields inferences which could not have been prompted when the figurative expression is only understood as serving very local discourse needs.

6.6   Alternative spaces, simile, and metaphor

In Chapter 4, we briefly introduced our earlier work (Dancygier and Sweetser 2005) on the class of constructions which build *alternative* mental spaces – that is, pairs of mental spaces which cannot coexist in the same space/time slot. Interestingly, these constructions have particular uses in figurative language, which we will discuss in this section.

Negation is the most obvious example of Mental Space alternativity. It cannot, for example, simultaneously (at the same time and in the same space) be the case both that there is milk in the refrigerator and that there is no milk in the refrigerator. Negative constructions, treated by Fauconnier (1985[1994], 1997) as *space-builders*, are understood by cognitive linguists to evoke the corresponding positive mental space, in a way that positive constructions do not evoke the corresponding negative space. This is why Nixon's famous *I am not a crook* was so unsuccessful as a rhetorical strategy: it could not fail to evoke the mental space of his being a crook. Someone who says *There's no milk in the refrigerator* is specifically comparing the current situation with an alternative (expected, perhaps) situation wherein some milk is in that refrigerator. Although true, it would be extremely strange to say, *There's no milk in the refrigerator*, of a newly delivered refrigerator which was entirely empty and was not expected to have milk in it.

The use of negation to evoke a positive alternative thus automatically commits the speaker not just to a belief or stance about a situation, but to a chosen network of alternative situations with which that situation is being contrasted. Moreover, negation can further serve a different function – rather than simply profiling an alternative space, it also profiles an alternative epistemic stance (Dancygier 2012b, Dancygier and Sweetser 2012). For example, one can reject the opinion of another participant in a discussion by saying *I do not **think** I am right, I **know** it*. In such a context, a stance best represented by *think* is presented as having been attributed to the speaker, and is then rejected by her. So-called metalinguistic negation, as in *It's not "a bit of a problem," it's a disaster*, where the speaker opts for a much stronger description of the situation (cf. Horn 1985, Dancygier 1998), belongs to the same category of alternative Mental Space setups. In sum, negation is a construction which sets up alternatives – alternative situations, stances, expressions, etc.

It is thus not surprising that negation constructions can be used to reject a metaphorical or simile-based construal emerging from the preceding context. Some such constructions are in fact lexically entrenched. For example, *It's not exactly rocket science* suggests not only that someone might (wrongly) compare or equate the relevant domain to rocket science, a paragon of abstruse and intellectually challenging areas of knowledge, but also that the addressee had better look elsewhere for his analogy, whether or not he had been considering this one. Similarly, the expression *It's not brain surgery* suggests that the task at hand is, contrary to what may have been suggested, not delicate, demanding, nor potentially dangerous. These negations follow a pattern: the negated comparison or metaphoric projection was to a paragon (as we saw, this is a standard pattern in similes), and was thus over-the-top and inappropriate. These examples of negation are figurative, in fact they are negated limited-scope blends: they reject an exaggerated frame, rather than using it as a basis for comparison.

Manipulation of alternative frames also lies at the core of some conditionals – and can be exploited figuratively as well. Standard predictive conditional constructions (Dancygier and Sweetser 2005) are another example of a class of constructions whose literal job is to work with alternative spaces. When someone says, *If it rains, they'll cancel the game*, it could only be a sensible utterance under the assumption that the alternative space (wherein if it doesn't rain, they won't cancel the game) is also assumed to be cognitively present as a contrast to the one overtly mentioned. These two spaces fall under our original definition of *alternative spaces*: that is, it cannot simultaneously be the case that it rains and the organizers cancel the game, and that it doesn't rain and they don't cancel the game. A conditional prediction only makes sense if these two alternative spaces are constructed; if we knew that they were planning to cancel the game in any case, regardless of rain, it would make no sense to use a conditional prediction.

Some conditional constructions can build or evoke alternative metaphoric construals (Sweetser 1996a, 1996b, Dancygier and Sweetser 2005). *Meta-metaphorical* conditionals build alternative relationships between metaphoric construals of a domain. One particularly nice attested example, cited by Dancygier and Sweetser, is given in example (16).

(16)   If the beautiful Golden Gate is the thoroughbred of bridges, the Bay Bridge is the workhorse.[9]

The Golden Gate Bridge (the route into San Francisco from the north) is an icon shown in San Francisco tourist advertising and visited by millions; the Bay Bridge, which is the route into San Francisco from the east, carries far more daily traffic but gets far less publicity. This example suggests that thinking of the Bay Bridge as a workhorse would not be the expected metaphor *unless* one were in the business of metaphorically thinking of bridges as different kinds of horses. Otherwise, just saying *The Bay Bridge is a workhorse* would not make much sense.

Once one starts looking for meta-metaphorical conditionals, there are quite a few to be found. Just to give one more attested example, the *Vancouver Sun* provided us with the conditional in example (17).

(17)   If public transit is the lifeblood of a dynamic city, Vancouver's in a coma.[10]

And it makes sense that these constructions should be useful enough to come up frequently, since we have already seen in earlier chapters that mappings between domains are constrained by other mappings, generally ensuring the coherence of the structure as a whole. For example, in the Grim Reaper blend, if one metaphorically maps the beginning of the grain's life onto the beginning of a human life, one is then obliged to map the end of the grain's life (reaping) onto human death. Conditional constructions allow one to consider alternative possibilities in the metaphoric mapping world, as well as in other worlds.

Conditionals and negatives are not in themselves figurative constructions, but they are constructions whose semantics is inherently alternative. So they can comment on possible alternative figurative construals, rejecting or accepting a construal, or balancing different possibilities. The fact that these very basic constructions – often thought of as the building blocks of logic – are pervasively and conventionally recruited to compare and assess figurative construals is certainly a tribute to the basic status of figurative construal in human thought and language.

---

[9] *San Francisco Chronicle*, Nov. 11, 1996, p. A13.
[10] *Vancouver Sun*, July 5, 2001, p. A11.

6.7   Nominal-Modification Constructions and frame metonymy

In Chapter 4, we discussed the nature of the meaning-emergence process called *blending*, but we did not look specifically at the role it plays in the extended figurative uses of constructions. In this section we will focus on a range of Nominal-Modification Constructions, where noun phrases use adjectives and prepositional phrases as modifiers.

Adj–Noun Modification Constructions were mentioned above, in examining the nature of metaphoric uses such as *bloodstained wealth* and *spiritual wealth*. In this section, we will consider some types of constructions which do not necessarily yield metaphorical meanings but which are processed as figurative. We argue that blending explains much of the meaning emergence in such contexts, and that the blending processes involved are evoked not only through lexical choices, but also through grammatical form. We will also show how viewpoint is relevant to the analysis of these constructions. Additionally, we will use this discussion to show how some processes of meaning-emergence rely on partially compositional mechanisms.

6.7.1   *XYZ Constructions*

In Chapter 4, we discussed examples such as *Hillary was Bill Clinton's First Lady*. We argued that this example is a simplex blend, in that the roles profiled in one of the inputs – United States President and his wife (the First Lady) – are filled by the values available in the second input – the actual married couple. We will return to genitive constructions later in this chapter, but first we will discuss another closely related construction, which can be schematically described as *X is the Y of Z*, as in *Sheila is the wife of Ron* or *Paris is the capital of France*. This construction is now known as the *XYZ* Construction, a label given to it by Turner (1989, 1991) (Brooke-Rose had previously labeled it *A is B of C*); Sullivan (2013) also treats *XYZ* Constructions at some length. In each example, there is a predicative construction that uses three referential expressions (*Paris, the capital, France*), but ultimately profiles four slots in the input spaces and links them through a simplex blend filling roles with values. In the Paris example, then, one input provides the roles (Country, Capital City) while the other provides the specific paired values, available in a mental space they share (France, Paris). Thus the type of relationship linking a country to its capital is now predicated to hold between France and Paris. The interesting point is that even though the meaning relies on two linked roles and two values linked by the same relation (Country-and-Capital City and France-and-Paris) the construction itself mentions two values and one role. The second role is not mentioned, but is accessible in the meaning of the construction as a whole, based on the hearer's knowledge that the role of a Capital City is profiled as part of the Country frame. Assuming that the hearer is not familiar with the geography of Europe, the construction is informative exactly by projecting the relation into the France–Paris input and thus providing the missing knowledge.

However, the nature of the construction requires in many cases that the hearer fill in the details of the relation in the Roles input – in other words, much of the meaning-construction process depends on how the speaker and the hearer construe the frames. In an example like *The Rockies are the Alps of North America*, the frame evoked is that of major mountain ranges as important features of continents, but the more specific frames might provide the required role/value link in a particular context – the expression might refer to the nature of the terrain, the recreation possibilities (for climbing, skiing, etc.), favorite vacation spots for skiers, etc., etc. The general frame of a Mountain Range provides all these options, but the specific choice to be made in interpreting the construction depends largely on the cross-mapping between the two frames. Thus the specific role the Alps play in Europe is projected onto the Rockies–North America input, describing the Rockies as playing a specific role with respect to North America.

Importantly, unlike the Capital or First Lady cases, the construction matching the Alps and the Rockies is figurative, and relies on a different use of the copula construction. *Paris is the capital of France* specifies a role/value mapping (it is a Specificational Copula Construction) and thus can be reversed (*The capital of France is Paris*). For comparison, *The Rockies are the Alps of North America* is a Predicational Copula Construction. The subject (*the Rockies*) is autonomous, while the predicate (*the Alps of North America*) is dependent – the Alps are not connected to North America other than through the analogy with *the Rockies*. And the sentence yielded by reversing the construction is hard to process: *The Alps of North America are the Rockies*. Similarly to the cases of metaphorical copula constructions we considered above, figurative *XYZ* Constructions also show an asymmetry of autonomy between the subject and the predicate.

It should also be clear from this discussion that this construction relies heavily on frame metonymy. The frame evoked could belong to common knowledge (countries have capital cities), or rely on the specific framing available to the speaker and, presumably, also the hearer (what makes the Rockies similar to the Alps). The frame-metonymic aspect of the construction is best seen in the examples which prompt a construal of the input frame which is unusual or not easily accessible. In Chapter 4, we discussed the example in which Richard Burton was described as *the Frank Sinatra of Shakespeare*. We argued that the meaning of that expression is not necessarily the same for everyone. When we now look at the context of the expression, given in example (18), we can see that what was intended was primarily popularity and financial success.

(18)   Burton played 136 performances of Hamlet over 18 weeks. The production grossed $1,250,000 and Elizabeth hailed him as the Frank Sinatra of Shakespeare.

The blend is thus constructed as follows: the Sinatra input profiles the performer who is artistically and commercially the most successful representative of his genre. The second input profiles Burton and his performances of Hamlet; it is initially structured only in terms of Burton and his work as an actor. The construction projects the status of being the best performer of the genre onto the Burton input.

Many of the examples we have been discussing involve proper names; we argue below that these have special status with respect to frame metonymy, and thus appear especially often in *XYZ* Constructions. Let us add, though, that examples with common nouns are easy to find, and are also often figurative, as in *Vanity is the quicksand of reason* (discussed by Turner 1989). The crucial factor, however, is the nature of the constructed connection between the elements in the frames evoked. The connection between the office of the US President and that of First Lady, as well as the connection linking countries and capital cities, is a matter of factual knowledge about roles determined by culturally available frames and filled by specific values. But the connection between two performers, or between vanity and quicksand, has to be constructed on the basis of how the frames are used, and the process of construction may involve setting up a previously unavailable role–value connection. As Turner remarked, *Vanity is the quicksand of reason* demands that we *extend* our frame for Reason to include a role corresponding to the role of Quicksand in another frame (presumably physical Travel). In this sense, *XYZ* Constructions may be more like simplex blends, assigning values to roles, or may be more like single-scope blends, constructing cross-domain links to highlight a specific aspect of the frames being evoked.

Examples like these show that constructions indeed carry meaning (the *XYZ* Construction profiles a relationship among four entities), but figurative meanings are built on the basis of the specific selection of frame structure and the accessibility of cross-mappings between input spaces. If two clearly distinct frames are involved, then a single-scope or metaphoric blend will be the result (*Vanity is the quicksand of reason*), while if a single frame is involved, then a simplex blend will be built (*Paris is the capital of France*). Where two very similar frames are involved (*The Rockies are the Alps of North America*), we may feel some clear unidirectional restructuring of one domain by another, but perhaps not enough to feel the power of major metaphoric reconstrual.

6.7.2   Nominal modification

Earlier in this chapter, we discussed Sullivan's interpretation of the adjectival modification of nouns, explaining the correlation between such constructions and metaphoric mappings. We should add here that the meaning of adjective-plus-noun combinations has also been described (Sweetser 1999) in terms of interactions between frames. In particular, Sweetser discusses the case of the adjective *safe*, which has typically been talked about as being ambiguous between two meanings, represented by examples such as *a safe solution* (a solution which is not expected to *cause* harm) and *a safe trip* (one in which the traveler is *protected from* potential causes of harm). As Sweetser shows, these meanings result from the different ways the frames interact. The concept of safety relies on the frame of Harm, which involves three roles – that of an entity which may cause harm, that of a valued entity which may be harmed, and that of some factor or entity which protects the vulnerable entity from harm. Saying that a baby is *safe* is likely to be understood as meaning that the baby is the vulnerable entity being protected. But a house can be framed as a valued possession, a potentially dangerous environment, or a protection against outside forces; so *a safe house* might be one that has been reinforced to protect it against earthquake damage, or one which has been appropriately prepared to avoid hurting small children (electrical outlets covered), or one in which inhabitants are safe from other entities (e.g. from the police, or possibly from fellow criminals, as in the conventional *safe house* compound). Many adjectival ambiguities can be explained via similar patterns.

The interpretation becomes more complicated in cases where modified nouns appear in specific types of copula constructions. Consider examples (19) and (20).

(19)   Water is the new oil.

(20)   Green is the new black.

In context, the readings of sentences such as examples (19) and (20) (discussed in Dancygier 2011) suggests that they are examples of another construction, which we will call the *X-is-the-new-Y Construction*. Like other *XYZ* Constructions, this one relies on frame metonymy and implied cross-mappings which need to be supplied by the hearer from accessible knowledge or context. In example (19), one possible interpretation might be that we expect water to become a new kind of fuel. But in fact the intended interpretation of the frame is not membership in the category Fuel; instead, it is intended to evoke the idea of a natural resource which may become scarce and expensive, and can thus cause various international tensions. The sentence in example (20) has often been applied to fashionable colors of clothing, but one of us recently saw it on a sign outside a café encouraging customers to drink matcha tea (which is indeed bright green) rather than coffee. As in *XYZ* Constructions, the meaning depends on the type of cross-mapping that links *X* to *Y*. Importantly, the meaning of the adjective *new* is constructionally determined, and marks a change in framing. Specifically, the preexisting frame for *Y* (a resource which causes problems, a popular color or drink) is now newly applied to *X*. What the construction thus does is describe an application of a preexisting frame to a new mental space.

Note that the X-is-the-new-Y Construction in itself does not specify whether the resulting blend is metaphoric. The expression *Weird is the new normal* appears to be a literal statement, and suggests that there is a 'normal' slot in the frame Life Situation Evaluation, and that the filler of that slot has been changed. A fashion editor saying that navy, or fuchsia, is *the new black* does not seem to be making a metaphoric statement, but to be specifying that there is a new filler for a role (Top Fashion Color) within a stable frame. And the status of that role is determined by the metonymic salience of the named filler (here, *black*). But a café-ad slogan for matcha drinks, *Green is the new black*, is a mapping from a fashionable-color frame onto a caffeinated-beverage frame, and this cross-domain mapping does feel metaphoric.

Further complexities can be seen in the quotation in example (21), from an online news item. It would not even make immediate sense, in a general context, to call something *accidental horse meat*, much less *new accidental horse meat*. But the text was published in the context of much-publicized ongoing European and North American scandals over sales of meat mixtures containing horse meat that had been falsely labeled as beef.

(21)   The good news: we don't have to worry about accidental horse meat
            anymore. The bad news: accidental pork is the new accidental horse meat.
            Swedish retailer IKEA has been forced to stop sales of its elk-meat lasagna
            in stores across Europe after testing showed that the lasagna contained over
            1 percent pork, which is the limit for contamination.[11]

In this case, the frame element evoking the scandal is not *horse meat*, but specifically *accidental horse meat*; the countries where the mislabeling scandal has played out are quite disparate in their attitudes towards eating and selling horse meat, but united in their demand that meat be truthfully labeled, without unknown additions (accidental or otherwise). And although there are North American and European Muslims and Jews who don't eat pork, the new scandal is clearly not that IKEA is selling pork but that there is *accidental* (and unlabeled) *pork* in a product labeled as being elk meat. So *accidental pork* is the element in the New Scandal frame which corresponds to the *accidental horse meat* in the earlier frame.

A class of cases of modification which have attracted much attention are NPs with domain-specifying denominal adjectives: *political dinosaur, mental detox, intellectual sleeping pills*, etc. Their central feature is that the noun is not understood in its standard way, so that the phrase *a political dinosaur* typically describes a person with outdated political views, rather than a type of dinosaur which is relevant to politics in some way (though the latter is also possible, in the right context). We have discussed some such examples (e.g. *mental detox*) in Chapter 4, but here we want to point out how modification constructions of this kind manipulate frames. If the noun *dinosaur* is used literally, in reference to a biological dinosaur, then there is also something about it that makes the creature (or its representation) relevant in some political context. In other words, in that case, the Dinosaur frame is basically unchanged and is applied to some aspect of the domain of politics (perhaps a fictional movie, where a dinosaur is given voting rights); it also has the syntactic autonomy required for it to remain the

---

[11] Levine, *Breaking News*, Apr. 6, 2013.

referent of the phrase. But if *dinosaur* refers to a person with outdated political views, then the meaning relies on an implied Predicational Copula Construction (such as *My honorable opponent is a political dinosaur*), and in that construction, the subject (*my honorable opponent*) has the syntactic autonomy. As a result, the word *dinosaur* provides an aspect of the frame that can now be predicated about the subject referent (a species which has become extinct, even though it once ruled the earth), but does not itself point to a referent who qualifies as a representative of some specific dinosaur species (triceratops or velociraptor or some such). As in the other types of constructions discussed above, the frame and the referent can become constructionally independent. This usage manifests one basic aspect of figurative language structure: it selects aspects of one domain to apply them to a different domain.

6.7.3   Proper names: framing and reference

We noted above that proper names are very common in the general family of *XYZ* Constructions. Considering that they have typically been described as having unique reference, what makes them so useful in the contexts where they are primarily used to provide framing? (Consider the role of *Sinatra*, *Shakespeare*, or *the Alps* in the examples above.) Following Vandelanotte and Willemse's usage analysis (2002) and Dancygier's frame-metonymy interpretation (2009, 2011), we argue that in fact the use of proper names in these constructions should be primarily characterized as evoking rich framing, rather than reference to individuals. A name like *Shakespeare* does indeed refer uniquely to the early modern English playwright and actor, but in fact most of us think of the name primarily in terms of the plays we know, the characters whose plight touched us at some point, the concept of genius, the nature of the Elizabethan and Jacobean theatre, famous Shakespearean actors, etc. There is of course a major body of scholarship that tries to reconstruct Shakespeare's life, but reference to an individual is still just one aspect of what the name does, and not the aspect most relevant to interpretation of these constructions.

Proper names are perfect fillers for the frame-dependent *XYZ* Construction because they can easily be used to evoke the framing, rather than making a reference. A 2013 article in *Slate Magazine*, "The Saudi Arabia of Sashimi,"[12] discusses the tiny Pacific nation of Palau, whose primary economic activity is tuna fishing. The waters where Palau fishermen fish are as rich in tuna as the land of Saudi Arabia is rich in oil. And since we have a clear frame of Saudi Arabia as a nation that is wealthy from selling its oil resources, we can transfer the framing to Palau's tuna resources (tuna being a kind of fish favored by restaurant customers in sashimi dishes). To make the framing complete, the article later claims that *tuna is the oil of the Western and Central Pacific* – another *XYZ* Construction based on the manipulation of those same frames.

---

[12] Shannon Service. 2013. "The Saudi Arabia of Sashimi," *Slate Magazine*, April 2.

We can easily find proper names in X-is-the-new-Y Constructions as well – consider the expression *Iraq is the new Vietnam*, which appeared in political commentaries during the most recent war in Iraq. While this refers clearly to the reality of post-Saddam Iraq, the framing is imported from the familiar case of the Vietnam war (whichever specific associations a reader chooses to rely on). Familiarity with the frame seems to be a crucial factor in the production and comprehension of such expressions.

We commented above on the role of alternative construals in the negotiation of figurative meanings. Alternativity can also have interesting effects in the domain of proper-name use. Some time ago, one of us saw an advertisement for a foundation seeking to promote self-confidence in students. The visual image was the well-known photo of the face of Albert Einstein in which he is defiantly sticking out his tongue. The accompanying text says, *As a student, he was no Einstein*, where *he* clearly refers to Einstein – who had well-publicized problems with the standards imposed by formal education. At the same time, the text plays on a common remark (*He/She is no Einstein*) that is used to describe someone as not very bright. The proper name in the text is thus used both as a referring expression (evoking the real Einstein, his genius, and his educational troubles) and as a frame-metonymic expression using negation to set up a space which is the alternative to "genius." The impact of the ad is much enhanced by the simultaneous evocation of two frames – that of a person who was not appreciated in his school years, but still very smart, and that of a person who is not too smart; evoking both frames prompts the viewer to assume that there is a potential Einstein/genius in every student considered to be *no Einstein*/not a genius. The whole ad thus relies heavily on the richness of the frame evoked by a proper name and on alternative construals.

The simple use of a proper name with an indefinite article causes a constructional clash between the definite and unique reading of the proper name and the indefinite constructional meaning. This demands further interpretation, just as the use of a count noun in a mass context forces reinterpretation (as in *I've got cat all over my skirt*, discussed in Section 6.2). *She thinks her daughter's an Einstein* (or *a Shakespeare*) cannot mean that she thinks her daughter is the unique person Einstein (or Shakespeare) – so the proper names are reinterpreted to mean some class of similar scientific (or literary) paragons, defined by metonymic relation to the superparagon mentioned. Alternatively, the indefinite article can mean that this is a particular temporal phase or instance (among many) of a unique and definite individual. When journalists wrote about *a tired Margaret Thatcher* or *a not-so-happy Tom Hanks*, the modifiers picked out temporary features of behavior that the referent displayed on a given occasion, so it was presumably not assumed that Mrs. Thatcher was always tired or that Tom Hanks was never happy (Dancygier 2011; see also Marmaridou 1991). Examples like these support the claim we are making here that proper names represent rich frames which make unique reference possible, but which also open possibilities for various types of uses which rely on only certain aspects of the frame – for example on the general cultural accessibility of the referent's frame or the temporary state of the referent individual. This kind of focus on culturally salient aspects of a frame is often seen as nonliteral, because the referent is not evoked. We argue that such interpretations result from patterns of frame evocation and selective projection, both of which accompany the emergence of figurative meanings, but do not uniquely determine them.

6.7.4   Genitives and experiential viewpoint

An overview of the family of constructions we are considering here would not be complete without a brief look at the role of genitive forms. In sentences such as *Iraq was going to be Bush's Vietnam* or *The presidency was going to be Hillary's Everest*, a construction resembling the X-is-the-new-Y Construction uses the genitive possessive construction. The noun typically represents a participant from whose perspective the frame evoked is viewed (see Dancygier 2009, 2011). The first sentence suggests that a potential lack of success in the Iraq war would be felt by then-President Bush as a liability of the kind that the Vietnam war was to President Johnson. Similarly, assuming that the noun *Everest* evokes a frame of a goal which is difficult to reach but represents the ultimate achievement, the presidency would have been, from the perspective of a presidential candidate, the ultimate success. Considering the steps in Hillary Clinton's political career, the presidency might indeed have seemed the final crowning achievement.

The English genitive construction is quite schematic as to what role relations it expresses: as grammarians have noticed, it can express different roles with respect to events as well as the possessor–possessed relation: e.g. *the army's destruction of the city, the city's destruction by the army, and Joe's book.* But none of these express participants' "experiential viewpoint" as such. For example, *Hillary's success* would not necessarily assume that the situation was being viewed from her perspective – it appears that all that is being said is that Hillary succeeded in some endeavor. The experiential-viewpoint meaning requires that the construction also metonymically evokes a frame which is selected with respect to how the participant mentioned feels about the situation. The *XYZ* and X-is-the-new-Y Constructions are not the only ones with experiential-viewpoint meaning, as it is also found in constructions such as *One person's X is another person's Y* (Dancygier 2009). Sentences such as *One person's trash is another person's treasure* follow a pattern in which the objects in question are framed differently from the perspective of different people – in this case, some frame them as precious possessions, others do not. Clearly, *one person's trash* does not refer to garbage collected by a person, but to a framing of an object or objects normally considered trash which is reframed as having great value from someone else's viewpoint. The genitive form participates in aligning the framing with a participant.

6.7.5   Constructional compositionality

In the sections above, we were looking at various types of evidence of how constructions rely on frame metonymy and selective projection, and how constructional meaning can affect the understanding of frames. But we have also shown that constructions do not necessarily evoke meanings as indivisible wholes. First, we have noted repeatedly that the Predicational Copula Construction is particularly open to figurative interpretation. But it is only a basis on which various specific constructions are built (metaphorical predication, *XYZ*, *X is the new Y*, *X is Z's Y*, etc.). Also, we saw that some constructions may share a mechanism whereby frame-rich nouns like proper names are used to evoke culturally salient meanings, but do not also provide referential connections. Further, we saw that adjectives like *new* or *another* can play a special role in manipulating the frames evoked by the nouns in the construction, and that the genitive form can add experiential viewpoint to the frame-metonymy pattern.

In earlier work (Dancygier and Sweetser 2005, Dancygier 2009, 2011) we talked about such phenomena as *constructional compositionality*. We are not claiming that constructional meanings are purely compositional: constructions have meanings as wholes, or we would not need to refer to them as *constructions*. But we also think that in many cases the Construction Grammar approach could be enriched by the addition of more than one level of generalization. It is an important fact that the genitive can construct experiential viewpoint in the presence of other constructional features, or that the adjective *new* means something different in *my new dress* and in *Green is the new black* because these expressions represent different constructions. It is also an important generalization that there exists a family of constructions which rely on frame-rich nouns and on frame-metonymic evocation of selected aspects of the frames. As we have said, some meanings which emerge in this way would often be perceived as figurative, but that depends on the extent to which different domains are evoked, and on what mappings are built. In all cases, however, the specific constructions involved contribute meaning to that blending process.

6.8   Constructions and the nature of figurative meaning

Throughout this chapter, we have argued that there is a very close connection between grammatical structure and figurative meaning. Accepting this point has many important consequences for the study of figurative language, in any approach. First of all, one cannot maintain that there is a clear opposition between the literal meaning of an expression on the one hand and the figurative one on the other. Figurative meaning is not just a matter of lexical choices or of polysemy, but a matter of meaning construction, which proceeds through all the levels of linguistic structure and involves syntactic as well as lexical meaning. In the range of constructions discussed above, we saw how figurative meaning emerges constructionally on the basis of morphological form (e.g. the genitive), lexical choices (e.g. proper names or adjectives like *new*), and syntactic form (e.g. Predicational Copula Construction). These choices are supported by meaning-based mechanisms such as frame metonymy. The resulting picture is one of a family of constructions which share the feature of operating on frames via selective projection and blending preexisting frames into new configurations.

The range of such constructions is very broad, depending on the levels of linguistic form involved, the nature of the figurative process, and the complexity of the configurations emerging through constructional compositionality. The result is that a syntactic pattern cannot provide sufficient data to distinguish patterns of meaning emergence; for example, looking at adjective–noun constructions would yield examples as varied as *a bright student, a bright lamp, a political dispute, a political dinosaur, the new dress*, and *the new oil*. But there are several different constructions involved here, as we have seen: *bright student* and *political dinosaur* are not examples of the same construction, and *X is the new Y* is a construction of its own. Searching for specific lexical items is not always helpful in identifying figurative patterns. In the case of adjectives like *political* or *new*, one needs to consider their role in the relevant constructions to appreciate the nature of their meaning. And focusing on the proper name *Einstein* alone would not lead to an appreciation of the double meaning of *As a student, he was no Einstein.*

These comments should make it clear why previous discussions of the difference between literal and figurative meaning have not led to a clear distinction (for an overview, see Gibbs and Colston 2012). Figurativity will not be understood properly as long as it is not seen as an integral part of a meaning-emergence process and remains the "afterthought" of literal-minded linguistics. It also cannot be sufficiently described merely by searching various corpora, or via mechanisms such as the Metaphor Identification Procedure proposed by the Pragglejaz Group (2007). Rather, it relies fundamentally on constructional mechanisms (and not just on some generally defined "context") and involves meaning-emergence processes which consist of much more than somehow deciding that the phrase cannot mean what it literally means. In the view of figurative meaning we have been building throughout this book, the common intuitive distinction between literal and figurative meaning results from the specific ways in which frame structure and Mental Space topology are manipulated, selected, and reconstrued in new ways. We cannot properly describe or predict what meanings will come up or not come up, but we can attempt to describe the nature of the *processes* which make the manipulation, selection, and reconstrual possible.

Figurative meaning is something which can be attributed specifically to a construction based on its literal meaning, as in the case of metaphoric uses of the Caused-Motion and Ditransitive Constructions or in the metonymic meanings of deverbal nouns. And figurative meaning can be built using constructions, with their particular meanings – copula clauses, comparison constructions, and genitives are useful for building particular kinds of Mental Space blending patterns, and thus have particular conventional roles in prompting metaphor, simile, and other blends. Of course, the actual power of figurative language can only be appreciated in broader discourse context, where the full range of inferences and conceptual structure is brought into play. In Chapter 8, we will bring together many of the concepts presented thus far, to show their functioning in extended discourses.

6.9   Summary

Constructions are typically not included in the analysis of figurative language. But in this chapter we have shown that such exclusion depends on a specific approach to the meaning of sentences. We have assumed, along with Construction Grammarians, that syntactic structures are meaningful. But we have also shown further that grammatical meaning is part and parcel of meaning overall, including figurative meaning. For example, we have discussed the role of copular constructions in the emergence of metaphors and constructional blends; moreover, we have clarified the difference between figurative meanings emerging through copular constructions and those emerging through interactions across domains within lexical forms.

We have also proposed a definition of simile which distinguishes it from metaphor but which also shows the similarities between similes, metaphors and blends. We have treated simile as a limited-scope blend relying on specific constructional features. Also, we have demonstrated the relation between mappings such as simile and alternative mental spaces.

We have devoted much attention to the emergence of figurative meanings in Nominal-Modification Constructions. There is quite a range of such constructions, and they jointly show the potential of grammatical manipulation of frames. To conclude that discussion we have brought up constructional compositionality – a theoretical concept which allows us to be specific about the roles of various constructional components. Overall, we have argued here that figurative forms have much to contribute to our understanding of linguistic structures and their emergent meanings.

7   The crosslinguistic study of metaphor

7.1   Introduction: the crosscultural comparison of language and cognitive patterns

Metaphor studies – like the rest of linguistics and cognitive science – has been a locus of debate as to how much of human language and cognition is universal and how much is culture specific. The very word *cognitive* is enough to evoke a frame of culture-independent cognition in many readers' minds. And yet a large proportion of the serious studies of metaphor have been conducted by literary analysts and anthropologists, who are very dubious about the existence of universals of human cognition – while formalist schools of linguistics strongly believe in formal linguistic universals, but generally consider metaphor to be a decorative add-on rather than an essential part of the structure of language. As the linguistic relativists point out, what could be more unique than Shakespeare's particular metaphoric understanding of love, or (to generalize to a culture) some particular language community's metaphoric understanding of time, or of emotions? Even if metaphor is a universal human capacity, why should there be universals of metaphoric structure? But on the other hand, if metaphor is part of an embodied human cognitive potential, why should we assume that variability is unconstrained?

This debate parallels the general Sapir–Whorf debate in linguistics, anthropology, and cognitive science. Edward Sapir and Benjamin Lee Whorf both, in different ways, expressed strong beliefs in cultural shaping of human cognition – in particular, they believed that culture-specific *linguistic* systems could shape cognitive patterns. Modern experimental psychology, on the other hand, is largely based on the (still often-unspoken) assumption that human cognition follows general shared principles – and if it were strongly shown that European and North American college students were fundamentally different from other humans in terms of basic cognitive patterns, most of experimental psychology would be in question. So the debate about potential universals of metaphoric structure is only one part of a much larger debate.

In this chapter, we will discuss what kinds of criteria might be used to examine crosslinguistic variation and universals of metaphoric structure. It is challenging to do crosslinguistic comparative work on metaphor systems. Typological work –

broad comparative work – is almost impossible, since a researcher cannot look at even a very good dictionary or grammar of a random language and expect to find sufficient data on even some particular subpart of its metaphor system. So in general, researchers need to either be native speakers of the language being analyzed, work on extensive corpora, or do in-depth field work. Fortunately, in some areas – notably in the area of metaphors for time – we have in-depth work on sufficiently different languages to begin to talk about a crosslinguistic typology.

7.2   Examining linguistic variation and universals

One "parade example" in the debate on universals is the examination of linguistic color categories. It was once the assumption (unexamined) that differences in linguistic color systems reflected differences in perceptual and cognitive categories of colors. For example, the fact that some languages (such as Irish, Welsh, or many languages of North America) have a single color label covering the categories labeled by English as *green* and *blue* (sometimes known as the GRUE category) was taken in the nineteenth century to indicate that speakers of those languages simply lacked perceptual distinctions between green and blue hues. But by the mid-twentieth century, linguistic research had broadened to cover more non-European languages, and vision research had advanced to show that human perception appeared to have universal constraints and abilities – in particular, retinal cells in all non-color-blind humans respond to the blue/yellow contrast and the red/green contrast, independent of culture and language. This was followed by the Berlin/Kay World Color Survey, which examined hundreds of languages (beginning with Berlin and Kay 1969; see reviews in Hardin and Maffi 1997) and showed that there are very strong universal constraints on naming of color categories: there is no language that has a separate word for PINK but does not have separate words for RED, YELLOW, and WHITE, and this is presumably because red, yellow, and white are more perceptually basic colors.[1]

On the other hand, recent research has shown that speakers' regular use of color terms does affect their judgments of color similarity: under some circumstances, speakers of languages with separate BLUE and GREEN terms are more sensitive to differences in color close to the blue/green boundary than are speakers of languages with so-called GRUE terms covering blue, green, and gray. But only in some circumstances. In particular, these differences between speakers are found if the contrast is displayed in the right visual field – so it is processed in the left hemisphere, the dominant processing area for language. But the same speakers, if the same contrasts are displayed in the left visual field (processed in

---

[1] The all-capitals format here (as in GRUE, RED) refers to a designated semantic class – the range of colors designated by *red*, for example – separately from the particular linguistic labels attached to that meaning class.

the right hemisphere) demonstrate no perceptual differences between language communities (see Franklin et al. 2008, Gilbert et al. 2008, Regier and Kay 2009). Color, it seems, is an area where humans have access to language-independent perception, and *also* may be influenced by their native language's categories (depending on context). And the nature of universal human color perception places strong constraints on the structure of those linguistic categories (see Regier et al. 2007).

In other areas, linguistic differences have been shown to correlate with much more major cognitive contrasts. For example, linguistic systems of spatial terms around the world are generally divided into two broad classes, *Absolute* and *Relative* spatial systems. These two kinds of systems have been studied in detail by the Spatial Cognition Group headed by Stephen Levinson at the Max Planck Institute for Psycholinguistics at Nijmegen (e.g. Levinson 2003). **Absolute spatial terms** like *east*, *west*, *north*, and *south* do not demand that their interpretation take into account some person's viewpoint location. *San Francisco is west of Berkeley* is true regardless of the speaker's location. But **Relative spatial terms** such as *in front of*, *in back of*, *to the right of*, *to the left of* are different: I cannot decide what is *in front of* a person without knowing which way the person is facing, nor can I decide whether or not something is *in front of* a tree in English without knowing where the describing viewer is located (English uses *in front of the tree* to refer to being situated between the tree and a viewer who is facing towards the tree). Most crucially, *in front of* could correspond to any compass direction at all; it is not anchored in Absolute directional parameters. Although most Relative-spatial languages, such as English, do have Absolute spatial terms, they don't use those terms for everyday small-scale spatial description. In English it would be extremely odd to say that *the cup is west of the plate on the table*, or that someone has *an ant on her north shoulder* (one would say *next to* or *to the right of the plate*, and *left* or *right shoulder*). But in Absolute languages such as Kuuk Thaayorre or Guugu Yimithirr, everything – including small-scale spatial relations of these kinds – is expressed in terms of absolute cardinal directions. Besides cardinal-direction Absolute systems, there is another class of Absolute systems based on local landscape features (upriver vs. downriver or uphill vs. downhill) (Levinson 2003) – but in all these cases, spatial relations are expressed independent of the viewer's location.

Absolute directional languages are a minority on the world scene, and are found predominantly in rural areas among relatively culturally traditional, small-scale communities. We might want to know why that is the case – and at present, it is unclear. It seems intuitively that an Absolute spatial system would be easier to develop and maintain in a community with a stable, relatively small shared space (where *uphill* or *upriver* meant the same thing for all); and indeed, such systems do not seem to occur in larger urbanized language communities. But while urbanized national and world languages apparently don't maintain Absolute systems, small traditional societies can and clearly do develop and use Relative spatial systems – as was apparently the case in earlier strata of modern European languages. We do not know why no traditional European society, nor any preliterate Indo-European society, seems to have used *your north leg* to refer to the one that is currently facing north, while such usages are the standard in many native languages of Australia.

One might well wonder whether this difference between linguistic systems results in major cognitive differences. And as the Levinson team has shown (Levinson 2003), it does. Absolute language speakers solve spatial problems differently; when asked to set up an array of objects "the same way" as the one they saw on another table in another room, they do so with respect to cardinal directions (e.g. from east to west if the original array was arranged east–west). English speakers (for example) will tend to arrange the objects from right to left if, in the original setting (no matter what the cardinal directions) they saw the array arranged facing from their right to their left. Haun and Rapold (2009) noted that speakers of a Namibian Absolute-spatial language even learn dance movements in cardinal terms; that is, if rotated physically, they replicate the cardinal direction of the moves they learned, rather than left–right or back–front orientation. It has been solidly demonstrated that Absolute language speakers have generally much more accurate judgments about cardinal directions, and a better memory for the arrangement of events with respect to cardinal directions (Levinson 2003).

Remarkably, then, colors were thought to be a particularly variable area of cognitive and linguistic categorization, but turn out to be quite constrained in variation – although there do seem to be some genuine cognitive-perceptual effects of linguistic color categories. But, on the other hand, spatial systems, which might seem obvious candidates for universals – what could be more universal than our experience of physical space? – not only seem to differ significantly between languages, but also to correlate with significant cognitive differences between the relevant communities.

Perhaps you can see where this is leading. The vast majority of linguistic descriptions of time are in some way based on descriptions of space – TIME IS SPACE, while not a specific metaphoric mapping, is a description of a large class of metaphoric mappings in the vast majority of the world's languages. And fortunately, spatial metaphors for time have been well researched in a number of languages with quite different spatial linguistic systems. So they are a good test case for our questions about universals of metaphor. But first, a brief discussion of Primary Metaphors and universals.

7.3   Crosslinguistic contrasts in metaphor – and crosslinguistic universals?

If we had to take a bet on one metaphor being a crosslinguistic universal, we might pick MORE IS UP. In all the conference sessions on metaphor we have attended, nobody has ever raised a hand and said, "Oh no, in the language I study, MORE IS DOWN" – whereas it is obvious that, in countless languages, MORE IS UP and LESS IS DOWN. This is plausibly explained by the kind of primary scene discussed in Chapter 2, where the quantity of liquid in a container correlates with the height of the surface, and the quantity of goods in a pile correlates with the height of the pile. Only a child living in a culture with no containers, or no piles, would fail to assimilate these correlations – and thus most children presumably acquire early the cognitive bases for MORE IS UP.

Another good bet might be POWER IS UP/STATUS IS UP. There has been no systematic crosslinguistic tally on this one, but it recurs in many languages, and there don't seem to be languages where the reverse holds – POWER is not DOWN. Again, a very basic primary scene appears to be the basis for this metaphor: taller adult caregivers loom over small children and inevitably also have power over them, and children learn early that the taller contestant (or the one on higher ground) has an advantage in a struggle. There is no doubt that this metaphor plays itself out in different cultures in different ways. Bickel (1997) has detailed the pervasive ways in which status is marked by up/down spatial differences in the Belhare culture of the Himalayan foothills: to name a few, Belhare houses are oriented with the hearth (next to which the most prestigious family members would generally be seated) at the uphill end, temples are always on local heights, and if a junior and a senior member of a Belhare community meet on a path, the junior member is obligated to take the downhill side of the path and give the uphill side to the senior. Stec and Sweetser (2013) detail the relevance of POWER IS UP and HOLY IS UP in the architecture of two religious structures from very different cultures, specifically Chartres Cathedral and the Buddhist monument of Borobudur in Java. Alongside this crossculturally shared structure, the two buildings also manifest plenty of culturally unique structure – just as the POWER IS UP metaphor motivates English speakers to seek penthouse offices but not to orient their houses with the hearth on the uphill side.

Some might now mention KNOWING IS SEEING, or KNOWLEDGE IS VISION. Indeed, this metaphor seems pervasive in the world's languages – across many unrelated languages. However, Evans and Wilkins (1998) have pointed out that in the languages of Australia, KNOWING IS HEARING appears to be the dominant metaphor, instead of KNOWING IS SEEING. So we couldn't call KNOWING IS SEEING a *universal*. But, as typologists, we would still want to note the broad dominance of this metaphor across the world's languages, and to consider whether that widespread shared pattern is due to universal cognitive correlations – the kind of primary scene discussed in Chapter 2, where vision is a hugely dominant source of new knowledge in sighted children's experience.

Needless to say, during the recent decades of research on figurative language and thought, cultural models of many other domains have been investigated. Anthropologists have long been investigating metaphoric understandings of emotion; and Kövecses (1986, 1995, 2000, 2005), Lakoff (1987), Lutz (1987) are among the leaders in investigating metaphoric models of Emotions in English and European languages. Yu (1998, 2009) has shown that Chinese models of Emotions share certain structures with English ones: HAPPY IS UP, SAD IS DOWN, for example, and also the understanding of emotions as liquids filling a Container (which is the Self or a part of the Self). But there are also major differences. As Kövecses and Lakoff would have expected, both Chinese and English speakers construe anger in terms of heat and pressure, presumably due to the rises in body heat and blood pressure which accompany anger. But Chinese primarily construes anger as a hot, explosive gas filling a container, while English thinks of it as a pressurized, heated liquid. And it is well recognized that specific body parts associated with emotions differ across cultures: no English speaker would guess that Chinese speakers associate fear with the gall bladder (Yu 2009), nor would they guess that Classical Greek associates the diaphragm with reflection and cognition. However, Yu convincingly argues that many aspects of the Chinese Emotion metaphors fall out naturally from traditional Chinese medical models of the body.

Taking a step back from these examples, we might say that, crossculturally, there is a very strong tendency to understand the abstract Self as the Human Body; this is the broad class of metaphors which Sweetser (1990) referred to with the label MIND IS BODY. The body being a physical domain, and one whose basic structure is common to all humans, we might expect some constraints on MIND IS BODY mappings due to our shared experience of the body. But as we have just noted with respect to the Chinese and Western medical models, different cultures do construe basic aspects of the human body in quite different ways. We are still very far from having a full typology of cultural models or metaphors for Emotion, Cognition, or Selfhood. But studies such as Yu's, or Avrahami's (2012) careful examination of Biblical Hebrew metaphors for Perception and Emotion, are making it more possible for us to see the broad landscape of cultural models in these areas. Casasanto's recent pioneering work on the relationship between bodily practices and metaphoric mappings also sets an example. Casasanto (2009) and Casasanto and Jasmin (2010) have shown that positive and negative associations with the right and left sides of the body are reversed for right-handed gesturers (for whom right is good) and left-handed gesturers (for whom left is good). And perhaps just as fascinating, these associations can be reversed by reversing someone's functional handedness temporarily in the lab (Casasanto and Chrysikou 2011).

Color-naming systems are perhaps the only semantic domain which has been more thoroughly researched across languages and cultures by cognitive scientists and linguists than spatial systems. They might therefore be imagined to be another possible domain for the exploration of these issues of figurative usage. However, despite their superstar status in the examination of crosscultural cognitive and perceptual differences, words for hues appear to manifest very few broad patterns of metaphoric usage – though there are certainly some metonymic ones, some crossculturally accessible (like *greens* meaning 'leaf vegetables,' for example) and others very culture specific (like English *in the red* meaning 'in debt,' because European accountants once wrote debts in red ink).

Dark and Light show more consistent crosslinguistic patterning: for example, metaphors for SADNESS AS DARK and HAPPINESS AS LIGHT or BRIGHTNESS are found in a wide range of languages; Yu documents such usages in Chinese. But it is unclear what we should make of the scattered figurative senses of color terms at large. Some Northern Europeans at some point assigned pink as a feminine clothing color, and blue as a masculine one; this contrast makes no sense to Chinese speakers, who prefer to dress all their children in red, the color of life. The Western white wedding and baptismal dresses are metaphoric for purity; we can see the basis of this metaphor in the fact that dirt makes a white cloth less white, and washing it makes it both clean and (once again) white. But for Chinese speakers, white is the color of death, and red the color of life. Again, we can see a basis for this metaphor, in the ruddy tones given to living skin by flowing blood, and the paleness of dead skin by comparison. But we don't know why a culture would choose one of these correlations over the other. Nor do we so far have any evidence to show that cultures' color metaphors are systematically related to the structure of their literal color systems.

We cannot in this chapter survey the immense literature on metaphors in different cultures. But we can address, for the case of figurative language, the general question of how to understand a case where there is not a universal pattern in some domain of human languages and cultures, but the data is clearly and strongly skewed in favor of some patterns rather than others. We noted above that MORE IS UP may be universal, while KNOWING IS SEEING seems to have dramatically wide currency in the world's languages, but is not a universal. It seems worthwhile to look more closely at cultural constraints and universal constraints on figurative construals, even if we cannot (in our present state of knowledge) do this for "the big picture" of all of cognition and culture.

One way to think about this problem would be to look at a test case where languages and cultures vary in their models of the source domain, and see whether that variation is systematically related to differences in their metaphoric construals of target domains. Spatial metaphors for time will be our test case. Linguistic spatial systems have been particularly well documented, thanks to the above-mentioned work of the Spatial Cognition Group at the Max Planck Institute. Spatial systems vary significantly across cultures and languages, but Absolute systems are clearly the minority and Relative systems the majority (Levinson 2003). But as more Absolute-spatial languages are better documented, it has recently become possible to examine the linguistic systems of time expressions in languages with differing spatial systems, and see not only what variation we find among figurative models of time, but whether that variation correlates with contrasts between languages' spatial systems.

7.4   Spatial metaphors for time: the TIME IS RELATIVE MOTION family

It has long been informally observed that most of the world's languages take their vocabulary for time from their spatial vocabulary. But there is by no means a single metaphor which accounts for this generalization. There is not a single mapping between space and time, but several dominant ones – and therefore more than one "superhighway" of linguistic change. It is important to distinguish these metaphoric patterns with precision, especially given that several of them have the same source domain, namely vocabulary referring to the back/front distinction.

One common metaphor is the understanding that EARLIER EVENTS ARE IN FRONT OF LATER EVENTS. The correlation in experience here is not hard to identify: a person who is in front of another person in line, or on a road, will arrive at the head of the queue, or at the end of the road, earlier than (before) the person behind them. English *before* and *after* are historically examples of this metaphor: the *fore* in *before* is the same as that in *forehead*, and the front and back ends of a ship are still called *fore* and *aft*. Bowerman and Choi (2001) noted the example of a Korean child who referred to the time *before* a meal as *in front of* the meal – using the Korean word for 'front' incorrectly in this case, but as would be predicted by the relevant Primary Metaphor.

Another very frequent metaphor, sometimes manifested in the same languages, is FUTURE IS IN FRONT OF EGO, PAST IS AT BACK OF EGO, NOW IS EGO'S LOCATION. As discussed by Moore (2000, 2011) and Núñez and Sweetser (2006), this metaphor has a necessary viewpoint from the Ego's Now, while the previous metaphor does not. A given time is before or after another time regardless of their relationships to Ego's Now; 2009 remains *before* 2020, whether we are speaking in 2000, in 2013, or in 2030. But Future and Past are defined with respect to Now. If I am speaking in 2013, the events of 2009 are now in the past (metaphorically, *behind us*), while those of 2020 are still in the future (metaphorically, *ahead of us*).

Again, the experiential basis for this metaphor is relatively clear. Suppose that I am walking along a path. The locations which are up ahead of me are those which I will encounter in the future, while the locations behind me are the ones where I have already been. Admittedly, this is local: assuming a long road or path, there could well be distant locations behind me on the path where I have never been, and distant locations ahead of me which I will never see. But *within the scope of the stretch of path I am traveling*, from my current start to my destination, the past locations on the path are behind me and the future locations are in front of me.

Again, we should note that each of these metaphors is a Primary Metaphor in the sense established by Grady (1997) and Johnson (1997), and discussed in Chapter 2. As discussed by Moore (2000, 2011) and Núñez and Sweetser (2006), any child moving along a path would experience both the fact that (1) moving people who are *ahead* on the path reach a particular destination *earlier*, and the fact that (2) a traveler on the path has *past* experiences of locations *behind* her on the path, and anticipates *future* experiences of locations *in front of* her. There are close correlations between Time and Motion in every person's experience from babyhood, and these do not diminish as the child grows up. Notice that, like other primary scenes, these are strong, salient correlations in particular contexts.

Of course Time still happens if we sit still rather than moving on a path – but this scenario does not give rise to the same salient correlation between times and locations, so this situation is not a primary scene with potential to give rise to a Primary Metaphor.

As we have noted elsewhere, it is very common to have multiple metaphors within a given language for any important target domain. And indeed, in English, these two metaphors are both centrally involved in conventional time expressions. *December is coming* and *November is almost gone* suggest a Moving Time metaphor (well recognized since Lakoff 1993), wherein times are understood as moving past observing Egos. The English term *past* is in fact a manifestation of this metaphor, since it is in origin merely a variant spelling of the word *passed*. We can also note conventional usages like *bygone days* or *upcoming events*. In this metaphor, of course earlier moving events are ahead of later ones, which are behind the earlier ones as the queue of events passes the observing Ego. English usages such as *after* and *before* are further evidence for this metaphor: etymologically, they mean 'behind' and 'in front of.' As we mentioned above, the temporal sequence is independent of Ego's perspective – events remain before and after each other independent of the construed Now.

On the other hand, the Moving Ego metaphor is involved in cases such as *We're coming up on Thanksgiving* or *Thank goodness we've left our disputes behind us*. In these examples, we see the observing Ego as moving through a static metaphoric landscape of Time; past events are behind Ego, and future events still in front of Ego. This metaphor takes Ego as its landmark – times are understood as being "in front of" or "behind" Ego, which means they are Future or Past with respect to Now. Thus, we refer to such metaphors as Ego-based (since Ego is the landmark), while the Time Queue metaphor cited above is Time-based, in the sense that there is no Now involved in calculating the before and after relationships which it models – times are landmarks, relative to which other times are earlier or later.

The Moving Time and Moving Ego time metaphors in English are both part of the family of what we might call TIME IS RELATIVE MOTION metaphors. Whether we understand time in terms of times moving on a path past us, or in terms of ourselves moving along a temporal path, we're understanding it as relative motion. As we mentioned above, both our experiences of motion on paths and our experiences of watching people move on paths in relation to each other are primary scenes correlating relative motion with time.

As well as distinguishing Moving Ego from Moving Time metaphors, we must also distinguish (Moore 2000, 2011, Núñez and Sweetser 2006) groups of metaphors according to which entity is the landmark for back/front orientation. Supposing Ego to be looking forward (towards the Future), as times stream past her along a path, this is a Moving Time metaphor. But there are two different landmarks whose orientations could be involved. Ego has a front and a back, and the stream of times also has a front and a back – individual times progress "forward" along a path from far future through present towards past. Words referring to fronts and backs of humans may therefore be quite ambiguous with respect to time expressions. An event's being *in front of* Ego means (via Ego-based metaphors, which refer to Ego's orientation) that it is in the Future relative to Now. But an event or time being *in front of* some other event simply means it is before that event, with no commitment as to the relationship of the events to the Ego's Now: this is a Time-based mapping, which refers to the Time's orientation. Note that a Moving Ego metaphor has no such ambiguity: if Ego is moving through time, there is no reason to necessarily attribute front/back orientations to times, so *in front* is unambiguously 'in front of Ego.'

Boroditsky (2000, Boroditsky and Ramscar 2002) decided to test this ambiguity in English. She chose the sentence *The meeting has been moved forward two days* as her ambiguous case. Supposing that a speaker is using the Moving Ego metaphor, which is necessarily Ego-based, she would imagine the meeting to have been moved two days forward with respect to Ego's oriented motion – i.e. two days farther into the future, hence two days *later* than planned. But in the case of a Moving Time metaphor, she could imagine *forward* to mean 'further along the trajectory of the moving Time,' which is moving past the observing Ego – thus, two days ahead of the projected time, hence two days *earlier* than planned. Indeed, English speakers are divided with respect to the reading of this sentence. But although the division may be random across speakers, it is not random across contexts. Boroditsky showed that priming a particular source domain also primed the speakers' metaphoric interpretation of the sentence one way or the other. Boroditsky asked speakers *The meeting was on Wednesday, but it has been moved forward two days. What day is it now?* Fascinatingly, speakers who were just getting off a plane (thus, involved in a scenario of Moving Ego) predominantly responded *Friday*, the Moving Ego metaphoric response (Friday is "up ahead" or "coming" on Wednesday). And speakers waiting for someone else to get off a plane (thus, involved in a scenario with something else saliently moving with respect to Ego) predominantly responded *Monday*, the Moving Time-appropriate response (Monday is earlier, "ahead of" Wednesday in the sequence of times).

Boroditsky's work is significant because it demonstrates a surprising correlation between source-domain (spatial motion) context and metaphoric (target-domain) interpretation: it seems clear that one can prime metaphoric construal by priming the relevant source-domain context. This possibility of priming provides added confirmation of the cognitive reality of the connection between source and target domains. If the temporal use of *forward* was a purely arbitrary linguistic choice – if the temporal use of this word was cognitively unrelated to its physical spatial uses – then there would be no reason for particular spatial motion situations to prime particular metaphoric construals of *forward*.

At this point we have covered some of the most crucial aspects of the world's temporal-metaphor systems. We have shown that, whether one sees Ego as moving through a temporal landscape or sees Times as moving past Ego in a queue, in both cases our experience of Time is understood as relative motion. Either Ego moves, or Times move, but in either case the relationship is one of spatial change. And, as it turns out, the vast majority of the world's languages use one or more of the TIME IS RELATIVE MOTION metaphor family members as described above.

Before going further, we do need to weigh in on one area of disagreement in the literature. As Moore (2000, 2011) and Núñez and Sweetser (2006) have pointed out, a great deal of confusion has arisen in crosscultural descriptions of time systems because cultural anthropologists, literary analysts, and historians did not have available the distinction between Ego-based and Time-based metaphors. There are thus relatively frequent claims in the literature that various languages differ from English (and Western European languages at large) in treating the Future as Behind. But the question here is, behind *what*? Of course, future times are (necessarily) later than present and past times, and hence "behind" them in a Time-based calculation of front and back relative to the stream or path of Moving Times. But, on the other hand, they are not typically "behind" Ego: Ego is mostly understood as facing forward, towards the future. Much of the evidence for FUTURE IS BEHIND metaphors boils down to evidence for the (very common) metaphor that understands later events as being behind earlier events (the Time-based Moving Time metaphor), rather than for a metaphoric understanding that FUTURE IS BEHIND EGO.

We should add that TIME IS RELATIVE MOTION is not inevitably about front/back orientation. Chinese, for example, appears to have both of the front/back time metaphors described above: Yu (1998, 2009; see also Gentner et al. 2002) describes the treatment of Past as being behind a Moving Ego, and Future as being ahead of a Moving Ego, as well as the Time-based model wherein earlier times are in front of later ones. However, Chinese also has up/down metaphors for time: EARLIER TIMES ARE HIGHER, LATER TIMES ARE LOWER. Whether vertical or back/front metaphors are used apparently depends on the time unit involved. Thus English *last week* translates into Chinese as UP- (or ABOVE)-WEEK, and *next week* as DOWN- (or BELOW)-WEEK, while *last year* translates as FRONT YEAR and *next year* as BACK (or BEHIND)-YEAR. The back/front metaphors seem to be standard Time-based ones: an earlier year is "in front of" a later one. The up/down metaphors at first look more surprising. However, we can see small pieces of a similar mapping in European languages: in French *haut(e)* 'high' refers to the earlier part of some time period, while *bas(se)* 'low' refers to later parts of a time period. For example, French *basse antiquité* 'low antiquity' would translate into English as 'Late Antiquity,' and *haut/bas moyen âge*, literally 'high/low Middle Ages,' would translate as 'early' or 'late Middle Ages.' (This is confusing for English speakers, since Anglophone medieval scholars use the term *high Middle Ages* to refer to either the "core" of the Middle Ages period, or the end of it, which is closer to the "high" culture of the Renaissance.) In both Chinese and French, one might attribute the vertical dimension to reverence for the past: for Classical culture in the case of Europeans, and for older Chinese culture in the case of the Chinese. Since

GOOD IS UP and STATUS IS UP, and certain aspects of the past are understood to be good and high-status, we can now map time onto a vertical dimension, and think of ourselves as gradually moving downwards on a temporal path through history.[2]

Our readers have most likely noticed that this class of time construals shares much with some of the mappings in the Location ESM – especially metaphors involving motion through space towards a destination. When someone talking about a project says, *We'll get there, for sure*, she is construing progress on the project as motion along a path which leads towards a destination. The construal can additionally include the mention of obstacles: *We'll get there, whatever stands in our way*. But being aware of obstacles is correlated with an expectation of a temporal delay: *We'll get there sooner or later, whatever stands in the way*. In our experience, achieving destinations involves a temporal dimension, and so expressions such *The end of this investigation is still way ahead* are as much about the amount of time needed to complete the investigation as they are about imagining reaching the goal. Also, because both the Location ESM and the TIME IS RELATIVE MOTION metaphor rely on the concept of directional motion along a path, it is natural, if not automatic, not only to correlate motion through space with time, but also to correlate the time spent achieving a destination with the experience of covering the distance. Consequently, achieving one's goal quickly is also about needing very little time, whether because of the lack of obstacles, the length of the path, the ability of the Ego, etc.

The experiential dimension of time has also been discussed by Fauconnier and Turner (2002) in terms of very personal perceptions of whether something takes more or less time. When we say that *The appointment was over in a blink*, we are mostly being told that the speaker felt the appointment did not take much time relative to some expectation, while in fact it could have been quite long. Expressions like *the days were crawling/whizzing by* or *it took forever* are common; they add an experiential dimension to time which does not conflict with the mappings we just discussed. If one experiences time as *crawling* or *whizzing by*, one is still using the Moving Time metaphor, with Ego stationary and Time moving past. Often the choice of verb is central to the construal. When we talked in Chapter 3 about expressions such as *We were dragging our feet through the process*, we noted the Event Structure aspects of their construal (motion along a path, obstacles, states as locations, events as bounded regions), but we can now add that the verb *drag* adds a further inference that the obstacles slowed us down, and so the process may have taken a long time, or it may at least have felt as if it was taking a long time.

The experiential aspects of time were used to excellent humorous effect in an article in *The Onion*, "It only Tuesday." The magazine's genre of humor

[2] For further studies of time metaphors in a variety of languages, we suggest looking into the following. English: Clark (1973), Lakoff and Johnson (1980, 1999), Lakoff (1993), Gentner et al. (2002). Wolof: Moore (2000) (which also has useful crosslinguistic references). Chagga: Emanatian (1992). Chinese: Yu (1998), Ahrens and Huang in press. Turkish: Özçaliskan (2002). Japanese: Shinohara (1999). American Sign Language: Cogen (1977), Emmorey (2001, 2002).

exaggerates the construal in ways that also display its structure very vividly for analysts:

(1)   Tuesday's arrival stunned a nation still recovering from the nightmarish slog that was Monday, leaving some to wonder if the week was ever going to end, and others to ask what was taking Saturday so goddamn long.

        The National Institute of Standards and Technology, which oversees the official time of the United States, is flatly denying that it has slowed or otherwise tampered with Tuesday's progression.[3]

We now have a picture of the broad distribution of the TIME IS RELATIVE MOTION metaphor among the world's languages, with variation as to what is construed as moving and what the orientational base is, and even as to whether the movement can be understood as being along a vertical dimension. One might now ask two questions. The first is: Are there languages which do not metaphorically construe time as motion, but in some other way? After all, primary scenes are universal, but particularly in cases like this one (where there are multiple primary correlations, which give rise to a range of metaphoric construals), languages do not necessarily regularly reflect some particular Primary Metaphor as a result. And the second question is: What about Absolute-spatial languages? We have been talking about time systems which involve mapping *relative* space onto time: times are understood as "in front of" or "behind" each other or Ego. But how would a language talk about time if it described space solely in terms of cardinal directions rather than front/back relations? Recent research has begun to answer those two questions, as we shall see in the next section.

7.5   Beyond TIME IS RELATIVE MOTION

        First, there does seem to be at least one clear case of a linguistic system and culture whose spatial model of time is relative, but *static* rather than dynamic. The Aymara culture construes time as a static physical landscape, within which FUTURE IS BEHIND EGO, and PAST IS IN FRONT OF EGO (Núñez and Sweetser 2006). Aymara speakers use terms for BACK to mean 'future' and FRONT to mean 'past' – the Aymara phrase for 'last year' translates literally into English as FRONT YEAR, and the phrase for 'next year' is literally BACK YEAR. One hypothesis to be eliminated here is that this is a Time-based model, and that in some way speakers are construing earlier times as being in front of later times, rather than past as being in front of Ego. This does not seem to be the case. Not only are these terms systematically used to indicate relationship to Ego's Now, rather than just to other times, but speakers even gesture behind themselves as they refer to future times (a point backward over the shoulder

---

[3] "It only Tuesday," *The Onion*, Oct. 16, 2007.

accompanies a reference to tomorrow) and forward to refer to past times (a point forward from the body for a reference to last year, and a point farther forward in referring to the year before last).

Most interestingly, this is not in any sense an "inversion" of the familiar Ego-based Time metaphors involving TIME AS RELATIVE MOTION. Instead, Aymara speakers view time as a *static landscape*. Native Aymara motion verbs are not used to describe time in any of the configurations we have discussed. Aymara speakers don't say that they are APPROACHING some event, or that one event FOLLOWS another, or that time PASSES, or IS COMING, or HAS GONE. (Though younger speakers using borrowed motion verbs from the local Andean Spanish dialect, Castillano Andiño, may use those borrowings to speak of time PASSING or COMING, under the influence presumably of Spanish-style TIME AS RELATIVE MOTION construals.)

There are some indications that the Aymara time model may be shared areally with some neighboring Andean languages which have not yet been as fully analyzed, but a static temporal metaphor is typologically quite unusual on the world scene. What motivates this particular mapping? At first glance, one might say that a static metaphor for time is simply less useful than a dynamic one, since it will be missing a rich set of inferences. For example, as an English speaker, I might say that *Summer is coming*, meaning that summer is in the relatively near future. The physical-motion verb *come* allows inferences about future locations: something which *is coming* (towards Ego's location) is not co-located with Ego but will presumably be co-located with Ego at a future time. This maps onto the fact that future times will in the future be Ego's present. Similarly, something which is *passing* is currently co-located with Ego and will not be co-located in the future, while something which *has gone by* was once approaching Ego, then was co-located with Ego, and will not be co-located with Ego in the immediate future because it will have moved away. These inferences map onto the understanding that present times will not always be present, and that past times once were Ego's present but will not be again. None of these inferences are accessible from a static front/back metaphor system. The fact that something is at the back of an unmoving Ego in a static landscape does not allow the inference that it will be co-located with Ego in the future, nor does the fact that something is in front of Ego allow the inference that it was once co-located with Ego, in the past. Inferences about past and future locations do not follow from knowledge of a present static location, but can only arise from knowledge of the present location and direction of an entity moving along a path.

Anthropologists discussing the Aymara system have quoted Aymara speakers as saying that the past is known, and the future unknown (Miracle and Yapita 1981); the known status of the past corresponds to the visibility (for Ego) of the space in front of Ego, while the unknown status of the future corresponds to the invisibility of the space behind Ego. KNOWING IS SEEING thus appears to be the most important metaphoric mapping involved in this model. We should therefore take a moment to note the different ways in which KNOWING IS

SEEING interacts with static and dynamic scene construals. In a static scene, a person can presumably see what is in front of her, and not what is behind her; the space around her is divided into approximately two halves, an invisible half behind Ego and a visible half in front of Ego. And indeed, Ego is more likely to *see* (and thus *know* about) events occurring in the space in front of her. In a dynamic situation of motion along a path, this is still of course true within the immediate space around the traveler, but now we have a different experiential correlation between location and sight. Along the path being traversed, we can infer that the traveler *has seen* (and thus *knows*) locations where she has been *in the past*, which are now *behind* her; and on the other hand, she has not yet been at locations *in front of her* on the path – she will only reach them in the *future*, and thus *has not seen* (and *does not know*) them.

In any spatial situation, including a static one, we thus have the correspondence between being locally in front of Ego and being visible (hence knowable); to this we may add the correlation between Future and Unknown, and between Past and Known, and we get an Aymara-type system. But in a dynamic situation of motion along a path, we also have a correlation between a Location being behind Ego on the path and its having been seen/being known, and between its being in front of Ego on the path and being unseen/unknown (or not yet seen or known). Notice that temporal correlations are already built into this frame; the known and seen locations behind Ego are in fact past locations, and the unknown and unseen ones in front of Ego are future locations. These two different primary experiential correlations between spatial configurations and visual experience are presumably present for anyone who has vision and has moved along paths. But the Aymara temporal-metaphor system is apparently based on the first, while most other languages' temporal-metaphor systems are based on the second. It is important to realize that this apparent "inversion" of directionality (English speakers think the Future is ahead *of* them, the Aymara think of it as behind them) does not involve inversion of some one Ego-based metaphor, but rather involves two different Ego-based metaphors, based on different correlations inherent to static and dynamic situations.

We now turn to the second question asked at the end of the last section: what about languages with Absolute spatial systems? Relative-spatial languages seem to regularly talk about time in Relative spatial terms; times are seen as being in front or at the back of (or above or below) other times, or in front or at the back of Ego. But Absolute-spatial languages, you will recall, would use either cardinal directions or large-scale landscape features (such as mountain slopes or rivers) to locate even small objects in small-scale scenes. A speaker of an Absolute language might need to say, when typing at a computer, that *my computer screen is south of me* or *downhill from me*, not *my computer screen is in front of me*.

Some recent studies have brought us initial evidence that at least some Absolute-spatial languages construe time metaphorically in terms of absolute rather than relative space. Núñez et al. (2012) worked on Yupno, a language of the Finisterre Range in Papua New Guinea which has a landscape-based Absolute spatial system rather than a cardinal-direction-based one; specifically, they orient their spatial world around the mountain valley in which they live, with the crucial dimension being up or down the valley. Although the linguistic system for time is not very rich, speakers do talk about future times as being uphill and past times as being downhill from them, and they also reliably *point* uphill as they speak of future times and downhill as they refer to past times. Núñez et al. found that this was independent of what direction the speaker was facing at the time (subjects were deliberately set up facing different directions, to control for this); there was no correlation between time reference and pointing ahead of, or behind, or to the right or left of the speaker. Most fascinatingly, the Yupno spatial model of time does not seem to follow a single linear "arrow" along a single angle, but is spread over the three-dimensional topography of the valley: points towards the future were steeply upwards (sometimes practically vertical), reflecting the steep slope uphill of the community, while points towards the past were often quite horizontal, although pointing in the downhill direction along the valley.

Boroditsky and Gaby (2010) did experimental work with the Kuuk Thaay-orre speech community of Pompurraw, a native Australian language community located on the Cape York Peninsula. Kuuk Thaayorre is a cardinal-direction Absolute-spatial language. Although it was apparently difficult to find spatial language used temporally in conversation, Boroditsky and Gaby investigated the conceptualization of time by asking speakers to arrange pictures in front of them. Each group of pictures represented the temporal stages of some situation: for example, one set included pictures of a whole apple, an apple with one bite out of it, a half-eaten apple, and an apple core; another set showed a baby, a child, a young man, and an elderly man. The subjects were seated (on the ground) facing in different cardinal directions, randomly distributed over the subject group and the stimuli presented: thus subject trials happened with subjects facing east, west, north, and south. Subjects overwhelmingly preferred to arrange the pictures in a temporal progression from east to west (that is, the whole apple would be at the east end, and the core at the west end), no matter how that related to their own orientation. A north-facing speaker would thus have been arranging the apple photos in a line from her right to her left, while a west-facing speaker would have been arranging them in a line away from herself. The experiential correlation between east and earlier, and between west and later, is a clear one: the sun gradually moves (in our visual experience at least) from east to west over the course of a day.

Similarly, Le Guen and Balam (2012) found some Absolute directional point-ing gestures used to refer to the time of day among Yucatec Maya speakers, although they found no temporal linguistic uses of spatial terms. One might speculate that the basis for the Kuuk Thaayorre and Yucatec mappings is frame-metonymic, rather than metaphoric like those of the Yupno and other time models discussed so far: sequences of locations across the sky are metonymically asso-ciated with times when the sun appears in those locations, and in turn with sequences of locations in an area on the ground below.

7.6   Gesture and temporal metaphors

The temporal uses of spatial language have thus been a laboratory for understanding crosslinguistic variation in metaphor systems. They constitute a particularly interesting laboratory because this is also an area where researchers have been using multimodal data, not just linguistic data. Cienki (1998) pioneered this approach, showing very interestingly that English speakers often gestured metaphorically even when not using linguistic metaphoric expressions (e.g. gesturing down when mentioning a bad grade and up for a good one, even when saying *bad grade* rather than *low grade*: Cienki and Müller (2008) offer a collection of recent studies of metaphor in gesture). Núñez and Sweetser used Aymara co-speech gestures as one part of their evidence showing that the Aymara time metaphor system is Ego-based; as with Cienki's work, these gestures also provide added evidence for the cognitive (rather than purely linguistic) character of these figurative models.

And it is gestural evidence which has brought to the fore another dimension, literally, of English and European time metaphors. English speakers appear to have two ways of gesturing about time. One is to gesture forward in referring to the future, and backward in referring to the past – this is a gestural manifestation of the same metaphor observable in linguistic uses like *the weeks ahead* or *the years behind us*, namely FUTURE IS IN FRONT OF EGO, PAST IS BEHIND EGO, NOW IS EGO'S LOCATION. It is particularly remarkable that English speakers use the same kind of point downwards, towards the space immediately in front of their feet, when saying *Here* and when saying *Now* (Sweetser 2009). Calbris (1990) documents a front–back time line in French co-speech gesture, similar to the English one. English speakers' other gestural pattern is to gesture across the space in front of the body, from left to right: earlier events correspond to locations further to the left, later events correspond to locations further to the right. Casasanto and Jasmin (2012) found a preference among English speakers for this pattern in the tasks they gave their subjects. There is some evidence that speakers use the left–right pattern more in referring to a sequence of events relative to each other, while they use the back/front pattern more in referring to deictic time contrasts (Past and Future relative to Now). This makes sense, since Ego's location is inevitably part of an arc going from directly behind Ego to the space in front of Ego, while Ego's location is not a point on a path traversing the space in front of the speaker from left to right; hence, Now is inherently part of the back/front gestural model of time, while it is not inherently part of the left/right model.

It has been shown that side-to-side gestural models of temporal sequence vary culturally; the western European models are left–right and appear to correlate with the left–right writing systems used by all of these language communities. Hebrew and Arabic speakers (and writers/readers) seem to gesture from right to left to refer to temporal sequence, reflecting their right-to-left writing system

(Tversky et al. 1981, Ouellet et al. 2009). But should we really be talking about these metaphors as right-to-left and left-to-right models of time? Here, linguistic data may help us understand the gestural data rather than the other way round. None of these languages ever show any linguistic usages equivalent to *the left year* or *the further right-hand day* for referring to sequential relations between time periods. One possible hypothesis is that these are really "transposed" Moving Ego back/front metaphors. Writing or visual scanning moves across a page from earlier to later words, and from left to right or from right to left, as the case may be, but this is understood as moving *forward*, in either case. English speakers certainly talk about text this way: they speak of something as being *back* on an earlier line or page, or *ahead* on a later point in the text (again, not *left* or *right*). Scanning also progresses gradually downwards across a page, but the most immediate progression is left to right. Chinese writing traditionally went first downwards along a line, then left to right for the next line (unlike Western writing which goes first left to right across a line, and then downwards to the next line); this seems another potential motivation for the Chinese vertical temporal metaphors (alongside the observation about reverence for the past): where EARLIER TIMES ARE HIGHER, just as earlier-scanned characters in a text are higher than later ones.

7.7   Visual-gestural languages and figurative usage

Numerous researchers have documented the fact that signed languages are not only iconic but deeply metonymic and metaphoric in linguistic structure. Since their figurative uses are grounded in the iconic aspects of form, let us first give a brief definition of iconicity and then examine its figurative uses.

By **iconic**, we mean that the forms systematically resemble the meanings in structure (McNeill 1992, Taub 2001, Hiraga 2005, Müller 2008, Mittelberg 2008). For example, the American Sign Language (ASL) sign for TREE involves the signer holding up her dominant-side (right, for right-handed signers) forearm to represent a tree: the forearm is the trunk, the fingers are the branches. The ASL sign for HOUSE involves the signer using her two hands to trace a peaked roof and vertical walls in the air. In the one case, the articulators' shape resembles the shape of the represented object, the tree; in the other case, the shape traced by the articulators' motion in the air resembles some canonical image of a house. As Taub (2001) has argued, it is no accident that iconicity is so pervasive in signed languages. Spoken languages use sound, and sound patterns can of course be iconic for sound patterns; thus there are patterns of sound symbolism or onomatopoeia, such as the representation in English of a cat's vocalization as *meow* or a bell sound as *ding-dong*, as well as other instances such as *crack* or *thud* or *crash*. But a sound cannot directly represent some visual or spatial situation; it can only do so frame-metonymically. (And indeed the word *crash* not only refers to a certain kind of noise, but also to the kind of impact involved in events which might cause such a noise.) Nonetheless, a visual-gestural language is naturally equipped to iconically represent shapes, motion, and spatial relations in a way that spoken languages are not: we have already seen that ASL represents shapes with shapes, but it also represents the motion of an object using the motion of an articulator (an index finger representing a person can move across the signing space to represent the movement of that person), and spatial relations of objects by spatial relations of articulators.

How would such a language exploit its iconic system metonymically and metaphorically? The answer is, prolifically. All languages require some ingenuity to represent abstract concepts such as time. ASL has both metonymic and metaphoric aspects to its models of time. A very basic metonymic example is the sign for TIME itself, which consists of points to the wrist of the nondominant hand, the place where a watch would conventionally be worn. So the location on the wrist is frame-metonymic for the watch (though of course an actual watch might or might not be located there), and the watch is in turn frame-metonymic for the concept of time. Similarly, signs for lengths of time often involve use of the dominant signing hand to iconically represent part of a clock – with fingers representing the hands of the clock, and rotating to indicate the length of time. These signs don't of course "mean" motion of the hands, but passage of the relevant amount of time that is correlated with that motion, so they are frame-metonymic.

Metaphorically, ASL and a number of other signed languages have a time line extending along the front–back axis of the signer: Future times are located at points in front of the signer (farther future points are farther in front of the signer), Past times are located at points behind the signer, and the Present is located at a point right next to the signer's body and just in front of it. Like English-speaking gesturers, signers thus point downwards right in front of the body to mean Now. Presumably this is an articulatory constraint in both cases: if the speaker's or signer's location is metaphorically Now, one might expect the point to be downwards at the speaker's or signer's head. But that would be outside the normal signing or gesturing space, which is more or less a quarter-globe in front of the upper body of the communicator. It is articulatorily much easier to point at a location right in front of one's torso. Overall, this model fits readily into the Ego-based models which we are familiar with in some spoken languages: it is certainly not so unusual as the Aymara model. A second ASL time line travels from left to right across the space in front of the signer – earlier times are at locations farther to the left, and later times at locations farther to the right; the present time may or may not be on this timeline. Again, this is familiar to English gesturers, and may even reflect the ways in which signed languages recruit aspects of the surrounding visual and gestural culture.

As Taub (2001) has documented, ASL has pervasive metaphoric structure. This includes a strong spatial metaphor for communication, reflecting COMMUNICATION IS OBJECT EXCHANGE – verbs for TELL, ORDER, and ASK show

physical movement of articulators away from the locus of the imagined communicator and towards the location of the addressee. Similarly, MORE IS UP is also
pervasive; the sign for MAXIMUM shows a hand at held at an "upper limit"
at the top of the torso, while the sign for DECREASE involves moving a hand
downwards. INTIMACY IS CLOSENESS is manifested in the sign for 'close friends,'
which involves interlocking the two index fingers, and in the clasped hands which
constitute the MARRY sign. Notice that MARRY is also metonymic, since the
frame of a Marriage Ceremony often involves the two participants clasping hands
(in a metaphoric sign for their new unity), and only the hands clasping are represented, not the two whole individuals.

More space should ideally be devoted here to the fascinating structures of
signed languages, but it should at least be clear from this discussion that they
operate on many of the same principles structuring metaphor and metonymy
in spoken languages and co-speech gesture. The striking difference between
signed and spoken languages lies in the inevitable incorporation of visual-gestural
iconicity into both the lexical and grammatical structures of signed languages.

7.8   Conclusions

Perhaps the most important conclusion to take from this chapter is that
the general findings on crosscultural variation in figurative language and thought
have the same profile as findings in other domains of language and thought. That
is, there are deep commonalities in human perception and cognition which are
reflected in language and in figurative models – and there are deep and fascinating
cultural differences. It is obvious to any observer that humans share the correlation
between being in front of Ego and being visible, as well as the correlation between
locations that are ahead on a path and future times. But without the clear evidence
from Aymara, researchers might not have been certain that the first of these
two correlations could constitute the motivation for a full metaphoric model of
time.

Another important conclusion is that (as we mentioned in Chapters 2 and
3), source-domain cognitive structure is crucial in determining the possible
metaphoric mappings to a target domain. Even in an area as apparently crossculturally stable in experience as Space, culture-specific and language-specific
construals affect cognition, and powerfully affect potential metaphoric mappings
to other domains. Chinese Emotion metaphors appear to differ systematically
from English ones in ways that reflect different cultural models of the body. This
means that crosslinguistic metaphor comparison depends crucially on detailed
crosslinguistic study of the frames involved in the source semantic domain, to
provide a basis for examining the metaphoric models themselves.

And finally, the work done so far in this area is very much the tip of an iceberg –
even more so than the language-specific studies, crosslinguistic comparative

work on metaphor is in its infancy. But as crosslinguistic semantics at large progresses, further domains clearly await closer examination by comparative metaphor analysts.

7.9   Summary

We have focused here on the figurative construals of time, to show the crosslinguistic and crossmodal similarities and differences. Time is typically construed in terms of space, so much depends on the construal of space in the language of investigation. Furthermore, as we have shown, other related components of the construal may influence meaning in important ways. For example, spatial construals of time typically involve motion through space, but in the cases where they do not, the construal may yield different effects. As we saw in the examples from Aymara, the static nature of the space/time construal yields an understanding of time which is signaled through gestures pointing towards the back to mark the future, while in most known cases the future is in front. This supports the claim we have been highlighting throughout the book, namely that lower-level schematic aspects of a mapping matter significantly with respect to the final effects. It is not enough to note the correlation between the understanding of space and the understanding of time, but the specific treatment of the interaction with space may be crucially important too.

The chapter confirms the need for crosslinguistic study of figurative language. Not only do we need to consider the sources of construals which differ across languages and consider their role in conceptualization, we also need to see correlations between figurative choices and other aspects of the structure of a given language. We have signaled such needs through the consideration of time construals in languages which have either relative or absolute space systems.

Finally, the chapter confirmed the need for consideration of other communicative modalities. Whether through sign language or gesture, we can obtain specific and important evidence to support or supplement our hypotheses about the relation between cognitive concepts and the formal or semantic choices a language makes.

8   Figurative language in discourse

So far we have examined a wide variety of uses of figurative expressions, focusing primarily on the nature of the mappings involved and their interaction with other linguistic forms. In this chapter we move on to consider the role figurative language plays in the construction of a broader message, in a larger discourse context. Text analysts representing different theoretical frameworks have talked about similar issues, considering discourses of politics, science, literature, or advertising, especially from the perspective of the goals and specific features of discourse genres.[1] We cannot do justice to the range of the discussion here; instead, we will thus focus on several examples of analyses where we will look at the specificity of the mappings, constructional phenomena, and viewpoint, rather than broadly construed discourse phenomena.

Moreover, linguists, as well as literary scholars, have interested themselves not only in discourse structure but specifically in literary texts. Jakobson (1981[1960], 1987) treated literary-text analysis as a normal part of the job of structuralist linguistics; and some literary scholars have more recently led a movement towards cognitive linguistic approaches. The resulting range of text analyses is a diverse patchwork, attesting to the differing goals of the analysts – and these range from improving science education to critiquing objectivist stances in medicine, honing political rhetoric or arguing for policy positions, explicating religious texts or advocating theological views, analyzing the artistic structure of literary texts, understanding stylistic effects of linguistic structures, and more.

We will continue this interdisciplinary dialogue here, bringing a cognitive linguistic viewpoint to bear on some of the findings in these diverse areas. The kinds of phenomena which we have focused on in this textbook – mappings,

---

[1] For a broad overview of figurative discourse phenomena, see Semino (2008); some examples of linguistic (rather than discourse) analyses can be found in Dancygier et al. (2012[2010]). Analyses of discourse in terms of mental spaces can be found in Oakley and Hougaard (2008). Specific genres are discussed in a number of monographs and articles. Cameron (2003) is a good source on the discourse of education, while Deignan (2005) shows important aspects of the work on metaphor with the use of corpora. The discourse genre which has attracted possibly the most attention is the language of politics. From a broad cognitive perspective, frames in political discourse are discussed in Lakoff (2002, 2009); analyses which are more oriented towards discourse phenomena and ideology can be found in Charteris-Black (2004, 2005), Chilton (2004), Musolff (2004), Musolff and Zinken (2009), Ahrens (2009), Hart (2010). Discourse phenomena are only the focus of one chapter of this book, so we provide only these examples of the many publications we could cite.

constructional phenomena, and especially viewpoint – are equally relevant in all these domains.

8.1   Metaphor and viewpoint: the discourse of illness and addiction

Much of the conventional literature on illness involves metaphors based on Conflict and Combat. Doctors and journalistic writers alike have adopted these metaphors, which have then spread into popular discourse. Such descriptions abound at any level of medical discourse – from the description of our immune system as a *line of defense against disease* to self-help literature for cancer patients advising them to *fight back* and try to *win the battle against cancer*. This is not surprising, considering the basic fact that illnesses are bodily states which are unwanted and harmful and do not seem to result from our actions. But there has been a reaction to these "standard" metaphoric models by authors who feel acutely that the Combat discourse does not capture the subjective experience of patients. In what follows, we examine two writers' depictions of the personal and social dimensions of illness, as well as the irony evoked by some common metaphors.

8.1.1   The Boundary schema: two construals of illness

In her now-classic book on metaphors for illness, Susan Sontag refers to illness as *a more onerous citizenship*.[2] She claims that every human being holds *dual citizenship, in the kingdom of the well and in the kingdom of the ill*. In the extended use of these metaphors, Sontag argues that metaphorical thinking about illness creates stereotyped visions of certain diseases (such as tuberculosis or AIDS). Clearly, Sontag's own citizenship metaphor relies on the perception that the state of being ill puts one in a location separated from the general population of healthy humans by an invisible boundary. The boundary is permeable, but it does create sides, and, consequently, a sense of alienation for those who are forced to reside in the kingdom of the ill for a long time. The Boundary image schema is the foundation for Sontag's construal, and she describes all of the inferences of that construal – forced separation, difficulties in moving freely from one side to the other, and living in a situation where local perspective prevails. Ill people are often forced to feel like outcasts, members of an inferior group which "the well" do not want to know much about. Overall, Sontag's argument analyzes illness from a social perspective (though she herself was a cancer patient, which possibly made her more sensitive to the issues).

---

[2] Susan Sontag, *Illness as metaphor and AIDS and its metaphors*, New York: Picador, 2001, p. 3.

More recently, in 2010, Christopher Hitchens revealed that he had been diagnosed with cancer, writing a personal article entitled "Topic of Cancer" in *Vanity Fair*, to which he had been a longtime contributor, and later documenting his story in the book *Mortality*. (He subsequently died of the disease.) The article starts by describing the sudden onset of horrific symptoms. Hitchens calls emergency services; he notices the frightening amount of gear the crew is displaying, and then describes being transported to the hospital as *a very gentle and firm deportation, taking me from the country of the well across the stark frontier that marks off the land of malady*.[3] The emergency ward is referred to as a *sad border post*, and later he refers to himself as *a citizen of the sick country*. He seems to be deploying a construal very much like Sontag's metaphor, but in fact there are important differences. Where Sontag talks about *emigration*, Hitchens describes what is happening as a *deportation*, and makes no comment on the fact that illness is a part of everybody's life – what Sontag refers to as *dual citizenship*.

Having set up the boundary metaphors in these subtly different ways, the two writers go on to explore the state of being ill very differently – Sontag talks about social issues, while Hitchens talks about his own experiences. Deportation is different from emigrating; while Emigration is not necessarily voluntary, it does not deprive the person of their free will, but the frame of Deportation involves a sudden change, definitely against the will of the person being moved to another country. The personal viewpoint which permeates Hitchens's text (and which is practically absent from Sontag's) makes an important difference in the construal of illness. As in many other cases we have seen, metaphorical discourse develops differently and fulfills different goals depending on viewpoint. The difference between experiential viewpoint and analytical viewpoint is thus reflected in the different effects achieved by these two writers who are using the same general schema.

Further on in the text, Hitchens uses the Boundary schema in a different way – he talks about his cancer as *an alien* which *had colonized a bit of [his] lung*. The sense of an outside force penetrating the boundaries of the human body is a different use of the same schema, but it contributes further to the sense of powerlessness permeating Hitchens's account of the events.

8.1.2   Metaphor and irony

Illness is a serious subject, and a personal account of it is expected to be serious too. But the use of metaphoric language can certainly be affected by the context; in the case of Hitchens's text it is important that he published the piece in a magazine not known for seriousness, being interested mostly in fashion, pop culture, celebrities, and the like. Having set up the metaphor of being in a foreign country, Hitchens discusses the local flavor, talking about language (*Tumorville tongue*), customs, the egalitarian spirit, the humor – which is *a touch feeble and*

---

[3] Christopher Hitchens, "Topic of Cancer," *Vanity Fair*, Sept. 2010.

repetitive, almost no talk of sex – and *the cuisine . . . the worst of any destination I have ever visited.* This style would be more appropriate for the travel section of *Vanity Fair*, and is humorous in unexpected ways. It seems to be a prime case of the form of figurative language use known as **irony**.

Irony has been discussed by analysts primarily as a pragmatic phenomenon. Typical cases of irony are those where the primary meaning of the utterance is blatantly untrue, as when a speaker calls a mean-spirited acquaintance *a fine friend*, or when one praises the weather (*What a beautiful day!*) even though it is hopelessly rainy outside. Standard treatments of irony (Sperber and Wilson 1981, Wilson and Sperber 1992) rely on the concept of implicature and the distinction between *use* and *mention*. An utterance such as *You are a fine friend* is not genuinely *used*, rather, it is merely *mentioned*, and implicature-based reasoning allows the hearer to conclude that the intended meaning is in fact not praise but criticism. Croft and Cruse (2004) offer a metonymic treatment of both irony and understatement – and this is in some respects close to Sperber and Wilson's, since it is only in its particular context that an ironic statement can (frame-metonymically, one might say) evoke a particular imagined but nonadopted viewpoint.

Recently, Tobin and Israel (2012) have proposed an interpretation of irony which relies on the concepts of mental spaces and viewpoint. They argue that the nature of irony cannot be described merely in terms of comparison between the literal meaning of the utterance and the (intended) opposite one. These two meanings represent two different (alternative) mental spaces, one of which is aligned with the reality space. But in order to perceive the contrast between the alternatives, one needs a viewpoint space higher in the network, where the contrast between the alternatives and the reason for using irony can be resolved. In other words, irony does not reside in the fact that a person is saying something blatantly not true, but in the perception of the nature of the contrast between the actual utterance and the intended meaning.

This view of irony captures Hitchens's style well. When he complains about the hospital *cuisine*, he is using a term which is clearly not appropriate in the context (though one would not call it "not true"), as it typically refers to food of much higher quality, in the context of fine restaurants and local specialties. The topic of the text is illness and its harsh consequences, while *cuisine* references frames of enjoyment and relaxation. The contrast between the two viewpoints yields the irony, and can truly be appreciated only from a perspective outside of either one of the frames evoked.

Hitchens also addresses one of the most pervasive metaphors for cancer – the Combat metaphor (*People don't have cancer; they are reported to be battling cancer*). As he notes, clichés like *You can beat this* are used everywhere (in fact, the medical profession is apparently becoming worried about the emerging implications that the patient is responsible for the results of the treatment). Hitchens then describes the experience of chemotherapy, pointing out that its effect is the opposite of empowerment and does not inspire a combative mood – rather, it makes one feel one is *dissolving into powerlessness like a sugar lump in water.*

The simile has an interesting effect. It describes a state in which a body loses its shape, its very boundaries, and, consequently, all of the embodied qualities which make action of any kind possible. The image of a boundary in this case portrays the experiential viewpoint of a patient well, but it is also poignantly ironic in the context of the battle metaphor.

The above examples suggest that figurative devices are very effective not just in representing the facts intended, but in representing viewpoint – and perhaps this is even their primary effect. This is particularly salient for figurative devices like irony, which, in our interpretation, are viewpoint expressions first and foremost. Importantly, figurative devices that appear to be "the same" may be used for very different purposes, depending on viewpoint.

8.1.3 Viewpointed experience and metaphor: an addiction narrative

The subjective-experiential viewpoint constructed in Hitchens's text includes a rich construal of how he felt through the stages of cancer diagnosis and early treatment, but it does not generally include specific construals of the illness itself (other than the *alien* metaphor). In the text we look at in this section, the viewpoint construal is predominantly based in the Relationship frame, with addiction to chewing tobacco being viewed as a partner in a long-term personal engagement. The narrative, by John Hare, appeared in *Newsweek* in 2003. In it, the writer documents the whole story of his addiction from his first encounter with tobacco, through addiction, to becoming free of the habit.

Hare describes his years of addiction as *my affair with chewing tobacco*, and refers to episodes of use as *frequent rendezvous*.[4] Initially, he talks about *succumbing to the seduction*, but then gives the initiative to addiction. He writes, *it crept into every aspect of my life, methodically tricking me into wanting more and more while enjoying it less and less*. Eventually, he found himself in *the clutches of tobacco addiction*, and chewing *had become [his] security blanket*. Finally, he decides to quit; he describes how he *chipped at the foundation of addiction, freeing [him]self from its grip*. He gets rid of *the monster* and can now refer to it fondly as his *old best friend*.

It is interesting to observe how Hare portrays his "partner" in this affair. First, he is seduced, then tricked, until he is in the clutches of the monster – which still helps him remain calm in social situations. He eventually takes action and frees himself from the unfortunate relationship. In this story, the addict is first weak and overpowered, and then resolves to be strong and wins. The narrative is in fact quite flattering to the writer, who faced irresistible force at first and then fought back, despite having initially fallen in love with the evil power. The choice of the Relationship frame creates an experiential viewpoint which presents Hare as at worst gullible, but probably just naive and trusting, and generally strong. The

[4] John Hare, "My turn: finally tough enough to give up snuff," *Newsweek*, Sept. 23, 2003.

addiction, however, is given all the features of a predatory female, first attractive and then destructive. The metaphors used give the reader an understanding of the addict's experience, with all its conflicting emotions, and also his construal of addiction itself.

Hare's narrative differs from Hitchens's primarily in the degree of control he attributes to his past self. While Hitchens feels deprived of any influence over his fate (*deportation, a sugar lump in water*, invaded by an *alien*), Hare makes bad choices initially, but has control over the condition. What examples like these show is that figurative language can be used to construe a situation from multiple perspectives. The choice of the organizing figurative frame of such an extended piece of discourse is responsible for the construal of the entire narrative. The overall effect and specific choices of metaphors and similes often depend on construals at a different level of schematicity. In the cases we have seen, the Boundary schema yields different viewpoints in the texts by Sontag and Hitchens, and the concept of having or not having control makes major distinctions in the narratives written by Hitchens and Hare. Much of the research on the discourse uses of figurative forms focuses on major metaphors (especially those having to do with War or Journeys). We argue that the analyses should start at the most schematic level, and include the analysis of viewpoint which may be present at richer levels of mapping. Then the metaphors involved can be seen in their full effect.

8.2   Argumentation and linguistic choices

Political discourse is very rich in metaphors, and much has been said about their effects (Chilton 1996, 2004, Lakoff 2002, 2009, Charteris-Black 2004, 2005, Musolff 2004, Semino 2008). The focus in most of this work has been on how the choice of metaphors helps political agents in achieving rhetorical goals, in presenting policies, or in taking a stand on issues. The topic is extremely broad and important, and we cannot do it justice within the limits of this section. What we will focus on instead is how some categories of figurative language structure political speeches, and how grammatical choices help explain the special character of political oratory as a genre. In what follows, we will look at examples of constructions which appear to be more common in that genre than in other types of discourse, and how these constructions are useful in achieving discourse goals. We will use examples from US rhetoric, but we believe that the patterns we discuss can be found in instances of political discourse elsewhere.

8.2.1   Source-of-Target metaphors

One of the most famous speeches of the twentieth century was the "I have a dream" speech, delivered by Martin Luther King on August 28, 1963, at the Lincoln Memorial in Washington, DC. The speech is a powerful example of antidiscrimination rhetoric, and also an excellent example of King's style, combining his role of a preacher and his role as a political activist and visionary. Throughout the speech, King uses a great number of metaphorical expressions, describing slavery and inequality and his hopes for a better future. Some of them are quoted in examples (1)–(5) below:

(1)   the Negro is still sadly crippled by *the manacles of segregation* and *the chains of discrimination*

(2)   the Negro lives on *a lonely island of poverty* in the midst of *a vast ocean of material prosperity*

(3)   *the dark and desolate valley of segregation . . . the sunlit path of racial justice*

(4)   Let us not seek to satisfy *our thirst for freedom* by drinking from *the cup of bitterness and hatred*

(5)   *the quicksand of racial injustice . . . the solid rock of brotherhood*

The speech uses a great number of this formal class of expressions, which could be described as Source-of-Target metaphors. In an expression such as *the manacles of segregation*, the first noun evokes the domain of slavery or brutal imprisonment, including the cruel practice of chaining prisoners' hands or feet. The second noun, *segregation*, is the target domain; while one might think of it only in terms of consequences to personal freedom, it is here construed in terms of cruel restriction of one's freedom of motion and action. The abstract social concept is thus given rich embodied meaning.

   This seems to be the general strategy in all of the expressions King uses, though he also builds many of them into contrasting pairs – being restricted on an island is opposed to having the freedom of a vast space, being in a valley (BAD IS DOWN) and in darkness (KNOWING IS SEEING) is contrasted with being on a well-lit path (with many destinations possible and visible), a lack of footing (*quicksand*) with firm ground (*solid rock*). What is particularly interesting about these metaphors is the pattern of evoking basic embodied experiences to talk about aspects of social and material well-being. As a result, the social and economic freedoms that King calls for are presented as equal to the basic rights to movement, light, and solid ground under one's feet. Social well-being is equated with bodily well-being. Thus the effect of the whole speech is founded on repeated reference to the source domain of embodied health and well-being.

   In standard accounts of metaphor, we see either Predicational Constructions like LIFE IS A JOURNEY, which construct a link between the source and the target in ways open to the language users' framing and experience, or examples of polysemous usage – whether diachronically well-established (like *transparency*, referring to openness of information in political settings) or newly coined for the purposes of the discourse context (like the *information detox* example discussed in Chapter 4). In these cases, we interpret the source expression as referring to the target. The construction King uses so aptly profiles both the source and the target, and makes the connection between them meaningful beyond what the "invisible" metaphoric usage does – it yields additional inferences with regard to human well-being as relying on both embodied and social factors. It is a metaphoric construction which does a bit more than just make us connect the target to the source. It is thus appropriate to the discourse context of argumentative and inspirational discourse – the category in which King's speech belongs.

8.2.2   Compression as an argumentation strategy

On September 12, 1962, just one year before the "I have a dream" speech, President John F. Kennedy delivered a speech at the Rice University Stadium in Houston, Texas.[5] The speech became known as the "Moon speech," since in it Kennedy announced the US plan to land a man on the moon (and bring him safely back to earth) – a mission statement for a most ambitious project. After first commenting on how much science has allowed us to understand and how much there is still to be discovered, Kennedy says:

(6)   No man can fully grasp how far and how fast we have come, but condense, if you will, the 50,000 years of man's recorded history in a time span of but a half-century. Stated in these terms, we know very little about the first 40 years, except at the end of them advanced man had learned to use the skins of animals to cover them. Then about 10 years ago, under this standard, man emerged from his caves to construct other kinds of shelter. Only five years ago man learned to write and use a cart with wheels. Christianity began less than two years ago. The printing press came this year, and then less than two months ago, during this whole 50-year span of human history, the steam engine provided a new source of power. Newton explored the meaning of gravity. Last month electric lights and telephones and automobiles and airplanes became available. Only last week did we develop penicillin and television and nuclear power, and now if America's new spacecraft succeeds in reaching Venus, we will have literally reached the stars before midnight tonight.

Example (6) is an excellent example of compression. Kennedy compresses the fifty thousand years of human learning and technology into the span of fifty years. Suddenly, in this extremely compressed blend, everything in the emergence of science and technology happens impressively fast, at a pace which feels almost hurried. We have barely invented electricity and telephone communication, and we are already reaching for places which seemed unthinkable not long ago. Similar images of compression (such as the visual compression yielding the image of humans developing from apes) have often been used to represent the stages in development. But Kennedy does more – not only does he list all the highlights of technological progress, he creates the impression that nothing is

---

[5] We looked at another excerpt from the speech in Chapter 4.

impossible and the most distant goal can be achieved almost immediately. Why wait if you can "reach the stars" tomorrow? Here, reaching the moon seems to be a powerful metonymy for voyaging to extraterrestrial locations, including the stars – which of course were and are not likely to be reached soon. The temporal compression creates a blend that also eliminates all the complex developments in between the landmark achievements, and makes them look like inevitable steps in the history of technological progress. In this view, going to the moon seems to be the only logical consequence of the technological developments thus far, and it cannot wait – the time is already here.

This is a clear example of what Fauconnier and Turner (2002) refer to as achieving human scale: this construal makes the pace of progress understandable and human. But it does more than that. The discourse here is not aimed just at promoting a better understanding of the history of technology. It is meant to make the hearers believe that the goal of reaching the moon is accessible, natural, and inevitable, and indeed part of the grand goal of space exploration, "reaching the stars." At the same time, it metaphorically gives a visionary flavor to an otherwise mundane technological problem. Blending supports the speaker's rhetorical goals in a way that a single-space representation could not.

8.2.3   Frames and grammar in political speeches

Political rhetoric relies heavily on frame evocation. In this section, we consider two speeches by Barack Obama, his victory speech after the 2008 election and his 2009 inaugural address; both speeches represent the same moment in American history. We will look at the different ways in which he evoked particular frames – from direct quotation to frame metonymy to generalized statements. In particular, we will look at the role of determiners in the effects of frame metonymy.

Political oratory often tries to locate the current speaker's position against the background of historical events. It is thus common for political speeches to explicitly or implicitly quote the words of earlier texts, spoken or written. In his 2009 inaugural address, Obama said:

(7)   We remain a young nation, but in the words of Scripture, the time has come
        to set aside childish things. The time has come to reaffirm our enduring
        spirit . . . to carry forward that . . . noble idea, passed on from generation to
        generation: the God-given promise that all are equal, all are free, and all
        deserve a chance to pursue their full measure of happiness.

The first reference is to St. Paul's letter to the Corinthians in the Bible, evoking the words, *When I was a child, I thought like a child, and reasoned like a child. But when I became a man I put aside childish things.* The blend prompted by this frame is quite obvious – like Paul, Americans as citizens and America as a country should stop thinking about themselves as a young nation; different challenges should now be accepted. The second reference, to the Declaration of Independence, evokes the inalienable rights of equality, and also *life, liberty, and the pursuit of happiness* and the need for a renewed commitment to them. Both references, appearing in the same paragraph, prompt the hearers to blend the historical words evoked with the current situation, and so the start of the new administration is to be read as the opening of a new era, which, though new in its freshly acquired maturity, will build on the revered principles of the earliest moments of American history. The temporal compression these two quotes jointly suggest is crucial to the impact of the speech. The frames evoked are the inputs to a blend which guides the hearer's understanding of the meaning of the event. And further, in a higher contextual blend, the text from *Corinthians* offers a Biblical mandate for the new historical directions advocated by Obama.

Earlier, in his 2008 election-victory speech, Obama offered a long passage dedicated to Ann Nixon Cooper, a 106-year-old African-American woman who voted for him that day. He talks about the historical events which happened in her lifetime. Among other things, he says:

(8)   She was there for the buses in Montgomery, the hoses in Birmingham, a bridge in Selma, and a preacher from Atlanta who told a people that "we shall overcome."

The major events of the civil rights movement are evoked here through several phrases, all of them involving proper names (*Montgomery, Birmingham, Selma, Atlanta*). As we argued in Chapter 7, proper names are a particularly effective means of frame evocation (the first three refer to cities where major protests and demonstrations took place, and Atlanta is the city of Martin Luther King; the last reference also includes a quote from a well-known protest song of the civil rights movement). In this highly compressed chain of frame evocation, proper names play the role of structuring a powerful account of the history of the civil rights movement.

But let us also note that Martin Luther King is referred to here as *a preacher from Atlanta* – with an indefinite article, even though the frame evoked is very unambiguous, unique, and specific. In the next paragraph, Obama continues using the same strategy: *A man touched down on the moon, a wall came down in Berlin, a world was connected by our own science and imagination.* In each of these phrases, the reference is to an event or entity that is already established as unique (the Berlin Wall, Armstrong's landing on the moon, the world of Internet communication we all inhabit). And yet, the speaker uses an indefinite article, which typically suggests introduction of a new referent. In this case, the indefinite article seems to mark the treatment of this referent as "an" example from a *class* of such examples.[6]

This kind of usage manipulates the specific frames evoked to construct higher level, more general discourse frames. For example, the Berlin Wall was a very specific structure, richly framed as a material symbol of the Iron Curtain mentality.

---

[6] We want to thank Adrian Lou for drawing our attention to this phenomenon.

It was a physical barrier, erected to create political barriers. Ordinarily, it was referred to as *the Berlin Wall*, with the definite article, and functioned just like a proper name – unique reference as a result of a rich frame. The indefinite article, in this instance, changes the nature of the events and makes them merely instances of the historical and cultural progression that Obama is describing. He is not talking about any of these events specifically, to make references to them; he is simply setting up a bigger frame of change and progress, which leads to the unique moment of the election in which Ann Nixon Cooper casts her vote.

Importantly, as soon as Obama gets back to Ann Nixon Cooper, he switches from the instance-type reference with the indefinite article to using the demonstrative *this* – a clear expression of not only uniqueness but also contextual accessibility and discourse focus. When he goes on to say *And this year, in this election, she touched her finger to a screen, and cast her vote*, he returns to the proper topic of this fragment of the speech. The meaning of this type of shift is also clear in another reference to the Berlin Wall. In another political speech, Ronald Reagan, standing at the Brandenburg Gate, called on Mikhail Gorbachev to annihilate the symbol of divisive politics, saying: *Mr. Gorbachev, open this gate. Mr. Gorbachev, tear down this wall* – using the demonstrative determiner *this*, referring clearly not only to the gate and the wall in front of him, but also to their symbolic value. This grammatical choice of determiners, between the indefinite *a* and demonstrative *this*, manipulates the relationship of a stable frame to the discourse – the zooming in and the zooming out these determiners provide shows that frame metonymy in discourse contexts can be subject to manipulation via very specific linguistic means.

These examples also show that, in a complex discourse event like this one, frame metonymy functions as an effective and textually economical way to construct higher-level frames out of lower-level, more specific ones. Evoking the central events of the civil rights movement is not the discourse goal – the goal is using them in constructing the frame of Progress. The Progress frame is actually built out of two indefinite sequences of frame metonymies. One documents the history of the civil rights movement, the other shows how we are now living in a world without barriers – the Berlin Wall divided a city, a country, a continent, and the world; Armstrong crossed another barrier when he walked on the moon; and contemporary modes of communication know no bounds. All this needed to happen, says Obama, to lead someone like Ann Nixon Cooper from a segregated society to the contemporary one in which she can vote by pressing her finger to a screen, and vote for an African-American President. Note that the touch-screen voting is itself a frame metonymy for *recent* technological progress – that is, for the new era in which an African American can be elected President. Both lines of progress and change Obama constructs through frame evocation converge in the vote cast by a 106-year-old woman.

Frame evocation often has very specific discourse goals, and frames can be evoked not only as sources of content, but as the basis of further framing.

Additionally, one can identify grammatical phenomena which help speakers manipulate frames for discourse purposes. We thus believe that figurative language can be studied to reveal important mechanisms reaching from grammar, through lexical expressions, to the analysis of discourse genres.

8.3   Extended metonymy and viewpoint

Metonymy is typically quite focused – an expression evokes aspects of a frame, and in this sense it compresses the expression of the larger frame, economically evoking the whole complex structure. But sometimes the metonymic process itself becomes the focus of a stretch of text. One such example was discussed in Dancygier and Sweetser 2005. In *The Wind in the Willows*, Kenneth Grahame plays with readers' understandings of frames when he has his characters Mole and Rat discover a door-scraper in the Wild Wood. The two small animals are far from home in the Wood, it is growing dark and snowing, and large animals are hunting. So Mole and Rat need shelter. Mole discovers the door-scraper by hurting his foot on it; Rat, somewhat to Mole's annoyance, is ecstatic. The discussion continues, as Mole persists in seeing the door-scraper as a piece of junk which happens to have ended up in the Wood, while Rat sees it as part of the *frame* of a dwelling: where there is a door-scraper, there is a door. They dig, and eventually find first a door-mat and then the door of the underground house of Rat's friend Mr. Badger. Mole is amazed by Rat's perspicacity. Having considered the power of frame metonymy in constructional contexts and in political discourse, our readers probably now understand that Rat's ability to infer the presence of a house from the presence of a household object is not unusual. But the story still makes it clear that metonymic reasoning is not automatic.

We will next consider a textual example from Jonathan Raban's travel narrative *Passage to Juneau*. In the text, the author sets out to sail through the Inside Passage in a small boat. It is a long journey, and he has many books with him. But a boat is also not always stable, and so the books can be easily displaced from their shelves.

(9)   When the boat was under way, my still very incomplete library took on a shuffling, drunken life of its own . . . After a rough passage, I'd find Edmund Leach, Evelyn Waugh, George Vancouver, *Kwakiutl Art*, Anthony Trollope, Homer, and *Oceanography and Seamanship* in an unlikely tangle on the saloon floor, their pages gaping, their jackets half-off: Hannah Arendt in the sink with Myron Eels. I liked these chance couplings and collisions, and hoped that on the long trip north the entire library would be shaken, pitched, and pulled into a happy interdisciplinary ragout.[7]

---

[7] Jonathan Raban, *Passage to Juneau*, New York: Vintage Books, 2001[1999], p. 33.

It might seem that example (9) is primarily using some basic version of the AUTHOR FOR BOOK and TITLE FOR BOOK metonymies discussed in Chapter 5 – objects which fell from the shelves are identified through their titles or the names of their authors. But the vocabulary describing the result of the books' being misplaced is open to interesting ambiguities. Being *in a tangle on the floor*, with *jackets half-off* builds ambiguously on the frame setup in the first sentence – perhaps prompting an image metaphor of a *drunken life*. As a result, the author names are no longer simply evoking the physical representations of their work; they are also there as people, people behaving in a somewhat rowdy and undignified manner, suggesting an intense social life and the emergence of new and interesting *couplings* (*Hannah Arendt in the sink with Myron Eels*) – the physical mixture of the books in the heap being metaphoric for potential social and intellectual interaction. The evocation of authors also brings out the view of books as representing the thoughts of their authors. The *library* in the last sentence can thus be interpreted not as a collection of books but as a collection of thoughts and ideas, mixed into a new pattern by the motion of the boat. The results will hopefully be *a happy interdisciplinary ragout*, an intellectual dish consisting of thoughts of various people, merged into a smooth, tasty, and nourishing stew. This evocation of an IDEAS ARE FOOD metaphor completes the construal of the passage.

What examples like these confirm is that metonymy does not have to function as a reference device only. Raban is not just referring to books, he is construing the books as containers for the thoughts of their authors and mapping the disorganized and accidental interactions among the objects thrown off their shelves onto the unpredictable interactions among the ideas they express. Crucially, in this metonymic and metaphoric blend, the books are physically bumping into each other in the cabin of the boat, but the ideas will be thrown together, absorbed, and reorganized in the writer's head. A further metonymy connects the boat he is inhabiting for the duration of the trip onto himself, the inhabitant; and a metaphoric mapping (MIND IS A CONTAINER) maps the space of the cabin onto the intellectual "space" his mind will be inhabiting at the same time.

The blend is essentially built by moving the reader from one aspect of the Reading frame to another – the activity of reading involves books, written by authors and published as physical objects, but the result is that the ideas are transferred from the books into the reader's mind, where they may be processed in a way which gives them a new meaning. The blend also relies on various deployments of the Container schema – the boat is a container, and the human mind is naturally construed as one, while books are also containers for the ideas expressed in them. The process of reading itself can also be thought about in terms of transfer from one Container holding intellectual content (a book) to another (a human mind). Crucially, the passage does not mention reading even once, and yet vividly represents the process by evoking various aspects of the frame. Instances like this one confirm the power of frame metonymy as a meaning-construction mechanism.

8.4   Literature and figurative meaning

Literary discourse is often considered to be a particularly rich source of figurative language.[8] Indeed, many literary texts are examples of elaborate figurative construals. As Lakoff and Turner (1989) showed, this does not mean that the language of literature is entirely unrestricted in choosing novel and innovative linguistic uses. Furthermore, Lakoff and Turner suggested that there are mechanisms that lead from ordinary conventional mappings to more creative ones. They discuss *extension* (a more complete reliance on the source domain), *elaboration* (using the source in an unusual way), and *composition* of multiple simpler mappings. They highlight both the creativity of their literary examples, and the foundation of creative uses in convention. Of course non-literary discourse can be very creative and innovative – as can be seen from many of the examples in this chapter. But esthetic impact may be one of the primary intended effects of figurative language in literature. An elaborate study of the various types of literary usage is outside the scope of this book, but we want to at least raise some fundamental questions about the linguistic devices deployed in literary texts.[9]

8.4.1   Minimalism and maximalism in poetry

We have seen throughout this book that there is good reason to think that figurative language is by no means just ornamental, but an important part of guiding cognitive construal. But does it matter *how* a figurative construal is evoked? – that is, what language, or what rhetorical strategy, is used to prompt the listener or reader to entertain that construal? For example, one could say *You're just at the beginning of the road of life*, which explicitly mentions, and maps between, the two domains of Life and Journeys. Or one could say *You're just at the beginning of the road* – which the addressee might understand literally, if the interlocutors were engaged in a physical journey, or might also interpret as being about LIFE AS A JOURNEY – even though only the Journey domain is mentioned – or about the start of some project, if the project is salient in the context. How does metaphoric discourse differ depending on the explicitness with which it specifies inputs and mappings?

---

[8] The range of discussion of figurative language in literature is, naturally, extremely broad. We want to draw the readers' attention to an emerging field of cognitive poetics, which approaches the language of literature from the cognitive perspective (for some broad examples, see Steen 1994, Stockwell 2002, Semino and Culpeper 2002, Gavins and Steen 2003, Brône and Vandaele 2009, Schneider and Hartner 2012). A blending analysis of narrative texts was proposed in Dancygier (2012a).

[9] There is quite an immense body of work applying conceptual-metaphor analysis to literary texts. A few selected works of interest are Lakoff and Turner (1989, 1991, 1996), Freeman (1993, 1995), Stockwell (2002), Bradshaw, Bishop, and Turner (2004) (including papers by Sweetser and Turner), Dancygier (2006, 2012a), Sweetser (2006), and Cook (2010). Hiraga (2005) is noteworthy for combining analysis of metaphor with making important advances in our understanding of iconicity.

Sweetser and Sullivan (2012) have argued that the degree of explicitness of metaphoric mappings is part of a cline which has been labeled *minimalism* and *maximalism* by literary scholars (see Barth 1986, Delville and Norris 2007); Stockwell (2002) talks about it as a cline of effortfulness in reading. A minimalist literary style leaves much to the reader, giving only minimal guides to meaning construction; a maximalist style does rich and complex meaning construction, guiding the reader much more explicitly. The cognitive and stylistic effects are quite different at the two ends of this spectrum.

To exemplify these two styles, we will look at short texts from each end of the spectrum which were analyzed by Sweetser and Sullivan. Example (10) is from "The red wheelbarrow," a 1923 poem by William Carlos Williams, a modernist whose work was often minimalist. In this poem, only the words *so much depends* even hint at a meaning more abstract than the described physical scene. And even that does not get us far. One interpretation of the text is that the beauty of everyday physical things is important – perhaps more important than more esthetically admired things (cathedrals or roses) or more abstract things – and perhaps, then, much depends on humans appreciating that beauty.

(10)   so much depends
           upon

           a red wheel
           barrow

           glazed with rain
           water

           beside the white
           chickens.

And yet, as we look at the poem, other readings may occur to us. We may note the iconic visual structure of the line-pairs: the first line in each pair "hangs out" over the second like the handle of a wheelbarrow over the body. And we may consider other metaphoric mappings: for example, Williams could mean that we should think of poetry as craft, and a poem as a physical *vehicle* (a Container for meaning, following the Conduit Metaphor) – in particular, a wheelbarrow. If so, part of what he is saying is that, unlike poetic traditions (perhaps maximalist ones) which pursue elaborate formal beauty in the service of communicating meanings with high cultural status, his poetic tradition involves simple and understandable forms and everyday meanings. A wheelbarrow is not a golden chariot, and the form of this poem is simple rather than abstruse. Wheelbarrows don't haul princesses in fine gowns, but loads of functional gardening materials or vegetables; the beauty of the described scene (the wheelbarrow's "load") is moving, but not rare or elevated.

So "The red wheelbarrow" in this second reading is not only an example of the minimalist esthetic, it is also metaphorically *about* the minimalist esthetic. Nothing in Williams's poem forces this second reading on us – and we could enjoy the poem with just the first reading. But many readers have found it pleasurable to go beyond the "minimal" reading to the reading about minimalism.

Shakespeare, on the other hand, was an unabashed maximalist in a period of maximalism. He not only often specifies complex metaphoric mappings, but he comments on them. In Sonnet 130 (*My mistress' eyes are nothing like the sun / Coral is far more red than her lips' red...*) he engages in metacommentary on the conventional image-metaphoric descriptions of female beauty, mentioning the metaphoric mappings explicitly as he negates them. In example (11), his famous tour-de-force passage from *Macbeth* (V.v.19–28), he evokes at least seven metaphors in nine and a half lines.

(11)   Tomorrow, and tomorrow, and tomorrow
            Creeps in this petty pace from day to day,
            To the last syllable of recorded time;
            And all our yesterdays have lighted fools
            The way to dusty death. Out, out, brief candle!
            Life's but a walking shadow, a poor player
            That struts and frets his hour upon the stage
            And then is heard no more. It is a tale
            Told by an idiot, full of sound and fury
            Signifying nothing.

The metaphors evoked here include at least the following:

TIME IS RELATIVE MOTION (*creeps, pace*) (Note that here time moves, not the viewer)

TIME IS A WRITTEN RECORD (*syllable, recorded*)

LIFE IS A CYCLE OF LIGHT AND HEAT (*lighted, candle*)

LIFE IS A JOURNEY (Ego movement) into an underground location (*lighted fools to dusty death*)

LIFE IS A MOVING SHADOW (*walking shadow*)

LIFE IS A PLAYER (*player, stage ...*)

LIFE IS A STORY (*tale*)

Lesser artists are warned not to "mix" metaphors, perhaps with good reason. But this passage is one of the most-quoted ones in Shakespeare, and brilliantly achieves an artistic goal. Sweetser and Sullivan argue that readers or listeners are pulled into Macbeth's mental processes by this hurly-burly flow of shifting metaphors; we have the impression that Macbeth (whose wife is by now dead, and who realizes that he has ruined his life by his crimes) is looking desperately for a new metaphor to help him find a less despairing construal of his life. But since he is already in despair, each metaphor only turns out to give him back his own despairing inferences. There is nothing inherently tragic in conventionally understanding LIFE AS A JOURNEY (the journey could be to a desired destination, mapping onto the achievement of desired life purposes), or in seeing LIFE AS A STORY (the story could have structure and coherence and a happy ending). But Macbeth's journey has no destination other than dusty death, and his imagined story is a meaningless one told by an idiot. By the time we are done, we can see that there is no help for Macbeth. And it is the piling of metaphor on metaphor, explicitly stated with language from both domains (*Tomorrow creeps, Life is X*), which makes this text so powerful.

Few readers can resist either Williams's text or Shakespeare's – they grab us, in their very different ways. What grabs us about Shakespeare's text is the mappings themselves, and their combination; what grabs us about Williams's text is the inexplicitness of the mappings. Minimalist texts have been described as "open," lacking determined "closure" of meaning by the author. This is perhaps an overly strong statement, given that Shakespeare is anything but minimalist, and yet is loved partly for his multiple ambiguities and for the many readings which can be given to his plays. But still, the charm of minimalist metaphor use is precisely in its avoidance of overt specification of mappings. Williams and other twentieth-century Western minimalists admired Japanese haiku, poems which also traditionally follow this strategy: overtly, many haiku only describe nature, leaving readers to bring in human social meanings. It seems no accident that Emily Dickinson, who is often stylistically minimalist though she lived in far-from-minimalist nineteenth-century America, is much admired in Japan.

Dickinson's "Over the fence –" in example (12) appears to be about a small girl wishing she dared to be disobedient and climb over a fence to steal some strawberries. The final four lines intimate that something more important than childhood fruit picking is involved; it seems far more likely that God is concerned with judging the major life decisions of adults than with small children's mischief.

(12)   Over the fence –
          Strawberries – grow –
          Over the fence –
          I could climb – if I tried, I know –
          Berries are nice!
          But – if I stained my Apron –
          God would certainly scold!
          Oh, dear, – I guess if He were a Boy –
          He'd – climb – if He could!

Once we have decided that Life is one of the input domains, we notice that the content of the poem is about a difficult spatial Path, over an Obstacle (the fence), to a desired Destination (the strawberry patch). We could then readily construe this poem as evoking conventional metaphors such as PURPOSES ARE DESTINATIONS (and its related mappings PURPOSIVE ACTION IS DIRECTED MOTION, and DIFFICULTIES ARE OBSTACLES). None of these mappings are overtly stated; but they are conventional and the reader is nudged by the evidence that Life is the target domain. We might even guess that, since the speaker laments the fact that boys are allowed to climb (and steal strawberries) while girls are not, the poem may be about life purposes which are forbidden to women but allowed to men.

But most mysterious remains the precise identity of the forbidden life purposes, here mapped onto the desirable strawberries. The fact that the strawberries are literally forbidden fruit, together with the image of (presumably) red stains on the apron, suggests that sexuality could be meant – certainly it was more restricted for women than for men in Dickinson's culture, and Dickinson never married. On the other hand, the mention of *climbing* suggests that a career ("rising in the world") may be the forbidden purpose – nineteenth-century New England men were supposed to improve their status by working at their careers, while women were not. And, given Victorian expectations that authorship is a male job, and that women writers should only tackle certain topics (only some of Dickinson's more conventional and "womanly" poems were published during her lifetime), we might reasonably wonder whether the forbidden fruit is writing poetry. A very significant part of the poem's power is that Dickinson leaves it up to the reader to decide between these and other potential metaphoric read-ings of the strawberries – and to meditate on the range of gender issues thus evoked.

Finally, sometimes metaphoric mappings are so conventional that they force themselves on readers or listeners even without any overt specification of map-pings. In such a case, the author can afford the apparent luxury of underspecifica-tion, exactly because it is only apparent. We cannot really call these minimalist – they don't give the reader any special sense of discovery or active participation in the reading. An example is Robert Frost's "The road not taken" which says *Two roads diverged in a yellow wood / and sorry I could not travel both . . . I took the one less traveled by / and that has made all the difference.* Despite Frost's own insistence that this poem was about actual choices of paths during country walks (poking fun at a friend who treated these choices too seriously), generations of readers have consistently and automatically understood it as being about LIFE AS A JOURNEY (within which LIFE CHOICES ARE CROSSROADS). This makes us realize that mappings which are not explicitly labeled may or may not be genuinely left open to the reader.

In short, the same metaphoric mappings may be set up in different ways. Frost, Dickinson, and Shakespeare set up some of the same LIFE IS A JOURNEY mappings; but Shakespeare states the mapping, Frost's readers presume it, and Dickinson leaves it as a possibility. All three texts are highly successful, as their iconic and much-quoted status attests. But the cognitive and stylistic effects are radically different. The successful reader of a good minimalist piece feels the heady pleasure of independent meaning construction, while the successful reader of a good maximalist piece feels the fun of following a complex path to new places, with a good guide.

8.4.2   Narrative and blending

Another observation that can be found in accounts of literary figurative language is that poetry is richer in figuration than prose. We do not agree with that evaluation. Though it is clear that narrative prose is often more focused on description of events and situations, it is not true that these descriptions are always more literal. Travel narratives are especially expected to be less esthetically elaborate, as they are expected to give a faithful account of the author's travel experiences. However, this generalization does not seem to apply to all cases. Example (13) is from Jonathan Raban's travel book *Hunting Mister Heartbreak*.

(13)   The trees that had been skeletal and grey the day before were coming into leaf this morning . . . The harder I stepped on the gas, the faster I could make things grow. I made the first magnolia burst suddenly into flower, woke the first snake from hibernation . . . At the rate I was going, it would be fall by Tuesday morning.[10]

This brief fragment seems to be telling a rather sober story about what the narrator did, but we quickly realize that he could not have actually seen or done any of these things – plants usually need more than a day to go from winter gray to leaf, stepping on the gas can make the car, but not time, go faster; people do not cause seasonal changes in nature, etc. We have no choice but to conclude that the description is figurative.

The fragment relies on a rather elaborate and innovative blend. The narrator is describing his impressions while driving down from New York City to Alabama; he is going south, and observing the changes in the appearance of nature. While it is still wintry and gray up north, it is green and spring-like in the south. But because the transition is gradual and in fact correlated with the motion of the car caused by pressing the gas pedal, the blend constructed in the text attributes causation to the driver via the The X-er the Y-er Comparative Correlative Construction (Fillmore et al. 1988). This construction (as in *the more the merrier*) pairs two scales and construes the change in one as correlated with (and often the cause of) change in the other. Here, the construction pairs the speed of driving with the speed of changes in nature, thus attributing the change to the driver's actions. More explicit causative constructions (*make X happen*) support this construal.

Crucially, however, the blend represents not what the driver *does*, but the changes he *sees* outside the window of the car. It is thus an example in which a figurative construal is not meant to give a new understanding of the situation, but to make the direct experience of the events described accessible to the reader. This kind of construal abounds in creative travel writing and fiction in general, but is not unique to literary texts (Dancygier 2005, 2012a). The crucial point is that we often think of travel literature as a genre which is as close to "pure"

---

[10] Jonathan Raban, *Hunting Mister Heartbreak*, New York: HarperCollins, 1991 (first published in 1990), p. 112.

factual description as it is possible to be, but in fact, experiential meanings are common in all genres.

In example (13) above, the figurative construal represents the driver's experience of the trip, rather than the objective facts of it. It does so through the unconventional use of certain constructions, including the use of causation constructions where all that was in fact observed was change. This, in turn, is supported by the Location ESM, especially mappings such as CAUSATION IS FORCED MOVEMENT and CHANGE IS MOTION. While the reading of movement as change would have been justified by any one of these metaphors, the constructions used prompt the further reading of motion in terms of causation. In the reality of the trip, causing motion by pressing on the gas pedal also causes a change in the view outside. But the construal proposed does not refer to motion at all – just to change. It is a change in perception, but it is presented as a change caused by the actions of the driver (which are now decoupled from the fact that they are causing the car to move). In its use of figurative means, the narrative here is as innovative as works of poetry, and, like many instances of poetic discourse, focuses on experience, not facts.

8.5   The discourse of science

Metaphors and analogies abound in the discourse of science, whether in high theorizing or in pedagogy. It has often been noted that these are elaborate, extended construals, which are relational in nature and allow one to understand a complex or not-yet-understood phenomenon in terms which can be grasped with some ease. What we want to show in this section is that science metaphors provide specific models with testable inferences – in other words, metaphor in science is a scientific tool, not just an example of figurative language. At the same time, the examples show that conceptualization of one phenomenon in terms of another does not affect specificity or coherence – on the contrary, the inferential power of the construal increases. In fact, Lakoff and Núñez (2000) have argued cogently that modern mathematics, generally considered the paragon example of rigorous argumentation and inference in model-building, is essentially metaphoric in most of its structure. We will next examine some examples from physical science discourse.

Importantly, we may develop more than one model of a phenomenon and reason about it in different ways. Gentner and Gentner (1983) did a pioneering study in which they examined the relationship between subjects' analogical (metaphoric, in our terms) models of electricity and their ability to solve problems about electrical systems. In particular, they looked at two commonly used folk models, ELECTRICAL CURRENT IS FLOWING WATER (WIRES ARE PIPES OR CONDUITS) and ELECTRICAL CURRENT IS MOVING CROWDS OF OBJECTS (WIRES ARE PASSAGES, RESISTORS ARE NARROW GATES). The subjects were high-school and college students, and the problems they were given were circuit diagrams involving batteries and resistors; they were asked whether the current at some particular location would be the same as at another location, or twice as much, or half as much. The Moving Crowd model turned out to be helpful to students in understanding resistors: it brought out the source-domain inference that two doors side-by-side will let people out of an auditorium faster than one door, while passing through two doors in sequence will only slow things down. And this is the right answer in the target domain: two resistors in parallel pass through twice the current that would be passed by one, while two resistors in series pass half the current that would be passed by one. On the other hand, the Water model should have been ideal for batteries. Two serial reservoirs, one above the other, make for double the height of the water and thus double the resulting water pressure coming out, while two side-by-side reservoirs of the same height and connected to the same outlet will let out exactly the same water pressure as a single reservoir, but the flow will last twice as long. This corresponds to the fact that serial batteries produce twice the current produced by a single battery, while parallel-connected batteries produce the same current as a single battery for twice as long. Unfortunately, students mostly did not know about the relationship between water pressure and current, and hence did not have the right inferences about the source domain of hydraulics, so the Water model did not help them as much with the serial-battery problems as it could have. Nonetheless, consistent users of the Water model still did better than Moving Crowd modelers on parallel battery problems, and Moving Crowd users did better on resistor problems, as predicted.

One important point to take away from this study is that it not only takes seriously the question of how people apply figurative models to scientific domains, it also takes seriously the idea that some models may be good for different purposes than others. Both in teaching and in research, a given metaphoric model brings certain inferences into salience and offers certain affordances for further reasoning or questions, while another metaphoric model may have other affordances. In other words, in solving science problems, metaphoric models and their inferences play a big part in our understanding.

8.5.1   Modeling the atom and scientific creativity

The physicist Niels Bohr remains a paragon of scientific creativity, so let us use one of his models as an example of the ways in which metaphoric inferential structure is centrally involved in reasoning and conceptualization in the physical sciences. It is also a good example of a metaphor which does not involve mapping between a concrete source domain and an abstract target domain.

The Bohr model of the atom as a solar system was a major scientific step forward when it was introduced in 1913, and it is now known to many millions of science students. The Bohr model sees the atomic nucleus as a "sun" (composed of the more massive protons and neutrons) and the much less massive electrons as "planets" rotating the sun. It thus understands one very complex and perceptually inaccessible physical system, the Atom, in terms of another very complex physical system which is only partially perceptually accessible – a great deal of inference is involved in using physical observations to build a model of the Solar system. We cannot call this understanding an abstract domain in terms of a concrete one, though we can clearly say that the solar system was better understood at that time, more cognitively accessible to scientists, than subatomic structure.

The Bohr model ignores some very obvious differences between the domains. The mass ratio between the sun and the planets, although it varies with the planet, is not assumed to be the same as the precise mass ratio between the nucleus and the electrons. There is no precise analogy in the solar system to the opposite positive and negative charges of protons and electrons; it is assumed that mass, momentum, velocity, and gravitic forces are the determinants of actual planetary orbitals. However, the solar system model provided some crucial basic inferences about atoms – ones which physicists already knew to be right. For example, if atoms (originally thought to be the smallest physical unit, hence the Greek-derived name *a-tom*, 'un-splittable') really did have smaller parts of differing mass and charge (as Rutherford and others had discovered), then why and how did those smaller parts cohere, move together, maintain a stable internal structure, and so on? The original Rutherford "plum pudding model" of the atom did not really explain this – it just referred to the compact shared space of the parts. However, by the time subatomic particles were discovered, scientists were well aware that stars and galaxies are not immobile, and that solar systems do move as units in space – and they knew the basic cause of this kind of physical coherence, namely gravitational attraction between the sun and planets. They also had models of stable orbits, which explained why gravity doesn't just make the planets instantly fall into the sun, or the moon into the earth. And in order to get those models, physicists had had to take into account the fact that there could be gravitational interaction between any pair of bodies in a solar system – the planets interact with each other's orbits, as the sun's gravity interacts with them all. The solar-system metaphor thus further correctly suggested the possibility of more complex internal atomic structure than just the nucleus mass attracting each electron, and even the possibility of electrons being attracted away from an atom by the attraction of another atom.

As later physics modelers came along and modeled some more complex sub-atomic interactions – pairs of electrons in orbitals, and extremely different orbital forms for "excited" electrons or those more distant from the nucleus – there were no obvious solar-system analogies for those. There are no counterparts to quantized energy states in solar systems, nor can two or more solar systems form a new stable shared unit (as atoms can form a stable molecule). So more complex models followed. Schools still do use the Bohr model as students' first introduction to the atom, because the students have already learned about the solar system, and the metaphor is useful in starting to give them the right kinds of inferences.

The most important point here is that the Bohr model got scientists to transfer to the structures of atoms *not only* general aspects of solar-system structure, but also the *mathematical models* which had been developed to express precise understandings of larger physical objects and orbits, and to make predictions about their behavior. Those models proved insufficient for subatomic structure – but, as in many applications of insufficient models, their application changed the science. Metaphor is not just fuzzy conceptual transfer, it is precise conceptual mapping that includes specific inferences; and in scientific modeling, that often means the transfer of computational models from one domain to another.

8.5.2   The status of science metaphors

8.5.2.1   Theory-constitutive metaphors

In her monograph on metaphor in various discourse types, Semino (2008) refers to Boyd (1993), who proposes a distinction between *pedagogical* and *theory-constitutive* metaphors in science. The proposed claim is based on distinguishing between different types of starting points for construal. If there exists a technical, complete formulation of the problem, and metaphor is used to explain it in more accessible terms to students, then the use is merely pedagogical and does not affect the scientific view. If, for comparison, metaphor is used in formulating the original description of the phenomenon, then it plays a theory-constitutive role.

Intuitively, the distinction seems valid, simply because colloquial or pedagogical discourse may opt for a model that does not feel accurate – for example, the role of DNA has been talked about as that of a *code*, a *blueprint*, and a *book*, and none of these models seems to yield the exact inferences the theory requires (for more discussion, see Nelkin 2001 and Nerlich and Dingwall 2003). At the same time, Semino observes that Boyd's distinction may be hard to maintain because science concepts are talked about in so many contexts and for so many different reasons. However, other responses to Boyd's proposal seem to shed a different light on the problem.

For example, Steinhart (2001) fully supports the distinction. Steinhart's work focuses on Possible Worlds Theory and the logical interpretation of metaphors, but his theory also assumes that metaphoric statements achieve truth or falsehood in their own right, without reference to literal meaning. In this context, he focuses on what he considers to be theory-constitutive metaphors. Importantly, he presents theory-constitutive metaphors as those which can be tested like other hypotheses and are, at a given time, linguistically indispensable (the metaphorical terms are used as technical terms to describe a phenomenon) and accepted by a broader scientific community. Based on these assumptions, Steinhart describes modeling the atom in terms of the solar system as not being theory-constitutive, because our knowledge of the atom has progressed from that model, but the understanding of Electricity as Fluid as theory-constitutive. It seems to us that this suggests that metaphors may change their status over time (much as in Gentner and

Bowdle's [2008] hypothesis about the "career of a metaphor"). This seems right in the context of the other part of the description, concerning the acceptance in the scientific community: once scientists come up with a more up-to-date model, a metaphor loses its status. Most importantly, it seems to us that the linguistic status of "terminology" also plays a big role in the description of a metaphor as theory-constitutive.

We argue, then, that a somewhat more useful categorization of science metaphors would be in terms of the kinds of inferences the metaphors yield. Bohr's model of the atom, as we showed above, at least *was* theory-constitutive at the time, because it yielded important inferences which were considered testable. What is more, this criterion is independent of linguistic usage, which is our focus – the same linguistic forms could reflect a theory-constitutive metaphor at one stage in the history of science, and subsequently be used as part of a pedagogical one (like the Bohr Atom). Linguists can, however, discuss the inferences a metaphorical model yields, and both of the examples we looked at above (models of electricity and the atom) show that the metaphorical models in question do yield inferences used in problem solving, whether the context is pedagogical or theoretical. The criterion of theory-constitutiveness seems to be a criterion about the nature of science, not language.

8.5.2.2   Source domains in science

Semino raises another problem of importance – how is the source related to the target in scientific metaphors? Many metaphor analysts expect that the source will be a domain which is more familiar to the hearer, and more concrete – and that the source structure is then used in allowing us to reason about the less familiar target. As we have shown in Chapters 2 and 3, these generalizations are often overstated, and as we pointed out, language users can reason from quite different types of sources as long as the structure yields accurate inferences. Some of the examples Semino analyzes (2008, 2010 (see also Dancygier 2012a)) use sources which have been constructed specifically for the purpose of representing the target. Among other things, she discusses an example from a textbook in which a very elaborate scenario, describing completely unrealistic octopuses behaving in ways octopuses do not behave, is used to explain the nature of neural networks. The point of the example, at least in part, is that the source domain in a science metaphor can in fact be constructed to suit the target (rather than the other way around, as we would expect), giving it more flair and concreteness and allowing for the use of more colloquial vocabulary.

Semino's discussion leads to interesting questions. Perhaps the problem is in the general (often unstated) expectation of a strict unidirectional projection from the source into the target – in other words, the problem arises if we insist on the view of metaphor which assumes a *prior* understanding of the source. But the setting up of an original source input also creates a domain, which *then* can be used in reasoning about the target: as we discussed in Chapter 4, projection between domains is selective, and depends on a shared generic space. This in turn may require a particular construal of the source domain itself, or highlighting aspects of that domain which allow mapping to the target. The "unrealistic" scenario can yield the kind of generic space which can then guide the projections and inferences – we believe that such cases support the need for analysts to be specific about the generic space as the source of the coherence across domains. It is then still true that the speaker's/writer's understanding of the target dictates the choice of the nature of the source, but the formulation in the source has to be accessible to the hearer/reader, and allow for the right inferences. It does not matter whether the source scenario is in fact realistic or not, and it does not matter whether the goal is pedagogical or not. The differences that we see are in the lexical and constructional choices the scientists make, and these are selected with the reader/hearer in mind. In other words, being a discourse phenomenon, metaphor chooses not only the nature of the domain to be used as a source, but also the vocabulary which makes the source a good vehicle for understanding the target. Whether the goal is explanatory or theoretical, the choice of vocabulary is central to achieving that goal.

This goal sometimes yields results which are stylistically quite striking. Example (14) is from Richard Dawkins's famous book *The selfish gene*. The text is an explanation of a scientific standpoint, but it is often written in a style that seems to be trying to not only explain the phenomenon, but engage the reader emotionally – mostly by offering a view of humans that readers may find hard to accept. The gene, in Dawkins's text, is a miraculous creature:

(14)   It does not grow senile, it is no more likely to die when it is a million years old than when it is only a hundred . . . It leaps from body to body down the generations, manipulating body after body in its own way and for its own ends, abandoning a succession of mortal bodies before they sink in senility and death . . .
        [Genes] swarm in huge colonies, safe inside gigantic lumbering robots, sealed off from the outside world, communicating with it by torturous indirect routes, manipulating it by remote control.[11]

Genes are here modeled after humans, but they are more like gods – immortal, capable of moving anywhere, and always getting what they want. Humans, in this view, are deprived of any importance or agency; their illusions of selfhood and control are totally misguided. Beyond these emotionally loaded construals, the language actually yields a number of important scientific claims, describing evolution as the engine behind the scenes, explaining the role of molecular structure in the shaping of the living world, describing the hidden causes of processes that affect humans, individually and collectively. The metaphor of the Selfish Gene has enormous inferential power – it shifts the understanding of survival from the level of an individual to the level of the species, redefines the concepts of *causation* and *agency*, reconstrues our behavior as communication

[11] Richard Dawkins, *The selfish gene*, Oxford University Press, 2004.

among genes, etc. The text as a whole is both pedagogical and theoretical – as Hamilton said in his review published in *Science*:

(15)   It succeeds in the seemingly impossible task of using simple, untechnical English to present some rather recondite and quasi-mathematical themes of recent evolutionary thought.[12]

We might add that the choice of source domain in the fragment quoted above is unusual in many ways. It is impossible to say if it is realistic or not, but it is extremely clear and powerful – though it is also not too flattering to us humans. It was probably enough pedagogically to say that genes don't age, rather than to remind humans that, unlike genes, some of us become *senile*. We could have been described in terms more elegant than *gigantic lumbering robots*. In other words, the choice of the source domain is excellent here, but there are much more extensive consequences to the choice of the actual vocabulary to represent that domain. The relational nature of the Selfish-Gene metaphor does not play the same role in the text as the stylistic choices Dawkins has made. This reinforces the view we have been trying to express here – that metaphors, including those in science, construct conceptual configurations that yield inferences, but the choice of specific metaphorical expressions is also an esthetic, stylistic, and eventually also terminological choice. Words prompt the construals, but the construals go deeper than the reader's concepts of described events or situations – they also cause esthetic and emotional relations to those descriptions. And metaphors, as discourse choices, do the same things.

8.6   Religious metaphor

Although in other contexts, analysts have seen figurative language as an "extra" and literal language as the basic framework of meaning, this relationship is inverted in cases where literal language is seen as *radically insufficient*. Language about Divinity is a central example of such a situation, where metaphor is often seen as essential. Jewish and Christian theologians have very long agreed that God is only very partially accessible to human experience, while that partial experience in turn is impossible to fully express in human language. The Divine *transcends* (or "rises above and beyond") the limits of human thought and language, which are seen as containers too small to contain such a huge and high object (corresponding to an immensely important and powerful concept). However, if people have a communal concept of the Divine, they will need to talk about it. So, to talk about the transcendent and the ineffable, Judeo-Christian practitioners and thinkers have traditionally had recourse to metaphor – as have members

---

[12] W. D. Hamilton, "The play by nature," *Science*, May 13, 1977, pp. 757–9. Review of *The selfish gene* by Richard Dawkins.

of many other religious traditions, whether world religions or local ones. And this is because metaphor is seen as to some extent "transcending" literal meaning. We have already commented in Chapter 3 that Greco-Roman gods were often personifications of abstract qualities, and in Chapter 5 that Christian iconography for the saints used frame-metonymic markers to identify them; religious art and tradition are full of figurative structures. Figurative language is not only pervasive in religious discourse; certain metaphors (e.g. GOD AS SHEPHERD) may even be seen as defining characteristics of particular religious discourse genres.

We would like here to focus on a few issues, specifically (1) the relationship of religious metaphor to the general metaphor system of a culture, (2) cultural variation in religious metaphor, and (3) the ways in which the same metaphors permeate religious linguistic expression and religious art and architecture. But first we need to respond to readers who may be noticing that various world religions have strands (sometimes labeled *fundamentalist*) that emphasize the literal truth of holy texts, and thus may read Genesis to mean that the world was literally created in a week, whereas other strands of the same traditions may interpret the same text more figuratively. This debate is a very old one, and a particularly heated and high-stakes example of the kind of opposing views of figurative language which we mentioned in Chapter 1. Metaphor in particular has been understood both as subrational and as superrational: as a false, deceptive addition to the basically literal (truthful) nature of language, and also as a somehow transcendent "superlanguage" which allows artistic and spiritual expression of higher Truths beyond literal expression.[13] Theologians and users of religious texts are no exception to this division. The Romantic poets would align themselves with the theologians who see metaphor as transcendent, and it seems as if many logicians align themselves with the subrational view of metaphor; ironically, this puts the Romantics in a camp with St. Augustine, and the logicians in a camp with fundamentalists who may disagree with them deeply on other issues.

Cognitive Metaphor Theory has argued that neither of these opposing views can be right – rather, metaphor is such a pervasive aspect of human thought and language that it is part and parcel of human rationality. And indeed, fundamentalists don't actually seem to escape metaphoric interpretation and expression. The same people who say they take literally the claim that the Creation happened in seven days also pervasively address God as *Father*, *Shepherd*, and *King*; and they do not think that Christ's parables are to be read literally. They interpret *Do not hide your light under a bushel* (a reference to a parable which occurs in three of the Gospels) as advice about moral behavior, rather than about lamps and baskets. And many of them would agree that they need metaphors to talk about God – so they apparently espouse, for different texts, both the subrational and the superrational models of figurative language.

One thing which emerges saliently from the study of religious metaphor is how frequently religious language simply applies more general metaphors to

---

[13] A survey of this millennia-long debate can be found in Johnson (1981).

the domain of religion. Seeing the Divine as High, *above* humans – possibly on mountaintops or in the sky – is something that most world religions seem to share, as well as many local and regional ones (as Bickel [1997], documented for the Belhare). And this is exactly what we might predict from the Primary Metaphors POWER IS UP and GOOD IS UP. The more we are talking about a good and all-powerful deity, the more these metaphors seem inevitable; though we may note that powerful deities who are not good, or who are associated with Death, may be seen as being underground instead. Crosscultural associations between Cleanliness and Moral Purity are also pervasive (see Lakoff and Johnson 1999 on metaphors for Morality), and may be seen as part of a Primary Metaphor based on a correlation between cleanness and well-being. Of course, these metaphors play out quite differently in different cultural contexts. Dead bodies are specified as a source of ritual pollution in Jewish tradition, so traditionally Cohens (Jewish priestly tribe members) cannot even enter cemeteries, whereas it is one of the duties of a Catholic or a Shinto practitioner to visit family graves – focusing not on metaphoric pollution connected with the unpleasant decay of dead bodies, but on the frame-metonymic connection between a beloved or admired dead person and their grave (Fauconnier and Turner 2002 discuss graves as *material anchors*).

Metaphors for God are often better understood as metaphors for the Divine–Human Relationship; that is, it makes more sense to say that they are about human interaction with God, or God's interaction with humans. DesCamp and Sweetser (2005) point out that the source domains for the pervasive Judeo-Christian metaphors for God as Father, King, and Shepherd all evoke frames involving a positive and strongly power-asymmetric relationship between two participant roles. To understand God as a Father, humans must be God's Children; if God is a King, humans are Subjects; if God is a Shepherd, humans are Sheep. God as Mother or Queen seems particularly difficult for these monotheistic traditions to assimilate as a metaphor; Greco-Roman Mediterranean cultures, which were also patriarchal but polytheistic, had a strong mother-goddess tradition alongside their Divine Father Zeus. But some might argue that the place of the Virgin Mary in Catholic tradition (sometimes called the Queen of Heaven) is filling some of that need for a feminine and maternal understanding of the Divine. Of course, once again, the metaphor GOD IS A FATHER is culturally variable; one cannot imagine it meaning the same thing to a modern European or American Christian that it may have meant in ancient Hebrew or Greco-Roman culture, where a father could legally sell his child.

And finally, religious metaphors are not only linguistic; they are built into physical rituals, artifacts, and buildings. Why is the altar higher than the worshippers, and why do they bow or kneel to it? Presumably they are enacting POWER IS UP in both their architecture and their ritual. Much ritual involves metaphoric *performative* blends – that is, blends that are enacted not to describe but to *bring about* the situation depicted (Sweetser 2000). Eating bread and drinking wine – which (in the blend) are Christ's body and blood – brings about literal union of that bread and wine with the worshipper's body; the goal is thereby to bring about metaphoric and spiritual union of the worshipper's soul with Christ. Physical structures – high altars and steeples, or physical path structures such as the Chartres cathedral labyrinth – are built to instantiate metaphors such as POWER IS UP and ESSENTIAL IS CENTRAL for worshippers (Stec and Sweetser 2013).

We might naively think of religious discourse – particularly discourse about God – as highly abstract and disembodied. But examination of actual religious discourse shows us that it is spoken, written, and understood by embodied humans, using their Primary Metaphors and their cultural frames of experience. And, as with any disputed discourse mode, disagreement with some metaphoric religious mode of discourse (such as Father and King metaphors for God) normally means having full access to that mode of discourse, and probably the cognitive discomfort which can come from simultaneous access to conflicting models. Religious discourse and religious-text interpretation are hugely important aspects of human thought and culture, seen as basic in guiding humans' understanding of morality and behavior. Modern metaphor analysis has barely scratched the surface of this domain, but much more work can be hoped for in the future.[14]

8.7 Conclusions

Studying the use of figurative language in various discourse types is important. It may illuminate the specific strategies used in discourse, help us obtain a better understanding of discourse specificity, and add to our understanding of linguistic structure. We do not have space here to talk about literature in every genre of interest in any more detail, but we hope that this discussion has not only given readers a sense of the issues, but raised some important potential further questions. We have also not looked at types of discourse which are more often studied, such as journalistic prose or advertising (especially the visual use of metaphors in advertising). But our goal was not to give the broadest view possible of the role of figurative language in discourse; rather, we have tried to point out some possible directions of study which would yield conclusions useful to various areas of linguistics, not only to the study of a specific genre. In this, we have followed some of the directions outlined in Dancygier et al. (2012[2010]) and pointed out some other avenues of inquiry.

Rhetorical or stylistic text analyses are often thought of by linguists as "applied" usage of the theoretical models developed by linguists – particularly, perhaps, because analysts interested in linguistic structure may be more or less willing to plunge into the debates of other domains such as Science, Education, or Politics. But of course, in an era when practically all linguistic models are based on corpus data, it is crucial to understand the characteristics of genres and

---

[14] Biblical scholars have been developing an interest in cognitive linguistic models of literature. References to some of this work can be found in Howe and Sweetser (in press).

authors, not just of languages as a whole. And it is to be hoped that text-based models of figurative language will in turn prove useful in elucidating texts. As we have seen, the same *kinds* of mappings and structures do recur across genres and authorial purposes; it is the *choices* of mappings that are much more varied.

8.8   Summary

The role of figurative language in discourse is a vast and complex topic. In this chapter, we have looked at selected areas of discourse to illustrate some tendencies, but also at some discourse-specific phenomena. First, we noted that the effects of figurative expressions depend to a large degree on the viewpoint taken. We have shown that very similar metaphors may have different interpretive effects when viewpoint changes; we argued that the choice of metaphors may be less directed at the representation of the phenomenon in question and more focused on the ways in which an experiencer is affected. We also considered examples where irony is not just an independent trope but depends crucially on prior figurative construals.

In addition, we have looked at figurative construals used in political argumentation. Importantly, these may be expressed through figurative constructions found less often in spontaneous colloquial discourse. Furthermore, political argumentation often relies on frames in ways which are directed at constructing hierarchies of frames, rather than on simple frame evocation. We also considered the roles metonymy can play in discourse.

The final two sections of the chapter dealt with areas of discourse which are often contrasted – literature and science. What we saw was that the range of metaphorical choices in literature demonstrates differing expectations about reader involvement, while metaphor in science is more specifically directed at prompting accurate construals. We also noted that figurative language plays an extremely important role in the discourse of science, regardless of the context. Metaphoric and analogical models seem to be the "bread-and-butter" of scientific thought. Overall, figurative language and thought are an important aspect of a variety of discourse genres, illuminating both the role of discourse forms in the construal and the power of figurative forms of expression.

9   Concluding remarks

Throughout this book, we have been gradually building a picture of what figurative language is and what it does; we would like to highlight some of the main points here. The analyses we have proposed address two issues which are to some degree separate. On the one hand, we have been postulating a theoretical approach which seems to yield insightful analyses of figurative structures, and to allow us to generalize across these structures crossculturally and across modalities. On the other hand, we have been trying to clarify the ways in which the question of figurative language can most fruitfully be addressed within linguistics: the approach we have chosen allows us to give satisfying accounts specifically of aspects of the structure of language. We will review some of our general claims below.

9.1   Theoretical postulates

Theories of figurative language have often addressed only those levels of analysis which seemed central to the type of linguistic inquiry chosen. So, for example, in discussions of discourse goals, researchers often choose the level of figurative structure which is most apparent in the vocabulary choices of the text in question. As a result, especially in discussions of metaphor, the mappings identified are often special cases of much broader metaphors. Thus there are numerous discussions in the literature of X as a Journey, when a broad image of goal-oriented motion is actually evoked by the examples, or of X as War, when some conflicting forces are at stake. To do justice to the nature of figurative language, we need to claim and identify exactly the mappings instantiated by the text at hand – however specific or schematic those may be – rather than the mappings involved in a particular previously identified metaphor. The understanding of texts and discourse would be enriched by identifying the ways in which specific metaphoric structures fit into higher level schematic ones – or motivate specific subcases. Crucially, one level of analysis does not preclude another; if LIFE IS A JOURNEY is active, then more general mappings such as PURPOSES ARE DESTINATIONS and ACTION IS FORWARD MOTION are also *necessarily* active, not just simultaneously but as part of the activation of LIFE IS A JOURNEY.

9.1.1   Levels of schematicity and levels of interpretation

We have therefore been proposing a multilevel model of analysis, starting with image schemas, through Primary Metaphors, to more complex structural constructs relying on richer frames/domains (metaphors, metonymies, or blends) – which are evoked by linguistic forms and constructions. We tried to show that engaging with various levels of schematicity yields very specific benefits. First of all, it helps in structuring a more complex and more accurate understanding of figurative language. The practice of picking out cases of polysemy in a text and describing them all in terms of a single broad metaphor misses important points about the actual constructs represented by these vocabulary items – different words in a sentence or text may be making complementary contributions to fleshing out figurative mappings. Also, not every figuratively used expression is metaphoric, and the more specific we can be about what does and does not constitute a metaphoric expression, the better we will understand the expressions in which actual metaphors are used.

Secondly, being specific about levels of schematicity helps in avoiding the simplistic understanding of figurative meaning which sees the primary issue as the separation between literal and figurative, rather than the motivating relation between them. As we have shown throughout this book, figurative meanings build on literal concepts, and should be understood as systematically related to them. It is important to explain how the expression *get somewhere* can have both a literal spatial meaning, and a metaphoric sense of progress in achieving a purpose – and in order to understand that connection, we need to understand the spatial schemas involved and the Primary Metaphors within the Event Structure cluster. A rigorous description needs to explain how we conceptually get from one meaning to the other. This is what the linguistic study of figurative language should do.

In their recent book, cognitive scientists Hofstadter and Sander (2013) give an impressive overview of the range of instances in which analogical thought plays a crucial role in meaning emergence. We agree with them that broadly construed analogical patterns underlie much of the usage labeled as *figurative language* in this book and that, from a broader perspective, all of the usage described here relies on some level of analogical thought. However, we also believe that it is the linguist's job to look for specific patterns represented by specific language forms. The correlations between linguistic form and figurative meaning are not obvious, but they are there. What we tried to do throughout this book is to give as accurate a picture of such correlations as possible at this point.

One might ask, why make it so complicated? Why not just get at the meaning of an expression starting from the literal meaning via context? Context is crucial to all meaning interpretation, figurative and otherwise – and indeed, in context it is usually clear whether a speaker's use of *get somewhere* refers to spatial motion or to achieving an abstract purpose. But without other analytic tools, such an approach misses a large number of generalizations – and these generalizations are more appropriately handled within semantics, rather than being relegated to pragmatics. For example, talking only about the contexts of specific utterances would not capture the generalization that language referring to physical Goal-directed Motion is systematically used, in many different contexts, to refer to Purposive Action. It might also miss the relations between levels of schematicity which structure figurative language as dependent on networks of related and unrelated concepts at different levels. Looking at various levels of structure to arrive at the level appropriate for the explanation of an expression allows us to see how expressions are related, and also how figurative *meanings* can be related. Also, starting from the most schematic level allows us to develop explanations across communicative modalities – noticing parallel structures in spoken language, gesture, and sign language, and also across expressive modalities (visual art, architecture, and language). A complex construal of time may be supported by a simple spatial gesture, not because the gesture expresses any particular complex metaphor of the TIME AS RELATIVE MOTION family, but because both forms of expression rely on similar schematic levels of conceptual structure.

Finally, a careful choice of the schematic level of analysis helps in properly understanding the multiple interpretations various readers/listeners arrive at. Especially when one is discussing creative forms of language, one has to be particularly open to the idea that different viewers/listeners/readers will interpret figurative forms differently. This is not because the meanings of creative expressions are more unpredictable or more vague than those of literal expressions, it is because a variety of inferences can be derived depending on the level of schematic structure and the framing chosen. The more specific our analyses are, the better we can understand multiplicity of meaning. Our goal as analysts of language should be to describe linguistic structures in a way that allows for their multiple interpretations in different contexts – or even for a multiplicity of readings by the same reader in one context.

It is particularly easy to overgeneralize mappings when one particular level of mapping has become conventionally salient in a culture. One common example is the domain of a Journey, which has been identified as the source domain of mappings in extremely varied examples, contexts, and texts. We cannot help but be reminded of a *New Yorker* cartoon portraying a man and a woman having a drink in some elegant social space, looking like they might be starting a flirtation; the woman says excitedly to the man, *OMG, I'm on a journey too!* The cartoon seems to be pointing out that LIFE IS A JOURNEY has become a rather empty cliché, presumably suggesting higher goals and sensitivities. But because of its ubiquitousness, the phrase has lost its meaning. We are worried that the same might be happening to analysts – an undoubtedly common mapping is becoming the one mapping worth discussing. We believe that no two metaphorical journeys are the same, and we need to dig deeper to uncover the added specific mappings involved in a given text. The cartoon, appropriately, avoids even the suggestion of such richer mappings, since it is only trying to evoke the cliché.

Overgeneralization of figurative meanings misses important points about how such meanings are arrived at, in creative and colloquial contexts alike. In principle, there is no reason to separate the two, as the mechanisms are the same, but developing a specific understanding of the processes involved relies on an appreciation of different aspects of meaning arising at different levels. In this book, we did not have much space to talk about how broad historical or cultural frames affect varying interpretations. In attempting to appreciate texts from different languages and cultures, it is essential to identify and analyze culture-specific frames. These particular frames, not some generic frames, will be involved in literal semantics, and extended in figurative mappings between frames: as noted in Chapter 8, the metaphor GOD IS A FATHER is surely not the same blend for modern English speakers as it was for ancient Near Eastern cultures where a father could sell his children.

At the other end of the analytical spectrum, carefully considering the constructions typically used to support figurative meanings also adds to our understanding of syntax and its contribution to meaning. Constructional meaning integrates with word meanings, both contributing meaning to the larger utterance and sometimes overriding lexical meaning. Constructional meanings can themselves be extended figuratively, and particular grammatical forms can be used systematically in the evocation of figurative structures. It is a grammarian's task to investigate the structure of grammar, and the relationship between form and meaning. One thing we hope is clear is that the vast majority of linguistic usage has figurative aspects to it. So until we integrate our investigation of figurative meaning construction and composition with our investigation of literal meaning, we will not have an account of meaning. Figurative data contributes to our analysis of the lexicon, of grammar, and of the relationship between them.

9.1.2   Viewpoint and experience

In past chapters we have noted that figurative meanings, like literal meanings, are inherently viewpointed, whichever level we look at. Considering viewpoint phenomena has given us an opportunity to enrich our interpretations significantly. We started by observing that many metaphors rely on experiential viewpoint – usually of some participant in one of the scenes mapped. We talked at some length about the concept of Anger, but viewpoint is part of the structure of many other figurative patterns, including metonymy, blending, and constructionally bound grammatical forms like the genitive. Metaphoric mappings between frame roles have been discussed far more frequently than the viewpointed structures which are built by these mappings; but since frames are frequently viewpointed, it should come as no surprise that blends are too.

For example, the expression *My surgeon is a butcher* relies importantly on the fact that from the speaker's viewpoint as a patient, the surgeon cannot be trusted to consider the patient's welfare as the first goal (indeed, the potential added inference that the surgeon is incompetent seems, if anything, to come from this initial inference rather than the other way around). Similarly, *My job is (like) a jail* does not mean that the job itself is necessarily constraining the employee's actions (though presumably all jobs do that to some degree), but that the speaker *experiences* her employment as unpleasant and an excessive constraint. The metaphor works not because there are especially rich mappings between imprisonment and employment, but because the experiential viewpoint implied by the reference to a restricting barrier is mapped from the Jail domain to the Job domain. We argue that such instances are not sufficiently explained through the concept of *highlighting* (which acknowledges that all mappings are partial and highlight specific aspects of the structure), because it is not the general structure of the mappings and the domains which accounts for the inferences here, but specifically the viewpoint of some participant. Distinguishing the various ways in which mappings use domains deepens our understanding of figurative language, and viewpoint is certainly one of the important aspects we need to consider.

9.1.3   Analyzing discourse

Studies of figurative aspects of discourse (admittedly, largely focused on metaphor) have shown how broadly figurative language is applied, and what a central role it plays in the impact or accessibility of discourse genres. In addition to these general observations, we have tried to show that an approach which considers the impact of more schematic concepts (such as image schemas) also reveals the source of important differences in the construals prompted. In Chapter 8 we examined various texts relying on the concept of a Boundary, and noted that the metaphoric meanings built on that image schema in those texts are different. Sontag and Hitchens both use barriers to construe the experience of illness, but because they take different viewpoints, they come up with different construals. And when Barack Obama talks about overcoming barriers through history to make one small but significant act possible, he gives still another different meaning to the Boundary schema.

One could respond to this by saying that if Boundaries can mean so many different things, we should just look at the most schematic and least detailed level to describe the meaning: for example, just assume that barriers are impediments to motion and they will always therefore stand metaphorically for difficulties in action or in achieving changes of state. But doing this would limit our understanding of the conceptual phenomena involved. There is a difference between uncovering the meanings of particular discourse instances and uncovering the mechanisms that make those meanings possible. We have shown that, in addressing the mechanisms, the most schematic level of meaning is crucial in constraining the types of inferences a text can yield: a Boundary could not be thought of as facilitating action. But the schema of a Boundary yields different experiential inferences depending on participant viewpoint – one can be on the desirable side of the barrier or the undesirable one, the barriers could be purposely erected to protect us or to restrict us, we may want to overcome barriers or hide behind them, etc. Thinking of a specific situation – e.g. being shut out of a location where others are allowed to go, as opposed to being safely surrounded by walls that protect one from harm – could make all the difference in the inferences transferred to the target domain. All these inferences are based on enrichment of a basic schema by participant viewpoint, and the source of these inferences is what we need to understand in order to understand the emergence of meanings in each individual case. In other words, to give a linguistically satisfying analysis, we need to understand what the meaning is, and also how it has been constructed. And this involves many levels of schematicity.

9.1.4   The role of experimental work

We often hear colleagues say that any claims we make about the conceptual sources of meanings should eventually be confirmed through experiments. This is a justifiable expectation; social scientists and humanists alike need to be more aware of the relevance of cognitive science – and neuroscience – to their endeavors. If not, they risk proposing models of literature and society and language which could not be implemented by actual humans with actual bodies and brains. The inverse is also true, of course: cognitive science needs to be aware of the higher-level cognitive patterns observed by sociologists, linguists, and literary analysts. If not, they risk "explaining" only the phenomena which they have picked out, rather than the full range of cognitive phenomena. A feedback loop between experimental work and work outside the lab is necessary in any case; every intelligent experimental cognitive scientist knows that not every variety of complex human thought could happen in constrained lab settings, and every intelligent linguist should realize that it is useful to examine linguistic behavior and brain function in situations with fewer variables than rich social interaction.

We speak, of course, as linguists. Our primary goals are the systematic observation of structural patterns in language and the development of generalizations about those patterns. Some of these are easier than others for lab scientists to examine; at present, for example, there is no way to meaningfully observe the brain activities involved in "immersed" reading of a long, complex text. Discourse analysts have shown that textual viewpoint is an extremely complex and distributed phenomenon – so they are not interested primarily in the reading and comprehension of small, simplified texts created by experimenters. There is still a major gap between lab experiments showing that hearers of sentences construe described scenes in a viewpointed way and any future neuroscientific model of text viewpoint. This is exactly why the two sets of researchers should be talking to each other, and working on the feedback loop between their projects.

One aspect of this feedback loop is the way in which increased understanding of linguistic or social behavior can change the interpretation of lab results. For example, it has been shown that interpreting figurative language sometimes takes more processing time than understanding literal expressions. These results were used to support the claim that literal meaning needs to be computed first and then the incompatibility between the basic meaning and the figurative one needs to be resolved. However, the extended processing time could also be due to the need to construe frames and domains evoked in some of the complex ways we have been suggesting throughout the book. If an expression involves constructional meaning, frame metonymy, and blending (like many of the examples discussed in Chapter 6), it would not be surprising that more processing time is needed – though none of our specific examples have been experimentally examined, and it would obviously be challenging to tease out multiple aspects of figurative comprehension of a complex text in examining brain activity. In other words, the fact that certain types of expressions require more processing time does not tell us what that additional time is needed for. Linguists make hypotheses about how meaning emerges, but not about how that affects mental processing. It is not entirely clear to us to what degree the experiments are testing the specific hypotheses made by experimenters, or the general interpretive effort required. The more interaction there is between linguists and experimentalists, the more we will know about the validity of explanatory hypotheses.

In this chapter, we have so far discussed some general theoretical frameworks and issues that the work presented in this book puts in focus. In what follows, we will consider some of the specifically linguistic questions this book has raised.

9.2   Linguistic issues

At this point, we shall generally consider how the study of figurative language fits into the context of broader linguistic questions. It has been assumed quite often that figurative language eludes any disciplined discussion and is better left to those who study literature and other forms of creativity. But linguistic creativity is something that happens every day, as speakers work to express new meanings – and sometimes thus create new conventions. Our conviction was from the start that figurative language usage is a remarkable laboratory in which to see the creative potential of linguistic production, and that linguistic inquiries should start addressing such issues. We picked an approach based primarily in cognitive linguistic models (Cognitive Grammar, Construction Grammar, Conceptual Metaphor Theory, and Conceptual Integration Theory), and we have attempted to build a cohesive framework on the basis of all of them.

The single most basic issue is the difference between literal and figurative language. Quite often, the distinction is based on the language user's intuition – and, as a result, the work done on conceptual metaphor is dismissed by some, simply because they intuitively feel that extremely conventional and everyday usages cannot be figurative. We believe that these kinds of intuitions are not helpful, especially since they are not being tested in any rigorous way, but simply rely on common folk models of language. Trying to clarify the systematic nature of figurative meaning is the only sensible response, and this is what cognitive linguistics analysts have been doing. We have argued that meanings emerging through selective projections involving one or more frames generally qualify as figurative. Thus a metaphoric mapping, a simile, or a blend is figurative because it selects structure from two domains and reconstrues preexisting frames. Metonymy works within one domain (or across subdomains), but it also selects aspects of meaning to be focused on. Some of the modification constructions we discussed rely specifically on evoking frames and using their content in framing other referents. In general, cross-domain or cross-frame blending is by this understanding a basically figurative process, even when it is not metaphoric in nature. Overall, the manipulation and selective use of frames are at the core of the types of meanings that we refer to as *figurative*.

We have only been able to touch briefly on multimodality, but we believe that these patterns of figurative reconstrual are exemplified, even highlighted, in the multimodal aspects of language use. Much of our understanding of language finds support in the study of gesture, signed languages, or modes of expression which include pictorial as well as linguistic elements (comics, cartoons, ads, etc.). Also, the interaction between modalities is in itself a fertile object of study. For example, it has been observed that in cases of metaphor in advertisements, the visual part often represents the source domain while the text represents the target (Forceville 1996, Forceville and Urios-Aparisi 2009, Semino 2008); similarly, metaphoric gestures typically represent the source frame (e.g. spatial direction) and not the target frame (past or future). This is not surprising, since gesture and images can more readily represent more concrete domains. But such patterns reveal much about the structure and the interaction of the frames mapped, which needs to be reflected in the linguistic analyses. For example, if gestures use the spatial dimension to refer to temporal relations, this gives us added data on the use of space as a source domain for construals of time, and confirms the cognitively basic nature of those construals. Such correlations not only confirm the figurative nature of many linguistic expressions, but should also be used in testing our hypotheses concerning the nature of meaning.

To sum up, then, the picture we have been building assumes there are several levels of structure involved in meaning construction. All linguistic meaning relies on frames. When they enter into a figurative mapping pattern, such as a metaphor, frames become domains to be manipulated by the larger mapping pattern. Domains are manipulated in different ways by the different figurative patterns we have described; what the patterns share is the selection of material to be projected further, and the resulting reconstrual of the domain or domains, often accompanied by a viewpoint shift. Some of the more complex patterns require that a generic pattern be established prior to cross-frame mappings to guide the construal. These stages are shared by all of the figurative patterns we have discussed.

Some of the discussion of figurative language seems to be at base an argument over appropriate labels – is a given usage a metaphor or a blend? A simile or a metaphor? A metaphor or metonymy? We agree that these categories are all useful and should be clearly defined and distinguished – and we have tried to achieve that goal in the preceding chapters. But we also think that it is more important to pay attention to the patterns of reconstrual involved, as they can serve as the best criteria for making distinctions. The nature of figurative meaning should be the focus of the discussion – the choice of categorization and terminology needs to be justified by observations about the uses of the figurative patterns described, and how those usages are similar or different. Only by studying the patterns can we hope to ever integrate the study of figurative language into the study of language.

We have argued for an understanding of figurative language which addresses broad questions about the nature of the connection between form and meaning and proposes specific tools and patterns of analysis. Figuratively speaking, our enterprise was like making an elaborate quilt. We have tried to establish smaller patterns and select the right fabrics, but the bigger task was stitching the whole quilt together, giving it shape, color, texture, functional value, and esthetic appeal. On the other hand, it was also like a voyage of discovery, with inevitable dead-ends and detours, ups and downs. Perhaps one could say that we have been searching for the Atlantis of linguistic semantics. Or perhaps, along the way, we have become the Captain Cook of Simile and the Captain Vancouver of Metonymy. As a homework assignment, we invite our readers to launch their own expeditions in search of better figurative descriptions of what we have tried to achieve in this book.

References

Ahrens, Kathleen (ed.). 2009. *Politics, gender, and conceptual metaphors*. Palgrave Macmillan.

Ahrens, Kathleen, and Chu-Ren Huang. In press. Time passing is motion. *Language and Linguistics*.

Avrahami, Yael. 2012. *The senses of scripture: sensory perception in the Hebrew Bible*. Library of Hebrew Bible and Old Testament Studies 545. London and New York: T & T Clark.

Barcelona, Antonio (ed). 2000. *Metaphor and metonymy at the crossroads: a cognitive perspective*. Berlin: Walter de Gruyter.

Barth, John. 1986. A few words about minimalism. *New York Times Book Review*, Dec. 28, 1–3.

Benczes, Réka, Antonio Barcelona, and Francisco José Ruiz de Mendoza Ibáñez (eds.). 2011. *Defining metonymy in cognitive linguistics*. Amsterdam and Philadelphia: John Benjamins.

Bergen, Benjamin K. 2012. *Louder than words: the new science of how the mind makes meaning*. New York: Basic Books.

Bergen, Benjamin K., and Nancy Chang. 2005. Embodied Construction Grammar in simulation-based language understanding. In Östman and Fried (eds.), 147–90.

Berlin, Brent, and Paul Kay. 1969. *Basic color terms: their universality and evolution*. Berkeley: University of California Press.

Berlin, Brent, Dennis E. Breedlove, and Peter H. Raven. 1973. General principles of classification and nomenclature in folk biology. *American Anthropologist* 75(1), 214–42.

1974. *Principles of Tzeltal plant classification*. New York: Academic Press.

Bickel, Balthasar. 1997. Spatial operations in deixis, cognition, and culture: where to orient oneself in Belhare. In Jan Nuyts and Eric Pedersen (eds.), *Language and conceptualization*. Cambridge University Press, 46–83.

Bierwiaczonek, Bogusław. 2013. *Metonymy in language, thought and brain*. Sheffield, UK, and Bristol, CT: Equinox Publishing Ltd.

Boroditsky. Lera. 2000. Metaphoric structuring: understanding time through spatial metaphors. *Cognition* 75, 1–28.

Boroditsky, Lera, and Alice Gaby. 2010. Remembrances of times east: Absolute spatial representations of time in an Australian aboriginal community. *Psychological Science* 21, 1635–39.

Boroditsky, Lera, and Michael Ramscar. 2002. The roles of body and mind in abstract thought. *Psychological Science* 13, 185–89.

Bowerman, Melissa, and Soonja Choi. 2001. Shaping meanings for language: universal and language-specific in the acquisition of spatial semantic categories. In Melissa Bowerman and Stephen C. Levinson (eds.), *Language acquisition and conceptual development*. Cambridge University Press, 475–511.

Boyd, Richard. 1993. Metaphor and theory change: what is "metaphor" a metaphor for? In Ortony (ed.), 481–532.

Bradshaw, Graham, Tom Bishop, and Mark Turner (eds.). 2004. *Shakespeare studies today. The Shakespearean International Yearbook, vol. 4.* Aldershot, UK: Ashgate Publishing.

Brône, Geert, and Jeroen Vandaele (eds.). 2009. *Cognitive poetics: goals, gains, and gaps.* New York: de Gruyter.

Brooke-Rose, Christine. 1958. *A grammar of metaphor.* London: Secker and Warburg Ltd.

Calbris, Geneviève. 1990. *The semiotics of French gesture.* Trans. by Owen Doyle. Bloomington: Indiana University Press.

Cameron, Lynne. 2003. *Metaphor and educational discourse.* London: Continuum.

Casasanto, Daniel. 2009. Embodiment of abstract concepts: good and bad in right- and left-handers. *Journal of Experimental Psychology: General* 138(3), 351–67.

   2013. Development of metaphorical thinking: the role of language. In Mike Borkent, Barbara Dancygier, and Jennifer Hinnell (eds.), *Language and the creative mind.* Stanford, CA: CSLI Publications, 3–18.

Casasanto, Daniel, and Evangelia G. Chrysikou. 2011. When left is "right": motor fluency shapes abstract concepts. *Psychological Science* 22(4), 419–22.

Casasanto, Daniel, and Katinka Dijkstra. 2010. Motor action and emotional memory. *Cognition* 115(1), 179–85.

Casasanto, Daniel, and Kyle Jasmin. 2010. Good and bad in the hands of politicians: spontaneous gestures during positive and negative speech. *PLoS ONE* 5(7), e11805.

   2012. The hands of time: temporal gestures in English speakers. *Cognitive Linguistics* 23(4), 643–74.

Charteris-Black, Jonathan. 2004. *Corpus approaches to critical metaphor analysis.* New York: Palgrave Macmillan.

   2005. *Politicians and rhetoric: the persuasive power of metaphor.* New York: Palgrave Macmillan.

Chen, Mel Y. 2012. *Animacies: biopolitics, racial mattering, and queer affect (perverse modernities).* Durham and London: Duke University Press.

Chilton, Paul A. 1996. *Security metaphors: Cold War discourse from containment to common house.* New York: Peter Lang.

   2004. *Analysing political discourse: theory and practice.* London: Routledge Chapman & Hall.

Cienki, Alan. 1998. Metaphoric gestures and some of their relations to verbal metaphoric counterparts. In Koenig (ed.), 189–205.

Cienki, Alan and Cornelia Müller (eds.). 2008. *Metaphor and gesture.* Amsterdam and Philadelphia: John Benjamins.

Clark, Herbert. 1973. Space, time, semantics and the child. In Timothy E. Moore (ed.), *Cognitive development and the acquisition of language.* New York: Academic Press, 27–63.

Clausner, Timothy C., and William Croft. 1997. Productivity and schematicity in metaphors. *Cognitive Science* 21(3), 247–82.

Cogen, Cathy. 1977. On three aspects of time expression in ASL. In Lynn A. Friedman (ed.), *On the other hand: new perspectives on American Sign Language*. New York: Academic Press, 197–214.

Cook, Amy. 2010. *Shakespearean neuroplay: reinvigorating the study of dramatic texts and performance through cognitive science*. New York: Palgrave Macmillan.

Coulson, Seana. 2001. *Semantic leaps: frame shifting and conceptual blending in meaning construction*. Cambridge University Press.

    2006. Conceptual blending in thought, rhetoric, and ideology. In Kristiansen et al. (eds.), 187–210.

Croft, William. 2001. *Radical Construction Grammar*. Oxford University Press.

    2009. Connecting frames and constructions: a case study of *eat* and *feed*. *Constructions and Frames* 11, 7–28.

Croft, William, and D. Alan Cruse. 2004. *Cognitive linguistics*. Cambridge University Press.

Cuenca, Maria-Josep and Manuela Romano. 2013. Similes in interaction: beyond (metaphor and) compare. Paper presented at the 12th International Cognitive Linguistics Conference. Edmonton, Canada, June 23–28.

Dancygier, Barbara. 1998. *Conditionals and prediction: time, knowledge and causation in conditional constructions*. Cambridge University Press.

    2005. Blending and narrative viewpoint: Jonathan Raban's travels through mental spaces. *Language and Literature* 14(2), 99–127.

    (ed.). 2006. *Language and Literature* 15(5), special issue: *Blending and literature*.

    2009. Genitives and proper names in constructional blends. In Vyvyan Evans and Stephanie Pourcel (eds.), *New directions in cognitive linguistics*. Amsterdam and Philadelphia: John Benjamins, 161–84.

    2010. Alternativity in poetry and drama: textual intersubjectivity and framing. *English Text Construction* 3(2), 165–84.

    2011. Modification and constructional blends in the use of proper names. *Constructions and Frames* 3(2), 208–35.

    2012a. *The language of stories: a cognitive approach*. Cambridge University Press.

    2012b. Negation, stance verbs, and intersubjectivity. In Dancygier and Sweetser (eds.), 69–93.

Dancygier, Barbara, and Eve Sweetser. 2005. *Mental spaces in grammar: conditional constructions*. Cambridge University Press.

    (eds.). 2012. *Viewpoint in language: a multimodal perspective*. Cambridge University Press.

Dancygier, Barbara, José Sanders, and Lieven Vandelanotte. 2012 [2010]. *Textual choices in discourse: a view from cognitive linguistics*. Amsterdam and Philadelphia: John Benjamins. (First published as a special issue of *English Text Construction*, 3[2].)

Deignan, Alice. 2005. *Metaphor and corpus linguistics*. Amsterdam and Philadelphia: John Benjamins.

Delville, Michel, and Andrew Norris. 2007. Frank Zappa, Captain Beefheart, and the secret history of maximalism. In Louis Armand (ed.), *Contemporary poetics*. Evanston, IL: Northwestern University Press, 126–49.

DesCamp, M. Therese, and Eve Sweetser. 2005. Metaphors for God: why and how do our choices matter for humans? The application of contemporary cognitive linguistics research to the debate on God and metaphor. *Pastoral Psychology* 53(3), 207–38.

Dirven, René and Ralph Pörings (eds.). 2003. *Metaphor and metonymy in comparison and contrast.* Berlin and New York: Mouton de Gruyter.

Emanatian, Michele. 1992. Chagga 'come' and 'go': metaphor and the development of tense–aspect. *Studies in Language* 16, 1–33.

Emmorey, Karen. 2001. Space on hand: the exploitation of signing space to illustrate abstract thought. In Merideth Gattis (ed.), *Spatial schemas and abstract thought.* Cambridge, MA: MIT Press, 148–74.

2002. *Language, cognition and the brain: insights from sign language research.* Mahwah, NJ: Lawrence Erlbaum Associates.

Evans, Nicholas, and David Wilkins. 1998. The knowing ear: an Australian test of universal claims about the semantic structure of sensory verbs and their extension into the domain of cognition. *Arbeitspapiere von Institut für Sprachwissenschaft, Universität zu Köln (Neue Folge)* 32. Cologne: Institut für Sprachwissenschaft.

Fauconnier, Gilles. 1994 [1985]. *Mental spaces: aspects of meaning construction in natural language.* 2nd edn. Cambridge University Press.

1997. *Mappings in thought and language.* Cambridge University Press.

Fauconnier, Gilles, and Eve Sweetser (eds.). 1996. *Spaces, worlds, and grammar.* University of Chicago Press.

Fauconnier, Gilles, and Mark Turner. 1994. Conceptual projection and middle spaces. University of California-San Diego Department of Cognitive Science Technical Report 9401.

1996. Blending as a central process of grammar. In Adele Goldberg (ed.), *Conceptual structure, discourse, and language.* Stanford, CA: CSLI Publications, 113–30.

1998a. Conceptual integration networks. *Cognitive Science* 2(22), 133–87.

1998b. Principles of conceptual integration. In Koenig (ed.), 269–83.

2002. *The way we think: conceptual blending and the mind's hidden complexities.* New York: Basic Books.

2008. Rethinking metaphor. In Gibbs (ed.), 53–66.

Fillmore, Charles J. 1982. Frame semantics. In The Linguistic Society of Korea (ed.), *Linguistics in the morning calm.* Seoul: Hanshin Publishing Co., 111–37.

1985. Frames and the semantics of understanding. *Quaderni di semantica* 6(2), 222–53.

Fillmore, Charles J., and Paul Kay. 1999. Grammatical constructions and linguistic generalizations: the *What's X doing Y?* construction. *Language* 75(1), 1–33.

Fillmore, Charles J., Paul Kay, and Mary Catherine O'Connor. 1988. Regularity and idiomaticity in grammatical constructions: the case of *let alone. Language* 63(3), 501–38.

Fleischman, Suzanne. 1982. *The future in thought and language.* Cambridge University Press.

Forceville, Charles. 1996. *Pictorial mapping in advertising.* London: Routledge.

Forceville, Charles and Eduardo Urios-Aparisi (eds.). 2009. *Multimodal metaphor*. Berlin and New York: Mouton de Gruyter.

Francis, Elaine J., and Laura E. Michaelis (eds.) 2003. *Mismatch: form–function incongruity and the architecture of grammar*. Stanford, CA: CSLI Publications.

Franklin, Anna, Gilda V. Drivoniko, Ally Clifford, Paul Kay, Terry Regier, and Ian R. L. Davies. 2008. Lateralization of categorical perception of color changes with color term acquisition. *Proceedings of the National Academy of Sciences* 105, 18221–5.

Freeman, Donald C. 1993. "According to my bond": *King Lear* and re-cognition. *Language and Literature* 2, 1–18.

    1995. "Catch[ing] the nearest way": *Macbeth* and cognitive metaphors. *Journal of Pragmatics* 24, 698–708.

Fried, Mirjam, and Hans C. Boas (eds.). 2005. *Construction Grammar: back to the roots*. Amsterdam and Philadelphia: John Benjamins.

Fried, Mirjam, and Jan-Ola Östman. 2004a. Construction Grammar: a thumbnail sketch. In Fried and Östman (eds.), 11–86.

    (eds.). 2004b. *Construction Grammar in a cross-language perspective*. Amsterdam and Philadelphia: John Benjamins.

Gavins, Joanna, and Gerard Steen (eds.). 2003. *Cognitive poetics in practice*. London and New York: Routledge.

Gentner, Dedre. 1983. Structure-mapping: a theoretical framework for analogy. *Cognitive Science* 7, 145–70.

Gentner, Dedre, and Brian Bowdle. 2001. Convention, form, and figurative language processing. *Metaphor and Symbol* 16(3/4), 223–47.

    2008. Metaphor as structure-mapping. In Gibbs (ed.), 109–28.

Gentner, Dedre, and Donald R. Gentner. 1983. Flowing waters or teeming crowds: mental models of electricity. In Dedre Gentner and Albert L. Stevents (eds.), *Mental models*. Hillsdale, NJ: Lawrence Erlbaum Associates, 447–80.

Gentner, Dedre, Mutsumi Imai, and Lera Boroditsky. 2002. As time goes by: evidence for two systems in processing space time metaphors. *Language and Cognitive Processes* 17, 537–65.

Gibbs, Raymond W., Jr. 1994. *The poetics of mind: figurative thought, language, and understanding*. New York: Cambridge University Press.

    2005. *Embodiment and cognitive science*. Cambridge University Press.

    (ed.). 2008. *Cambridge handbook of metaphor and thought*. New York: Cambridge University Press.

Gibbs, Raymond W., Jr., and Herbert L. Colston. 2012. *Interpreting figurative meaning*. Cambridge University Press.

Gibbs, Raymond W. and Gerard J. Steen (eds.). 1999. *Metaphor in cognitive linguistics: Papers from the Fifth International Cognitive Linguistics Conference (Amsterdam, July 1997)*. Amsterdam and Philadelphia: John Benjamins.

Gilbert, Aubrey, Terry Regier, Paul Kay, and Richard Ivry. 2008. Support for lateralization of the Whorf effect beyond the realm of color discrimination. *Brain and Language* 105, 91–8.

Glucksberg, Sam, and Boaz Keysar. 1993. How metaphors work. In Ortony (ed.), 401–24.

Goldberg, Adele E. 1995. *Constructions: a construction grammar approach to argument structure*. University of Chicago Press.

2006. *Constructions at work: the nature of generalization in language*. Oxford University Press.

Grady, Joseph. 1997. Theories are buildings revisited. *Cognitive Linguistics* 8, 267–90.

1998. The "Conduit" Metaphor revisited: a reassessment of metaphors for communication. In Koenig (ed.), 1–16.

Grady, Joseph, Todd Oakley, and Seana Coulson. 1999. Blending and metaphor. In Gerard Steen and Raymond W. Gibbs, Jr. (eds.), *Metaphor in cognitive linguistics*. Amsterdam and Philadelphia: John Benjamins, 101–24.

Hardin, C. L. and Luisa Maffi (eds.). 1997. *Color categories in thought and language*. Cambridge University Press.

Hart, Christopher. 2010. *Critical discourse analysis and cognitive science: new perspectives on immigration discourse*. London: Palgrave Macmillan.

Haun, Daniel B. M., and Christian J. Rapold. 2009. Variation in memory for body movements across cultures. *Current Biology* 19(23), R1068–9.

Hiraga, Masako K. 2005. *Metaphor and iconicity: a cognitive approach to analyzing texts*. Palgrave Macmillan.

Hofstadter, Douglas, and Emmanuel Sander. 2013. *Surfaces and essences: analogy as the fuel and fire of thinking*. Basic Books.

Hopper, Paul J., and Elizabeth Closs Traugott. 1993. *Grammaticalization*. Cambridge University Press.

Horn, Laurence. 1985. Metalinguistic negation and pragmatic ambiguity. *Language* 61, 121–74.

Howe, Bonnie, and Eve Sweetser. In press. Cognitive linguistics and Biblical interpretation. In Steven L. McKenzie (ed.), *The Oxford encyclopedia of Biblical interpretation*. New York: Oxford University Press.

Hutchins, Edwin. 2005. Material anchors for conceptual blends. *Journal of Pragmatics* 37, 1555–77.

Israel, Michael, Jennifer Riddle Harding, and Vera Tobin. 2004. On simile. In Michel Achard and Suzanne Kemmer (eds.), *Language, culture and mind*. Stanford, CA: CSLI Publications, 123–35.

Jakobson, Roman. 1981 (1960). *Linguistics and poetics. selected writings*, vol. 3. The Hague: Mouton.

Jakobson, Roman. 1987. *Language and literature*. Ed. Krystyna Pomorska and Stephen Rudy. Cambridge, MA: Harvard University Press.

Johnson, Christopher. 1997. Metaphor vs. conflation in the acquisition of polysemy: the case of SEE. In Masako K. Hiraga, Chris Sinha and Sherman Wilcox (eds.), *Cultural, typological, and psychological issues in cognitive linguistics*. Amsterdam and Philadelphia: John Benjamins, 155–69.

Johnson, Mark. 1981. Introduction: metaphor in the philosophical tradition. In Mark Johnson (ed.), *Philosophical perspectives on metaphor*. Minneapolis: University of Minnesota Press, 3–47.

1987. *The body in the mind: the bodily basis of meaning, imagination, and reason*. University of Chicago Press.

Jostman, Nils. B., Daniel Lakens, and Thomas W. Schubert. 2009. Weight as an embodiment of importance. *Psychological Science* 20, 1169–74.

Koenig, Jean-Pierre (ed.). 1998. *Discourse and cognition: bridging the gap*. Stanford: CSLI Publications.

Kosecki, Krzysztof (ed). 2007. *Perspectives on metonymy*. Proceedings of the International Conference "Perspectives on Metonymy," Łódź, Poland, May 6–7, 2005. Frankfurt am Main: Peter Lang.

Kövecses, Zoltán. 1986. *Metaphors of anger, pride, and love: a lexical approach to the study of concepts*. Amsterdam and Philadelphia: John Benjamins.

  1995. Anger: its language, conceptualization, and physiology in the light of cross-cultural evidence. In John R. Taylor and Robert E. MacLaury (eds.), *Language and the cognitive construal of the world*. Berlin: Mouton de Gruyter, 181–96.

  2000. *Metaphor and emotion*. New York: Cambridge University Press.

  2005. *Metaphor in culture: universality and variation*. Cambridge University Press.

  2013. The metaphor–metonymy relationship: correlation metaphors are based on metonymy. *Metaphor and Symbol* 28(2), 75–88.

Kristiansen, Gitte, Michael Achard, Rene Dirven, and Francisco Ruiz de Mendoza Ibáñez (eds.). 2006. *Cognitive linguistics: current applications and future perspectives*. Berlin and New York: Mouton de Gruyter.

Lakoff, George. 1987. *Women, fire, and dangerous things: what categories reveal about the mind*. University of Chicago Press.

  1993. The contemporary theory of metaphor. In Ortony (ed.), 202–51.

  1996. Sorry, I'm not myself today: the metaphor system for conceptualizing self. In Fauconnier and Sweetser (eds.), 91–123.

  2002 [1996]. *Moral politics: how liberals and conservatives think*. University of Chicago Press.

  2009. *The political mind: a cognitive scientist's guide to your brain and its politics*. Penguin Books.

Lakoff, George, and Mark Johnson. 1980. *Metaphors we live by*. University of Chicago Press.

  1999. *Philosophy in the flesh: the embodied mind and its challenge to Western thought*. New York: Basic Books.

Lakoff, George, and Rafael Núñez. 2000. *Where mathematics comes from: how the embodied mind brings mathematics into being*. New York: Basic Books.

Lakoff, George, and Mark Turner. 1989. *More than cool reason: a field guide to poetic metaphor*. University of Chicago Press.

Langacker, Ronald W. 1990. *Concept, image, and symbol: the cognitive basis of grammar*. Berlin: Mouton de Gruyter.

  1987, 1991. *Foundations of Cognitive Grammar*. (2 vols.) Stanford University Press.

Le Guen, Olivier, and Lorena I. Pool Balam. 2012. No metaphorical timeline in gesture and cognition among Yucatec Mayas. *Frontiers in Psychology* 3, 1–15.

Lehrer, Adrienne. 1983. *Wine and conversation*. Bloomington: Indiana University Press.

Levinson, Stephen C. 2003. *Grammars of space: explorations in cognitive diversity*. Cambridge University Press.

Lutz, Catherine. 1987. Goals, events, and understanding in Ifaluk emotion theory. In Dorothy Holland and Naomi Quinn (eds.), *Cultural models in language and thought*. Cambridge University Press, 290–312.

Marmaridou, Sophia A. 1991. What's so proper about proper names? A study in categorization and cognitive semantics. *Parousia Monograph Series* 15. University of Athens.

Matlock, Teenie. 2004. Fictive motion as cognitive simulation. *Memory and Cognition* 32, 1389–1400.

McNeill, David. 1992. *Hand and mind*. University of Chicago Press.

Mervis, Carolyn, and Eleanor Rosch. 1981. Categorization of natural objects. *Annual Review of Psychology* 32, 89–115.

Mikkelsen, Line. 2005. *Copular clauses: specification, predication and equation*. Amsterdam and Philadelphia: John Benjamins.

Miracle, Andrew W., and Juan de Dios Yapita. 1981. Time and space in Aymara. In M. J. Hardman (ed.), *The Aymara language in its social and cultural context*. Gainesville: University Presses of Florida, 33–56.

Mittelberg, Irene. 2008. Peircean semiotics meets conceptual metaphor: iconic modes in gestural representations of grammar. In Alan Cienki and Cornelia Müller (eds.), *Metaphor and gesture*. Amsterdam and Philadelphia: John Benjamins, 115–54.

Moder, Carol. 2008. It's like making a soup: metaphors and similes in spoken news discourse. In Andrea Tyler, Yiyoung Kim, and Mari Takada (eds.), *Language in the context of use: discourse and cognitive approaches to language*. Berlin: Mouton de Gruyter, 301–20.

    2010. Two puzzle pieces: fitting discourse context and constructions into Cognitive Metaphor Theory. *English Text Construction* 3(2) 294–320.

Moore, Kevin E. 2000. Spatial experience and temporal metaphors in Wolof: point of view, conceptual mapping, and linguistic practice. PhD dissertation, University of California, Berkeley.

    2011. Ego-perspective and field-based frames of reference: temporal meanings of FRONT in Japanese, Wolof, and Aymara. *Journal of Pragmatics* 43(3), 759–76.

Morgan, Pamela S. 2008. Competition, cooperation, and interconnection: "metaphor families" and social systems. In Gitte Kristiansen and René Dirven (eds.), *Cognitive sociolinguistics: language variation, cultural models, social systems*. Berlin and New York: Mouton de Gruyter, 483–515.

Müller, Cornelia. 2008. *Metaphors dead and alive, sleeping and waking: a dynamic view*. University of Chicago Press.

Musolff, Andrea. 2004. *Metaphor and political discourse: analogical reasoning in debates about Europe*. Basingstoke: Palgrave Macmillan.

Musolff, Andrea, and Jorg Zinken (eds.). 2009. *Metaphor and discourse*. Basingstoke: Palgrave Macmillan.

Nelkin, Dorothy. 2001. Molecular metaphors: the gene in popular discourse. *Nature Review Genetics* 2(7), 555–9.

Nerlich, Brigitte, and Robert Dingwall. 2003. Deciphering the human genome: the semantic and ideological foundations of genetic and genomic discourse. In René Dirven, Roslyn May Frank, and Martin Pütz (eds.), *Cognitive models in language and thought: ideology, metaphors and meanings*. Berlin: Mouton de Gruyter, 395–427.

Nikiforidou, Vassiliki. 1999. Nominalizations, metonymy and lexicographic practice. In Leon de Stadler and Christoph Eyrich (eds.), *Issues in cognitive linguistics: proceedings of the 1993 International Cognitive Linguistics Conference.* Berlin and New York: Mouton de Gruyter, 141–63.

Núñez, Rafael E., and Eve Sweetser. 2006. With the future behind them: convergent evidence from Aymara language and gesture in the crosslinguistic comparison of spatial construals of time. *Cognitive Science* 30(3), 401–50.

Núñez, Rafael E., Kensy Cooperrider, D. Doan, and Jürg Wassmann. 2012. Contours of time: topographic construals of past, present, and future in the Yupno valley of Papua New Guinea. *Cognition* 124(1), 25–35.

Oakley, Todd, and Anders Hougaard (eds.). 2008. *Mental spaces in discourse and interaction.* Amsterdam and Philadelphia: John Benjamins.

Östman, Jan-Ola, and Mirjam Fried (eds.). 2005. *Construction Grammars: cognitive grounding and theoretical perspective.* Amsterdam: John Benjamins.

Ouellet, Marc, Julio Santiago, Ziv Israeli, and Shai Gabay. 2009. Multimodal influences of orthographic directionality on the "Time is Space" conceptual metaphor. In Niels Taatgen and Hedderik van Rijn (eds.), *Proceedings of the 31st Annual Conference of the Cognitive Science Society.* Amsterdam: Cognitive Science Society, Inc., 1840–5.

Ortony, Andrew (ed.). 1993. *Metaphor and thought.* 2nd edn. Cambridge University Press.

Özçaliskan, Seyda. 2002. Metaphors we move by: a crosslinguistic-developmental analysis of metaphorical motion events in English and Turkish. PhD dissertation, University of California, Berkeley.

Panther, Klaus-Uwe. 2006. Metonymy as a usage event. In Kristiansen et al. (eds.), 147–86.

Panther, Klaus-Uwe, and Günther Radden (eds.). 1999. *Metonymy in language and thought.* Amsterdam and Philadelphia: John Benjamins.

Panther, Klaus-Uwe, Linda Thornburg, and Antonio Barcelona (eds.). 2010. *Metonymy and metaphor in grammar.* Amsterdam and Philadelphia: John Benjamins.

Pascual, Esther. 2008. Fictive interaction blends in everyday life and courtroom settings. In Anders Hougaard and Todd Oakley (eds.), *Mental spaces in discourse and interaction.* Amsterdam and Philadelphia: John Benjamins, 79–107.

Piaget, Jean. 1985 (1975). *The equilibration of cognitive structures.* University of Chicago Press.

Pragglejaz Group. 2007. MIP: A method for identifying metaphorically used words in discourse. *Metaphor and Symbol* 22(1), 1–39.

Radden, Günther, and Zóltan Kövecses. 1999. Towards a theory of metonymy. In Panther and Radden (eds.), 17–60.

Reddy, Michael. 1979. The Conduit Metaphor – a case of frame conflict in our language about language. In Andrew Ortony (ed.), *Metaphor and thought.* Cambridge University Press, 284–97.

Regier, Terry, and Paul Kay. 2009. Language, thought, and color: Whorf was half right. *Trends in Cognitive Sciences* 13, 439–46.

Regier, Terry, Paul Kay, and Naveen Khetarpal. 2007. Color naming reflects optimal partitions of color space. *Proceedings of the National Academy of Sciences* 104, 1436–41.

Rips, Lance J. 1975. Inductive judgments about natural categories. *Journal of Verbal Learning and Verbal Behavior* 14, 665–81.

Rosch, Eleanor. 1977. Human categorization. In Neil Warren (ed.), *Studies in cross-cultural psychology*. London: Academic.

Sakahara, Shigeru. 1996. Roles and identificational copular sentences. In Fauconnier and Sweetser (eds.), 262–89.

Schank, Roger C., and Robert P. Abelson. 1977. *Scripts, plans, goals, and understanding*. Hillsdale, NJ: Lawrence Erlbaum Associates.

Schneider, Ralf, and Marcus Hartner (eds.). 2012. *Blending and the study of narrative: approaches and applications*. Berlin: de Gruyter.

Searle, John R. 1969. *Speech acts: an essay in the philosophy of language*. Cambridge University Press.

1975. Indirect speech acts. In Peter Cole and Jerry L. Morgan (eds.), *Syntax and semantics, volume 3: Speech acts*. New York: Academic Press, 59–82.

1990. A classification of illocutionary acts. In Donal Carbaugh (ed.), *Cultural communication and intercultural contact*. Hillsdale, NJ: Lawrence Erlbaum Associates, 349–72.

Semino, Elena. 2008. *Metaphor in discourse*. Cambridge University Press.

2010. Unrealistic scenarios, metaphorical blends, and rhetorical strategies across genres. *English Text Construction* 3(2), 250–74.

Semino, Elena, and Jonathan Culpeper (eds.). 2002. *Cognitive stylistics: language and cognition in text analysis*. Amsterdam and Philadelphia: John Benjamins.

Shinohara, Kazuko. 1999. *Epistemology of space and time: an analysis of conceptual metaphor in English and Japanese*. Nishinomiya, Japan: Kwansei Gakuin University Press.

Sperber, Dan, and Deirdre Wilson. 1981. Irony and the use–mention distinction. In Peter Cole (ed.), *Radical Pragmatics*. New York: Academic Press, 295–318.

Stec, Kashmiri, and Eve Sweetser. 2013. Borobudur and Chartres: religious spaces as performative real-space blends. In Rosario Caballero and Javier E. Díaz Vera (eds.), *Sensuous cognition: explorations into human sentience: imagination, (e)motion, and perception*. Berlin: Mouton de Gruyter, 265–91.

Steen, Gerard. 1994. *Understanding metaphor in literature: an empirical approach*. London: Longman.

Steen, Gerard, J., Aletta G. Dorst , J. Berenike Herrmann, Anna Kaal, Tina Krennmayr, and Trijntje Pasma. 2010. *A method for linguistic metaphor identification: from MIP to MIPVU*. Amsterdam and Philadelphia: John Benjamins.

Steinhart, Eric 2001. *The logic of metaphor – analogous parts of Possible Worlds*. New York: Springer.

Stockwell, Peter. 2002. *Cognitive poetics: an introduction*. London: Routledge.

Sullivan, Karen. 2009. Grammatical constructions in metaphoric language. In Barbara Lewandowska-Tomaszczyk and Katarzyna Dziwirek (eds.), *Studies in cognitive corpus linguistics*. Frankfurt am Main: Peter Lang, 57–80.

2013. *Frames and constructions in metaphoric language*. Amsterdam and Philadelphia: John Benjamins.

Sullivan, Karen, and Eve Sweetser. 2009. Is "generic is specific" a metaphor? In Fey Parrill, Vera Tobin, and Mark Turner (eds.), *Meaning, form, and body*. Stanford, CA: CSLI Publications, 309–28.

Sweetser, Eve. 1984. Semantic structure and semantic change. PhD dissertation, University of California, Berkeley.

1990. *From etymology to pragmatics*. Cambridge University Press.

1996a. Reasoning, mapping, and meta-metaphorical conditionals. In Sandra Thompson and Masayoshi Shibatani (eds.), *Grammatical constructions: their form and meaning*. Oxford University Press, 221–33.

1996b. Mental spaces and the grammar of conditional constructions. In Fauconnier and Sweetser (eds.), 318–33.

1999. Compositionality and blending: semantic composition in a cognitively realistic framework. In Theo Janssen and Gisela Redeker (eds.), *Cognitive linguistics: foundations, scope, and methodology*. Berlin: Mouton de Gruyter, 129–62.

2000. Blended spaces and performativity. *Cognitive Linguistics* 11(3/4), 305–34.

2004. "The suburbs of your good pleasure": cognition, culture and the bases of metaphoric structure. In Bradshaw et al. (eds.), 24–55.

2006. Whose rhyme is whose reason? Sound and sense in *Cyrano de Bergerac. Language and Literature* 15(1), 29–54.

2009. What does it mean to compare language and gesture: modalities and contrasts. In Jiansheng Guo, Elena Lieven, Nancy Budwig, Susan Ervin-Tripp, Keiko Nakamura, and Seyda Özçaliskan (eds.), *Crosslinguistic approaches to the psychology of language: studies in the tradition of Dan Isaac Slobin*. New York: Psychology Press, 357–66.

Sweetser, Eve, and Karen Sullivan 2012. Minimalist metaphors. *English Text Construction* 5(2), 153–73.

Taub, Sarah F. 2001. *Language from the body: metaphor and iconicity in American Sign Language*. Cambridge University Press.

Tobin, Vera, and Michael Israel. 2012. Irony as a viewpoint phenomenon. In Dancygier and Sweetser (eds.), 25–46.

Traugott, Elizabeth Closs. 1982. From propositional to textual and expressive meanings: some semantic–pragmatic aspects of grammaticalization. In Winfred P. Lehman and Yakov Malkiel (eds.), *Perspectives on historical linguistics*. Amsterdam and Philadelphia: John Benjamins, 245–71.

1989. On the rise of epistemic meanings in English: an example of subjectification in semantic change. *Language* 57, 33–65.

Turner, Mark. 1987. *Death is the mother of beauty: mind, metaphor, criticism*. University of Chicago Press.

1991. *Reading minds: the study of English in the age of cognitive science*. Princeton University Press.

1996. *The Literary mind: the origins of language and thought*. Oxford University Press.

2004. The ghost of anyone's father. In Bradshaw, Bishop, and Turner (eds.), 72–97.

Tversky, Barbara, Sol Kugelmass, and Atalia Winter. 1991. Crosscultural and developmental trends in graphic productions. *Cognitive Psychology* 23(4), 515–57.

Vandelanotte, Lieven, and Peter Willemse. 2002. Restrictive and non-restrictive modification of proprial lemmas. *Word* 53(1), 9–36.

Verhagen, Arie. 2005. *Constructions of intersubjectivity: discourse, syntax, and cognition*. Oxford University Press.

Wilkins, David. 1996. Natural tendencies in semantic change and the search for cognates. In Mark Durie and Malcolm Ross (eds.), *The comparative method revisited: regularity and irregularity in language change*. New York: Oxford University Press, 264–304.

Williams, Lawrence E., and John A. Bargh. 2008. Experiencing physical warmth promotes interpersonal warmth. *Science* 322(5901), 606–7.

Williams, Robert F. 2004. Making meaning from a clock: material artifacts and conceptual blending in time-telling instruction. PhD dissertation, University of California, San Diego.

Wilson, Deirdre, and Dan Sperber. 1992. On verbal irony. *Lingua* 87, 53–76.

Yu, Ning. 1998. *The contemporary theory of metaphor: a perspective from Chinese*. Amsterdam and Philadelphia: John Benjamins.

   2009. *From body to meaning in culture*. Amsterdam and Philadelphia: John Benjamins.

Further reading

The material covered in this textbook can be expanded in many directions. It would be close to impossible to follow all those paths here. Instead, we propose an eclectic and rather short selection of texts which provide basic methodological guidance in cognitive linguistics and in its applications to the study of texts and discourse types. They are all good starting points for an interesting journey, wherever the reader wishes to go.

Bergen, Benjamin. 2012. *Louder than words: the new science of how the mind makes meaning*. New York: Basic Books.

Charteris-Black, Jonathan. 2004. *Corpus approaches to critical metaphor analysis*. New York: Palgrave Macmillan.

Croft, William, and D. Alan Cruse. 2004. *Cognitive linguistics*. Cambridge University Press.

Gibbs, Raymond W. Jr. 1994. *The poetics of mind: figurative thought, language and understanding*. Cambridge University Press.

Goldberg, Adele. 1995. *Constructions: a Construction Grammar approach to argument structure*. University of Chicago Press.

Evans, Vyvyan, and Melanie Green. 2006. *Cognitive linguistics: an introduction*. London: Routledge.

Johnson, Mark. 1987. *The body in the mind: the bodily basis of meaning, imagination and reason*. University of Chicago Press.

   (ed.) 1981. *Philosophical perspectives on metaphor*. Minneapolis: University of Minnesota Press.

Kittay, Eva Feder. 1987. *Metaphor: its cognitive force and linguistic structure*. Oxford University Press.

Kövecses, Zóltan. 2002. *Metaphor: a practical introduction*. Oxford University Press.

Lakoff, George. 1987. *Women, fire and dangerous things: what categories reveal about the mind*. University of Chicago Press.

Lakoff, George, and Mark Johnson. 1980. *Metaphors we live by*. University of Chicago Press.

   1999. *Philosophy in the flesh: the embodied mind and its challenge to Western thought*. New York: Basic Books.

Lakoff, George, and Mark Turner. 1989. *More than cool reason*. University of Chicago Press.

Langacker, Ronald. 2001. *Concept, image and symbol*. Berlin: Mouton de Gruyter.

Ortony, Andrew. 1993. *Metaphor and thought* (2nd edn). Cambridge University Press.

Semino, Elena. 2008. *Metaphor in discourse*. Cambridge University Press.

Soskice, Janet Martin. 1985. *Metaphor and religious language*. Oxford University Press.

Stockwell, Peter. 2002. *Cognitive poetics*. New York: Routledge.

Turner, Mark. 1987. *Death is the mother of beauty: mind, metaphor, criticism*. University of Chicago Press.

   1991. *Reading minds: the study of English in the age of cognitive science*. Princeton University Press.

   1996. *The Literary mind: the origins of language and thought*. Oxford University Press.

Index